THE
MEATBALL
COOKBOOK
BIBLE

THE Meatball COOKBOOK BIBLE

Foods from Soups to Desserts—500 Recipes That Make the World Go 'Round

ELLEN BROWN

CIDER MILL PRESS

BOOK PUBLISHERS

This book is dedicated to my wonderful sister, Nancy Dubler,
whose enthusiasm for meatballs and love of food constantly delights me.

13-Digit ISBN: 978-1-60433-097-7
10-Digit ISBN: 1-60433-097-X

This book may be ordered by mail from the publisher. Please include $3.50 for postage and handling. Please support your local bookseller first!

Books published by Cider Mill Press Book Publishers are available at special discounts for bulk purchases in the United States by corporations, institutions, and other organizations. For more information, please contact the publisher.

Cider Mill Press Book Publishers
"Where good books are ready for press"
12 Port Farm Road
Kennebunkport, Maine 04046

Visit us on the web!
www.cidermillpress.com

Illustration by Sherry Berger
Design by Alicia Freile, Tango Media
Typography: Minion, PMN Caecilia, and Univers
Front Cover Images Copyright: Joe Gough, Barbara Ayrapetyan, Lulu Durand, RoJo Images, Alexander Remy Levine, Robyn Mackenzie, Jaimie Duplass, E. G. Pors, Tanya_F, 2009. All used under license from Shutterstock.com

Printed and bound in Malaysia for Imago

1 2 3 4 5 6 7 8 9 0
First Edition

CONTENTS

INTRODUCTION

Who doesn't like meatballs? Meatballs are fun food, casual food, and flavorful food all rolled into one easy-to-eat morsel. And meatballs are so easy to make.

There isn't a cuisine that doesn't have a meatball of its own, call them *pulpety* in Poland, *almondigas* in the Philippines, or *keftedes* in Greece. The world loves meatballs. And this book lets you sample them all. You'll find recipes from meatball-loving countries around the world, and you'll find meatballs made from a panoply of foods.

Meatballs are often thought of as "family fare" or "peasant food." And with good reason. Add some vegetables, breadcrumbs, rice, or any other number of ingredients, and meatballs are a way to stretch a limited amount of expensive meat to feed more people. Now that's a concept that appeals to us today with skyrocketing food prices. Meatballs, however, can have much loftier culinary connotations. Take the French *quenelle*; it's nothing more than a poached meatball made with fish.

This book also contains many variations on the meatball theme. My theory is that after you make a recipe once—and like the results —you'll want to make it again. You can make it exactly the same way, or change it to add variety to your table. For example, who doesn't love basic Italian-American meatballs on top of spaghetti? But I'll show you how to prepare one-step lasagna with leftover meatballs.

Unlike most foods, meatballs also have dual personalities. They can be plain. They can be fancy. The same meatballs your family enjoys for dinner one night can be made as miniatures and served to guests as part of the hors d'oeuvre at your next cocktail party. Meatball dishes work well at buffets because they're "fork-only food." Even if larger than bite-sized, they can be divided into smaller pieces without using a knife, so guests can eat them easily while standing up.

So read on and start making—and enjoying—meatballs.

BUILDING
THE BEST
MEATBALLS

Meatballs are good news for cooks. Why? It's almost impossible to mess them up. They're not like a soufflé that can turn into a flat pancake instead of reaching great heights. You don't need to be a professional chef with a battery of culinary skills. Meatballs are one of the easiest foods to make successfully, and in this chapter you'll learn the many ways there are to make them. You'll also learn ways to transform meatballs into other forms of foods such as a hearty meatball shepherd's pie or meatball lasagna, as well as general pointers on food handling that will make your kitchen a safer environment for all cooking.

ANATOMY OF A MEATBALL

My definition of "meatball" is a broad one; anything made from a mixture that is ground and ends up round is a meatball. Many of the recipes don't even use meat! There are meatballs made with poultry, fish, and vegetables. There are even balls made from sweet mixtures. Are they desserts?

Each ingredient in the ground mixture has a purpose, and that is to produce a flavorful meatball with an appealing soft texture. While many meatballs are made the size of marbles or the size of golf balls, no one wants them to taste like one. The ideal texture for a meatball is a soft interior; the exterior can be hard or soft depending on how they are cooked. Some of these ingredients play more than one role; for example, using rye bread for moisture adds flavor from the caraway seeds, and adding ketchup for flavor will also enhance the moisture in the mix. Here are the various categories of ingredients that comprise a meatball, with some variations given:

The Starring Player: The primary ingredient of a meatball is usually meat. But that can mean beef, veal, lamb, pork, poultry, or some combination of these. They can also be made with fish and shellfish. Grains, legumes, and vegetables can also take on the starring role, but with a different touch than meat or seafood.

The Flavor Boosters: This category includes herbs, spices, cheeses, vegetables, and prepared sauces and condiments. These ingredients vary in proportion by recipe; there are no hard and fast rules. If the meatball is intended to be eaten in a sauce, there will be fewer flavoring ingredients in the meatball itself, compared with those that are eaten off a toothpick as a stand-alone

item. In addition to adding flavor, cheeses and condiments such as ketchup, mustard, or soy sauce also add moisture to meatballs. The vegetables in the meatball mixture can be either raw or cooked. Some combination of onion, celery, garlic, and carrots are most frequently used, but chopped mushrooms or mashed potatoes can be added as well.

The Seasonings: Notice that specific amounts of salt and pepper aren't listed in the recipes because I believe this is a very personal decision. First make the meatball mix without salt and pepper because some of the secondary ingredients—such as seasoned breadcrumbs or condiments—may already include some salt and pepper. Season the mixture after all other ingredients have been added and blended.

The Texture Enhancers: Most meatball recipes include at least one whole egg, and sometimes an additional egg yolk or egg white. The egg serves as a binder for the other ingredients so the meatball holds its shape. The egg also offers a bit of fat and liquid to give the meatball a pleasing mouth feel when chewed. Some vegetables, such as cooked chopped spinach or shredded cooked carrots, also add texture to meatballs.

The Moisture Magnets: In addition to liking meatballs with a soft interior, we also like meatballs that have a moist interior. That's where some sort of carbohydrate enters the picture. It can be anything from torn bread, fluffy Japanese panko, crushed crackers, or plain breadcrumbs to grains such as raw or cooked rice, oatmeal, or bulgur. The purpose of the carbohydrate is to absorb moisture as the meat cooks and gives off liquid. Depending on what ingredient is used, the moisture magnet can also add flavor and texture to the meatball.

Some recipes have a low moisture content, so the moisture magnet is soaked in a liquid before adding it to the mixture. In recipes with a high moisture content the carbohydrate is added dry. The liquid in which it soaks can be as simple as water, to add only moisture to a recipe, or wine, stock, fruit juice, or tomato sauce to add flavor. While each recipe in this book specifies a particular carbohydrate, feel free to change it or use whatever is on hand. Experiment. The only caveat is to determine if the moisture magnet was also contributing to the flavor of the meatball and adjust accordingly. For example, Italian pre-seasoned breadcrumbs are one of the great convenience foods on the market, but if all you have are plain breadcrumbs, add ½ teaspoon of Italian seasoning (or some combination of dried basil, oregano, and thyme) to the mixture per ½ cup of breadcrumbs used.

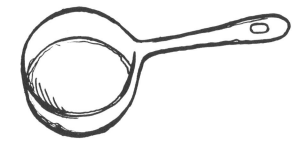

If you buy loaves of crusty bread on a regular basis, you can save money by making your own breadcrumbs. Once a loaf is a day old, and the texture is no longer optimal, cut some of it into one-inch cubes and let it sit at room temperature for a day or so. Then place the rock-hard cubes in a food processor fitted with a steel blade and process until you have fine breadcrumbs. The bread can be a white baguette or a multi-grain or flavored bread such as an olive or cheese loaf. Store the crumbs at room temperature in an air-tight container for up to one week.

THE DAILY GRIND

The quality and type of ground meat makes an enormous difference when cooking beef meatballs because some cuts of beef are more flavorful than others. The best beef meatballs are made with ground chuck that is 80 percent lean and comes from a very well marbled and flavorful cut. Should you want a leaner burger, look for ground sirloin. Avoid any packages generically labeled "ground beef."

The same distinctions are not made with other ground meats, such as pork or lamb. But in most supermarkets you do have the choice between ground turkey and all-white meat ground turkey. The all-white meat is a bit leaner but not as flavorful as the mixture that includes some dark meat. For meatballs made with a mixture of meats – usually beef, pork, and veal – many supermarkets carry a product called "meatloaf mix" containing all three meats in an equal proportion. I use this same proportion in many recipes in Chapter 7.

Almost no one actually grinds meat at home these days; my meat grinder lives in a box in the basement along with other culinary antiques such as my fish poacher and waffle maker. But chopping fish and seafood at home is necessary for some recipes, and there is no better friend than the food processor to accomplish this task.

For finfish, such as salmon, tuna, or cod, start by cutting the fish into 1-inch cubes, and arrange the cubes on a baking sheet lined with a sheet of plastic wrap. For shrimp, use the 21 to 25 shrimp per pound size. Remove and discard the shell, and devein the shrimp.

Place the baking sheet in the freezer for 20 to 30 minutes, or until the fish is partially frozen. Then transfer the cubes to the work bowl of the food processor and chop it either finely or coarsely, according to the directions in the specific recipe, using the on-and-off pulsing action.

In some recipes part of the chopped fish or shellfish is removed from the work bowl to add texture to the mixture, and the remainder is pureed with eggs to become the mousse-like base for the fish balls.

> There are actual recipes for meatballs from the time of the Romans. Marcus Gavius Apicius, better known as Apicius, was born in 25 CE, and his *De re coquinaria libri decem* (*Cuisine in Ten Books* for those who have forgotten their high school Latin) has an entire book devoted to "minces," or meat mixtures combined with other ingredients.

PUTTING IT ALL TOGETHER

There is an order in which the various categories of ingredients are combined to create the best meatballs, although this may change to some extent from recipe to recipe. But remember this isn't rocket science. It's meatballs. And if you combine ingredients in an order other than the one specified in the recipe, your results will still be delicious.

Most recipes start by combining the ancillary ingredients, and then adding the meat last. If the breadcrumbs or other carbohydrate are to soak in liquid, then that will be the first step. In a few recipes any liquid remaining is discarded after the initial soaking time. If you don't have to drain away excess moisture, the recipe will begin by beating the egg with liquid, and then adding the crumbs.

While the crumbs soak, the vegetables can be chopped and sautéed, if necessary, and the other ingredients can be assembled. If the vegetables are sautéed, they are then allowed to cool briefly so that they don't cook the egg when added to the mixing bowl. The last thing added is the meat itself, and then the mixture is formed.

The secret to achieving meatballs with lots of texture is to create a mixture with your fingertips—either wearing disposable plastic gloves or with well-washed hands. The ancillary ingredients are either chopped by hand or in a food processor using the on-and-off pulsing action so that the mixture is blended as briefly as possible and individual ingredients retain their characteristics. Using this method, the resulting meatballs are rustic, and rarely form a perfect sphere because they are patted into shape rather than rolled between your palms.

For smooth and satiny texture, the mixture is beaten either in a food processor or in a standing mixer using a paddle attachment; hand mixers do not have enough power to beat a meat mixture into a smooth paste. I used both methods, depending on the recipe. But if you like smooth meatballs regardless of ingredients or sauce, use the food processor.

Once the mixture is together, it's time to taste for seasoning and add more salt and pepper, if necessary. Because almost all mixtures contain raw eggs, do not sample it from the bowl. While it looks prettier if you fry up a small amount in a small skillet, I hate to dirty a pan for that task. I cook a few teaspoons, uncovered, in a microwave oven for 20 to 25 seconds. It will be pale and not very visually appealing, but it will be cooked through, and safe to sample.

If time permits, the flavor of meatballs is vastly improved if the mixture is refrigerated for at least one hour. In fact, it can be refrigerated for up to twelve hours, but after that should be cooked because it contains raw ingredients like meat and eggs which can be carriers of food-borne illnesses.

If you don't want to cook a meatball until it's well done, then make the mixture without an egg. There are some recipes in this book made without eggs because their flavors and textures are improved if the meat is slightly rare. You can omit the egg and add more liquid to the mixture to replace its role in providing moisture.

A baseball player at bat loves being thrown a "meatball pitch," one that travels slowly through the upper part of the strike zone. It's an easy pitch to time and hit, often resulting in extra bases or even a home run.

FROM MIXTURE TO MEATBALL

Whether your meatballs are the size of an egg yolk, the size of an egg, or the size of an orange, what's important is that the meatballs in each batch are all the same size so that they cook at the same rate. That might seem obvious, but it's actually harder to control than you think. With the repetition of forming meatballs they have a tendency to grow larger unless you're careful when portioning the meat.

It is faster to make meatballs—and forming them can take far more time than making the mixture from which they are formed—if you follow an assembly line process. First, measure your mixture out with an implement of specific size, and then turn the individual portions into balls.

For very small cocktail meatballs you can use the large side of a melon baller, and for slightly larger meatballs use a measuring tablespoon. Large meatballs can be formed in ¼-cup dry measuring cups, and there are specialized cookie dough scoops that come in a variety of sizes. These scoops are spring-loaded so they quickly discharge the mixture.

Once all the mixture has been portioned, it's time to form these blobs into meatballs. The easiest way is to *gently* roll the meat between the palms of your hands. Especially if you like meatballs with a lot of texture, the mixture should not be over-handled or it will negate all the good work you've done to give them texture. If you like meatballs with a smooth texture, roll the mixture into the perfect orb, but you will still have to do it gently because it is a soft mixture.

While serving cocktail meatballs on toothpicks – plain ones or those with frilly ruffles – is traditional, guests often don't know what to do with these sticks once the meatballs are consumed. Use pretzel sticks or very thin carrot sticks as edible picks for the meatballs instead.

COOKING STRATEGIES

In addition to being made from varied ingredients, meatballs are cooked in myriad ways. Some are fried; others are steamed. Some are grilled or broiled over very high heat while others are gently poached in barely simmering liquid.

Most meatballs are browned initially to create a crispy crust, but this can be done on a baking sheet in the oven or in a skillet on top of the stove. Some meatballs are coated with crumbs or a batter before they are cooked while others are cooked as they are.

The kind of mixture often dictates how the meatball should be eaten. Sometimes they are served without a sauce, so all the flavor is in the meatball itself. Other times they are simmered in a sauce (like the ubiquitous spaghetti and meatballs) or they are dunked into a dipping sauce.

One factor that remains constant is that meatballs are intended to be cooked through and not eaten rare, even those made from ground red meats that many people would eat rare as a steak or even as a burger. Since meatballs are made with eggs, eating uncooked or undercooked eggs can be dangerous from a health standpoint because eggs can be carriers of salmonella bacteria.

I am a firm believer that if one method requires constant attention while another method requires none of my attention, I'll always opt for the latter. I'd much rather be reading a book than turning meatballs in a skillet, and that's why the recipes in this book specify browning them in a hot oven. It happens all at once, and you're done with that step. If the meatballs are coated with crumbs, a light coating of vegetable oil spray will accomplish the same browning as the fat you would have in a skillet and the crumbs absorb less fat.

But if you like to be more involved with your meatballs, brown them or cook them completely on top of the stove in a skillet. Use a 12-inch skillet or larger, and begin by adding enough vegetable oil to generously coat the bottom. Heat it over medium-high heat until a meatball sizzles loudly when placed in the pan. Then add the meatballs in a clockwise fashion starting at the top of the pan, being careful to leave at least 1½ to 2-inches between each.

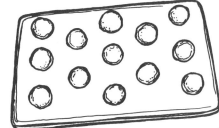

Adjust the heat so that there is a merry sizzling sound and turn the meatballs gently after a few minutes so that all sides brown. The best implement to use is either a soup spoon or a pair of soup spoons, and not a spatula, which is too large to maneuver gracefully around the skillet. Do not turn the meatballs until a dark brown crust has formed on the side touching the pan. Because meatballs are round and the pan is flat it is not easy to brown all sides evenly. Towards the end of the process, use one meatball as a prop for a neighboring meatball to keep it in the proper position.

SIZING UP THE SITUATION

Each recipe in this book tells you what size to make your meatballs, but you can make your meatballs any size you wish. Here is some guidance for measuring the mixture:

- The large side of a melon baller produces a 1-inch meatball.
- A level measuring tablespoon produces a 1½-inch meatball.
- A heaping measuring tablespoon produces a 2-inch meatball.
- A ¼ cup dry measuring cup produces a 2½- to 3-inch meatball.

Perhaps you want to try a recipe that yields 2-inch balls, but you want to serve them smaller and hors d'oeuvre-size at a cocktail party. Look for a similar recipe that makes 1-inch balls, which are a perfect size for a single bite meatball, and follow the cooking time of that recipe. But here are some tips:

- Cut back on cooking time by one-third when cutting the size of a meatball in half. There is not a direct proportion because of the density of most meat mixtures.
- If you want to make a dipping sauce out of a sauce you use for simmering meatballs, add five minutes of cooking time to the meatballs to compensate for the time they would have simmered.
- If you are planning on freezing meatballs, undercook them by a few minutes so that they will not become too dry when reheated. The reheating should complete the cooking.

MEATBALLS TO MEALS

The recipes in this book fall into different categories; some meatballs are meant to be enjoyed as snacks while others are geared to entire meals. A wonderful quality of meatballs is their versatility.

While a meatball sandwich is a tried-and-true favorite, meatballs can also be wrapped in flour tortillas and pita bread. For these types of bread, make the meatballs one inch in diameter.

Meatballs are to spaghetti what chocolate chips are to cookies; they are a natural fit, which is why they are so incredibly popular as combinations. But other carbohydrates and grains are equally good for sopping up a sauce, and many suggestions are given in specific recipes. Couscous, a tiny granular pasta hailing from North Africa, is excellent with Middle Eastern and Mediterranean meatballs; rice is a natural accompaniment for Asian meatballs.

SAFETY FIRST

The first—and most important—requirement for good cooking, whether the food is a few meatballs or a whole roast, is knowing the basic rules of food safety. This begins with trips to the supermarket and ends after leftovers are refrigerated or frozen at the end of a meal.

The sections that follow may seem like common sense, but after many decades as a food writer I've heard horror stories about very sick people, who did not follow basic food safety rules.

If you have any questions about food safety, the U.S. Department of Agriculture is the place to go. The Food Safety Inspection Service was designed to help you. The website, www.fsis.usda.gov, provides a wealth of information in a very user-friendly format.

Shop Safely: Most supermarkets are designed to funnel you into the produce section first. But that's not the best place to start. Begin your shopping with the shelf-stable items from the center, then go to produce, and end with the other refrigerated and frozen sections. Never buy meat or poultry in a package that is torn and leaking, and it's a good idea to place all meats and poultry in the disposable plastic bags available in the produce department if not in the meat department. Check the "sell-by" and "use-by" dates, and never purchase food that exceeds them. The case is always stocked with the least fresh on top, so dig down a few layers and you'll probably find packages with more days of life in them. For the trip home, it's a good idea to carry an insulated cooler in the back of your car if it's hot outside or if the perishable items will be out of refrigeration for more than one hour. In hot weather, many seafood departments will provide crushed ice in a separate bag for your fish.

Banish Bacteria: Fruits and vegetables can contain some bacteria, but it's far more likely that the culprits will grow on meat, poultry, and seafood. Store these foods on the bottom shelves of your refrigerator so their juices cannot accidentally drip on other foods. And keep these foods refrigerated until just before they go into the dish. Bacteria multiply at room temperature. The so-called "danger zone" is between 40°F and 140°F. As food cooks, it's important for it to pass through this zone as quickly as possible.

Avoid Cross-Contamination: Cleanliness is not only next to godliness; it's also the key to food safety. Wash your hands often while you're cooking, and never touch cooked food if you haven't washed your hands after handling raw food.

The "cooked food and raw food shall never meet" precept extends beyond the cook's hands. Clean cutting boards, knives, and kitchen counters often. Or if you have the space, section off your countertops for raw foods and cooked foods, as many restaurant kitchens do. Bacteria from raw animal proteins can contaminate the other foods. So don't place cooked foods or raw foods that will remain uncooked (such as salad) on cutting boards that have been used to cut raw meat, poultry, or fish.

Choose the Right Cutting Board: A good way to prevent food-borne illness is by selecting the right cutting board. Wooden boards might be attractive, but you can never get them as clean as plastic boards that can be run through the dishwasher. Even with plastic boards, it's best to use one for only cooked food and foods such as vegetables that are not prone to contain bacteria, and another one devoted to raw meats, poultry, and fish.

HOW TO USE THIS BOOK

All of the recipes are annotated with the number of servings, which is usually given as a range. If the dish is part of a multi-course meal—or if your table will be occupied by eaters with small appetites—the yield can be "stretched" to feed more people. The recipes for sauces and stocks are given as yields of cups or quarts.

"Active time:" the second annotation, is the amount of hands-on prep time needed in the kitchen when you're slicing and dicing. The third annotation is "Start to finish:" that is the amount of time needed from the moment you start collecting the ingredients to the time you are placing the steaming meatballs on the table. The actual cooking time, as well as any time for chilling, is included in this figure. The unattended time is when you can be reading a book or readying other components of the meal.

GETTING
SAUCY

Many of the individual recipes in this book include a sauce in which the meatballs are cooked or into which they're dipped; this chapter, however, contains some basic recipes for sauces to be used with many of the recipes.

In some recipes, I give you an alternative to making a sauce from scratch. To my taste, the Herbed Tomato Sauce has superior flavor to a purchased marinara sauce, but you may not agree; or you may decide to forego flavor for convenience from time to time. There's no question the supermarket yields a treasure trove of options for dipping meatballs. Here are some examples:

- Any dip used with a potato or tortilla chip can moisten meatballs, including ranch dip, blue cheese dip, or that old standby—onion dip.

- Hummus, the Middle Eastern dip made from chickpeas, now claims its own section in most supermarkets; it comes with many flavors, from roasted garlic to lemon.

- Thick salad dressings such as creamy Italian or Thousand Island work well because they don't drip en route from the bowl to the mouth.

- Barbecue sauces and chutneys can be used straight from the bottle.

- Dry sauce mixes for hollandaise, béarnaise, and brown sauce variations just need to be prepared according to the package instructions.

Herbed Tomato Sauce

Makes 2 cups

Active time:
20 minutes

Start to finish:
1 hour

VARIATIONS

Add basil, rosemary, or marjoram along with or instead of some of the herbs listed.

Add ½ teaspoon crushed red pepper flakes to make the sauce spicier.

Everyone needs a good, basic tomato sauce in his or her repertoire. Add other herbs, spices, and flavorings as you wish.

¼ cup olive oil
1 medium onion, finely chopped
4 garlic cloves, minced
1 carrot, finely chopped
1 celery rib, finely chopped
1 (28-ounce) can crushed tomatoes, undrained
½ cup dry red wine
2 tablespoons chopped fresh parsley
2 tablespoons chopped fresh oregano or 2 teaspoons dried
1 tablespoon fresh thyme or 1 teaspoon dried
2 bay leaves
Salt and freshly ground black pepper to taste

1. Heat olive oil in 2-quart heavy saucepan over medium heat. Add onion and garlic and cook, stirring frequently, for 3 minutes, or until onion is translucent.

2. Add carrot, celery, tomatoes, wine, parsley, oregano, thyme, and bay leaves. Bring to a boil, reduce the heat to low, and simmer sauce, uncovered, stirring occasionally, for 40 minutes, or until lightly thickened. Season to taste with salt and pepper.

Note: The sauce can be refrigerated for up to 4 days, or frozen up to 3 months.

Southern Barbecue Sauce

Makes 2 cups

Active time:
10 minutes

Start to finish:
40 minutes

1⅓ cups ketchup

½ cup cider vinegar

¼ cup firmly packed dark brown
    sugar

3 tablespoons Worcestershire sauce

3 tablespoons grated fresh ginger

2 tablespoons vegetable oil

1 tablespoon dry mustard

2 garlic cloves, minced

1 lemon, thinly sliced

½ to 1 teaspoon hot red pepper
    sauce, or to taste

1. Combine ketchup, vinegar, brown sugar, Worcestershire sauce, ginger, vegetable oil, mustard, garlic, lemon, and red pepper sauce in a saucepan. Bring to a boil over medium heat, stirring occasionally. Reduce the heat to low and simmer sauce, uncovered, for 30 minutes, or until thick, stirring occasionally.

2. Strain sauce, pressing with the back of a spoon to extract as much liquid as possible. Ladle sauce into containers. Refrigerate until ready to use.

Note: The sauce can be refrigerated for up to 2 weeks, or it can be frozen for up to 3 months.

Many companies apply a thin layer of wax on citrus fruits to keep them fresher longer during shipping and storage. That's why rather than just rinsing lemons, I suggest using a mild soap and washing them.

Southwestern Barbecue Sauce

Makes 3 cups

Active time:
15 minutes

Start to finish:
25 minutes

2 tablespoons olive oil

1 large onion, chopped

2 garlic cloves, minced

2 canned chipotle chilies in
   adobo sauce, drained and
   finely chopped

2 cups crushed tomatoes in
   tomato puree

½ cup firmly packed dark brown
   sugar

¼ cup cider vinegar

3 tablespoons freshly squeezed
   lime juice

2 teaspoons dry mustard

Salt and hot red pepper sauce
   to taste

1. Heat oil in a saucepan over medium-high heat. Add onion, garlic, and chilies and cook, stirring frequently, for 5 minutes, or until onion softens. Stir in tomatoes, sugar, vinegar, lime juice, and mustard, and bring to a boil over medium heat, stirring frequently.

2. Reduce the heat to low and simmer sauce, uncovered, for 15 minutes. Keep warm.

Note: The sauce can be refrigerated for up to 2 weeks, or frozen up to 3 months.

When dealing with chipotles in adobo sauce, be sure to scrape off all the sauce from the chilies before chopping them. Otherwise, you'll get even a more fiery flavor. But don't rinse them as that diminishes their smoky nuances.

Blue Cheese Sauce

Makes 2 cups

Active time:

10 minutes

Start to finish:

10 minutes

VARIATIONS

For a low-fat version, substitute non-fat yogurt for both the mayonnaise and sour cream.

Finely chopped scallion tops can be substituted in this or in any recipe in place of chives. Don't use the white part of the scallions; they're too strong.

¾ cup mayonnaise

½ cup sour cream

2 tablespoons white wine vinegar

½ pound blue cheese, crumbled

3 tablespoons chopped fresh chives

Salt and freshly ground black
      pepper to taste

Whisk mayonnaise, sour cream, and vinegar together until smooth. Stir in blue cheese and chives, season to taste with salt and pepper.

Note: The sauce can be refrigerated for up to 4 days.

Dill and Scallion Sauce

Makes 2 cups

**Active time:
10 minutes**

**Start to finish:
10 minutes**

VARIATION

*For a low-fat
version, substitute
non-fat yogurt
for both the
mayonnaise and
sour cream.*

1 cup sour cream

¾ cup mayonnaise

¼ cup freshly squeezed lemon juice

⅓ cup finely chopped scallions,
    white parts and 3 inches
    of green tops

¼ cup chopped fresh dill or
    2 tablespoons dried

2 garlic cloves, minced

Salt and freshly ground black
    pepper to taste

Whisk sour cream, mayonnaise, and lemon juice together until smooth. Stir in scallions, dill, and garlic. Season to taste with salt and pepper. Refrigerate until ready to use.

Note: The sauce can be refrigerated for up to 4 days.

When using dried rather than fresh herbs in a dish, factor in at least 1 hour of time to refrigerate the dish. This will allow the herbs time to infuse flavor in the food.

Sun-Dried Tomato Sauce

Makes 2 cups

Active time:
15 minutes

Start to finish:
15 minutes

1 (8-ounce) package cream cheese,
    softened
½ cup mayonnaise
½ cup sour cream
3 garlic cloves, minced
2 teaspoons herbes de Provence
½ cup sun-dried tomatoes packed
    in oil, drained and diced
4 scallions, white parts and
    2 inches of green tops,
      cut into 1-inch sections
Salt and freshly ground black
    pepper to taste

1. Combine cream cheese, mayonnaise, sour cream, garlic, and herbes de Provence in a food processor fitted with a steel blade. Puree until smooth.

2. Add sun-dried tomatoes and scallions to the work bowl, and chop finely using on-and-off pulsing. Season to taste with salt and pepper, and refrigerate until ready to use.

Note: The sauce can be refrigerated for up to 4 days.

If your sun-dried tomatoes are not packed in olive oil, rehydrate them in boiling water for 10 minutes, then drain them and continue with the recipe. If you use them as they are they will not be chewable in the sauce.

Tartar Sauce

Makes 2 cups

Active time:
10 minutes

Start to finish:
10 minutes

1½ cups mayonnaise

3 scallions, white parts only,
   chopped

¼ cup finely chopped cornichons

3 tablespoons small capers, drained
   and rinsed

2 tablespoons white wine vinegar

2 tablespoons chopped fresh parsley

1 tablespoon smooth Dijon mustard

1 tablespoon chopped fresh tarragon
   or 1 teaspoon dried

Salt and freshly ground black
   pepper to taste

1. Combine mayonnaise, scallions, cornichons, capers, vinegar, parsley, mustard, and tarragon in a mixing bowl. Whisk well, and season to taste with salt and pepper.

2. Refrigerate until ready to use. Note: The sauce can be refrigerated for up to 4 days.

Cornichon is the French word for gherkin, and these sweet-tart pickles are made from tiny cucumbers. You frequently see them served with patés or smoked meats. Small gherkin pickles can be substituted, but don't use commercial pickle relish. It just doesn't have the same depth of flavor.

Remoulade Sauce

Makes 2 cups

Active time:
10 minutes

Start to finish:
10 minutes

VARIATIONS

Add 1 or 2 grated hard-boiled eggs.

Add 2 tablespoons Worcestershire sauce.

1⅓ cups mayonnaise

6 scallions, white parts and
    2 inches of green tops, chopped

3 garlic cloves, minced

¼ cup freshly squeezed lemon juice

3 tablespoons grainy mustard

3 tablespoons chopped fresh parsley

3 tablespoons prepared white
    horseradish

2 tablespoons bottled chili sauce

Salt and freshly ground black
    pepper to taste

Combine mayonnaise, scallions, garlic, lemon juice, mustard, parsley, horseradish, and chili sauce in a mixing bowl. Whisk well, and season to taste with salt and pepper. Refrigerate until ready to use.

Note: The sauce can be refrigerated for up to 4 days.

Easy Aïoli

Makes 2 cups

Active time:
10 minutes

Start to finish:
10 minutes

VARIATIONS

Add 2 tablespoons chili powder.

Add ¼ cup pureed roasted red bell peppers.

1½ cups mayonnaise

6 garlic cloves, minced

3 tablespoons freshly squeezed
   lemon juice

2 tablespoons smooth Dijon
   mustard

Salt and freshly ground black
   pepper to taste

Combine mayonnaise, garlic, lemon juice, and mustard in a mixing bowl. Whisk well, and season to taste with salt and pepper. Refrigerate until ready to use.

Note: The sauce can be refrigerated for up to 4 days.

Aïoli is the most popular sauce in Provence, and it's used for everything from topping a piece of grilled meat to flavoring fish stews and as a dip for vegetables. It's as popular as mustard and ketchup combined in this sunny region of southern France. The only constant ingredients are mayonnaise and garlic. Then there are many variations from village to village.

Creamy Chipotle Sauce

Makes 2 cups

Active time:
10 minutes

Start to finish:
10 minutes

VARIATION

To make a low-fat version, substitute non-fat yogurt for both the mayonnaise and sour cream.

1 cup mayonnaise

⅔ cup sour cream

3 tablespoons freshly squeezed
     lime juice

3 scallions, white parts and
     3 inches of green tops, chopped

3 garlic cloves, minced

3 chipotle chiles in adobo sauce,
     finely chopped

1 teaspoon adobo sauce

Salt to taste

Combine mayonnaise, sour cream, lime juice, scallions, garlic, chiles, and adobo sauce in a mixing bowl. Whisk well, and season to taste with salt. Refrigerate until ready to use.

Note: The sauce can be refrigerated for up to 4 days.

One can of chipotle chiles in adobo sauce lasts a long time; it's rare to use more than three in a recipe. To save the remainder of the can, place three or four chiles with a teaspoon of sauce in ice cube trays. Once frozen transfer them to a heavy-duty resealable plastic bag, and wash the ice cube tray well.

Mexican Tomato Sauce

Makes 2 cups

Active time:
15 minutes

Start to finish:
40 minutes

VARIATIONS

For a spicier sauce, substitute 2 finely chopped canned chipotle chiles in adobo sauce in place of the green chiles.

Substitute red or white wine for the stock.

3 tablespoons olive oil
1 small onion, finely chopped
3 garlic cloves, minced
3 tablespoons chili powder
1 tablespoon ground cumin
1 tablespoon dried oregano
¾ cup chicken stock or vegetable stock
1 (15-ounce) can tomato sauce
1 (4-ounce) can chopped mild green chilies, drained
¼ cup chopped fresh cilantro
Salt and freshly ground black pepper to taste

1. Heat olive oil in a heavy saucepan over medium-high heat. Add onion and garlic and cook, stirring frequently, for 3 minutes, or until the onion is translucent. Reduce the heat to low, stir in the chili powder, cumin, and oregano, and cook, stirring constantly, for 1 minute.

2. Stir in stock, tomato sauce, and green chilies. Whisk well, bring to a boil, and simmer sauce, uncovered, for 15 minutes, stirring occasionally, or until the sauce is reduced by ¼.

3. Stir in cilantro, and season to taste with salt and pepper. Serve hot or at room temperature.

Note: The sauce can be refrigerated for up to 4 days, or freeze it for up to 3 months.

Greek Feta Sauce

Makes 1½ cups

- - - - - - - - - - - - - - -

Active time:
10 minutes

- - - - - - - - - - - - - - -

Start to finish:
10 minutes

VARIATION

To make a low-fat version, substitute more yogurt for the sour cream.

½ pound mild feta cheese, diced
½ cup sour cream
¼ cup plain whole milk yogurt,
    preferably Greek
¼ cup olive oil
2 tablespoons freshly squeezed
    lemon juice
2 garlic cloves, peeled
¼ cup chopped fresh dill or
    2 tablespoons dried
Salt and freshly ground black
    pepper to taste

Combine feta, sour cream, yogurt, olive oil, lemon juice, and garlic in a food processor fitted with a steel blade or in a blender. Puree until smooth. Scrape mixture into a mixing bowl, and stir in dill. Whisk well, and season to taste with salt and pepper. Refrigerate until ready to use.

Note: The sauce can be refrigerated for up to 4 days.

Tahini

Makes 2 cups

Active time:
10 minutes

Start to finish:
10 minutes

1 cup tahini paste

½ cup water

½ cup freshly squeezed lemon juice

3 garlic cloves, peeled

Salt and cayenne to taste

Combine tahini, ½ cup water, lemon juice, garlic, salt, and cayenne in a blender. Blend until smooth, scraping the inside of the jar as necessary. Refrigerate until ready to use.

Note: The sauce can be refrigerated for up to 4 days.

Tahini paste is made from ground sesame seeds, and it has a tendency to separate in the container. Stir it well before measuring. You may have to transfer it to a mixing bowl to stir if the container is very full.

Middle Eastern Yogurt Sauce

Makes 2 cups

- - - - - - - - - - - - - - - - - - -

Active time:
10 minutes

- - - - - - - - - - - - - - - - - - -

Start to finish:
40 minutes

VARIATIONS

Add ¼ cup very finely chopped tomato.

Substitute fresh chopped oregano for the mint.

2 cups plain yogurt
2 scallions, white parts only,
*   chopped*
3 garlic cloves, minced
2 tablespoons finely chopped
*   fresh mint*
1 tablespoon olive oil
Salt and freshly ground black
*   pepper to taste*

1. Place yogurt in a fine-meshed sieve over a mixing bowl, and allow it to drain for 30 minutes at room temperature, or up to 4 hours refrigerated.

2. Discard whey from the mixing bowl, and return yogurt to the bowl. Add scallions, garlic, mint, and olive oil. Whisk well, and season to taste with salt and pepper. Refrigerate until ready to use.

Note: The sauce can be refrigerated for up to 4 days.

Nomadic tribes in the Balkans are thought to have started yogurt-making thousands of years ago, and yogurt is still used extensively in dishes springing from that region. The process probably started by accident, but then the tribesmen realized that it preserved the freshness of milk.

Cucumber Raita

Makes 2 cups

Active time:
10 minutes

Start to finish:
10 minutes

VARIATIONS

Add 1 tablespoon ground cumin and 2 teaspoons ground coriander.

Substitute 3 tablespoons chopped fresh oregano for the dill.

½ medium cucumber, finely chopped

2 ripe plum tomatoes, cored, seeded, and finely chopped

2 scallions, white parts and 3 inches of green tops, finely chopped

2 garlic cloves, minced

1 cup plain yogurt

2 tablespoons chopped fresh dill or 2 teaspoons dried

2 tablespoons freshly squeezed lemon juice

Salt and freshly ground black pepper to taste

Combine cucumber, tomatoes, scallions, garlic, yogurt, dill, and lemon juice in a mixing bowl. Whisk well, and season to taste with salt and pepper. Refrigerate until ready to use.

Note: The sauce can be refrigerated for up to 4 days.

Sesame Honey Mustard Sauce

Makes 2 cups

Active time:
10 minutes

Start to finish:
10 minutes

1 cup Dijon mustard

⅔ cup honey

⅓ cup Asian sesame oil

½ cup chopped fresh cilantro

Salt and freshly ground black
   pepper to taste

Combine mustard, honey, sesame oil, and cilantro in a mixing bowl. Whisk well, and season to taste with salt and pepper. Refrigerate until ready to use.

Note: The sauce can be refrigerated for up to 1 week.

Asian Dipping Sauce

Makes 2 cups

Active time:
10 minutes

Start to finish:
10 minutes

¾ cup unsweetened applesauce

½ cup hoisin sauce

¼ cup firmly packed dark
  brown sugar

6 tablespoons ketchup

2 tablespoons honey

2 tablespoons rice wine vinegar

1 tablespoon soy sauce

1 tablespoon Chinese chili paste
  with garlic, or to taste (hot red
  pepper sauce can be substituted)

Combine applesauce, hoisin sauce, brown sugar, ketchup, honey, vinegar, soy sauce, and chili paste in a mixing bowl. Whisk well, and refrigerate until ready to use.

Note: The sauce can be refrigerated up to 1 week.

Certain foods can be stored for months in the pantry before they are opened but should be refrigerated after opening. Although many of them are marked with that instruction, others frequently are not. Refrigerate mustard, maple syrup, barbecue sauce, Asian condiments such as oyster sauce and hoisin sauce, tortillas, and bottled lemon and lime juice after opening. I also refrigerate expensive olive and nut oils after they've been opened to retard rancidity.

Spicy Thai Peanut Sauce

Makes 2 cups

- -

Active time:
10 minutes

- -

Start to finish:
10 minutes

1 cup chunky peanut butter

½ cup hot water

½ cup firmly packed dark
   brown sugar

⅓ cup freshly squeezed lime juice

¼ cup soy sauce

2 tablespoons Asian sesame oil

2 tablespoons Chinese chili paste
   with garlic

6 garlic cloves, minced

3 scallions, white parts and
   3 inches of green tops, chopped

¼ cup chopped fresh cilantro

Combine peanut butter, ½ cup hot water, brown sugar, lime juice, soy sauce, sesame oil, and chili paste in a mixing bowl. Whisk until well combined. Stir in garlic, scallions, and cilantro. Whisk well again, and refrigerate until ready to use.

Note: The sauce can be refrigerated up to 1 week.

To save time when making a recipe with many liquid ingredients, measure them into the same large cup, calculating what the level should be after each addition.

Sweet and Sour Sauce

Makes 1½ cups

Active time:
15 minutes

Start to finish:
20 minutes

VARIATIONS

Substitute mango or papaya for the pineapple.

Omit the chili paste if you want a sauce with no "heat."

2 tablespoons vegetable oil

4 scallions, white parts and
    2 inches of green tops, chopped

2 garlic cloves, minced

2 tablespoons grated fresh ginger

½ cup finely chopped fresh
    pineapple

½ cup rice vinegar

⅓ cup ketchup

¼ cup firmly packed dark
    brown sugar

2 tablespoons Chinese chili paste
    with garlic

1 tablespoon soy sauce

1 tablespoon cornstarch

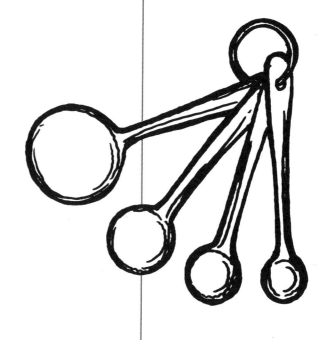

1. Heat oil in a small saucepan over medium-high heat. Add scallions, garlic, and ginger, and cook, stirring frequently, for 3 minutes, or until scallions are translucent.

2. Add pineapple, vinegar, ketchup, sugar, chili paste, and soy sauce to the pan, and stir well. Bring to a boil over medium-high heat, stirring occasionally. Reduce the heat to low, and simmer sauce, uncovered, for 5 minutes.

3. Combine cornstarch and 1 tablespoon water in a small cup, and stir well. Add mixture to the pan, and cook for 1 minute, or until slightly thickened. Serve sauce at room temperature or chilled.

Note: The sauce can be refrigerated up to 1 week.

Easy with the saltshaker if you're making a dish that also lists soy sauce as an ingredient. Soy sauce is very high in sodium and performs the same function as salt in cooking.

Thai Sweet and Spicy Dipping Sauce

Makes 2 cups

Active time:

10 minutes

Start to finish:

10 minutes

1 cup rice wine vinegar

⅔ cup fish sauce (nam pla)

⅓ cup firmly packed dark
   brown sugar

6 garlic cloves, minced

1½ teaspoons crushed red pepper
   flakes, or to taste

Combine vinegar, fish sauce, brown sugar, garlic, and red pepper flakes in a jar with a tight-fitting lid. Shake until sugar is dissolved. Serve at room temperature or chilled. Refrigerate until ready to use.

Note: The sauce can be refrigerated up to 1 week.

Brown sugar is granulated sugar mixed with molasses, and the darker the color the more pronounced the molasses flavor. If you have only light brown sugar and a recipe calls for dark brown sugar, add 2 tablespoons of molasses per half-cup of sugar to replicate the taste.

Ponzu Sauce

Makes 2 cups

Active time:
10 minutes

Start to finish:
10 minutes

½ cup soy sauce

½ cup mirin

½ cup freshly squeezed lemon juice

¼ cup Asian sesame oil

3 tablespoons grated fresh ginger

1 tablespoon grated lemon zest

Combine soy sauce, mirin, lemon juice, sesame oil, ginger, and lemon zest in a jar with a tight-fitting lid. Shake well, and refrigerate until ready to use.

Note: The sauce can be refrigerated up to 1 week.

Mirin is a sweet Japanese wine made from glutinous rice, and it's part of many traditional dishes. You can substitute sweet sherry, adding one tablespoon of granulated sugar to each quarter cup of liquid.

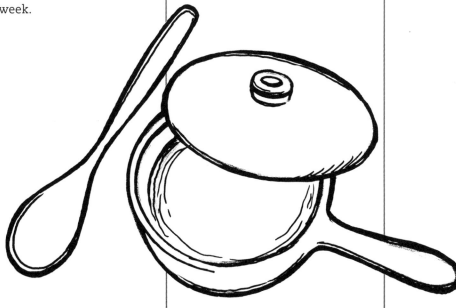

MEATBALLS IN BROTH:

MAIN COURSE SOUPS

There's an old Spanish proverb: "Of soup and love, the first is best." A bowl of steaming soup says "comfort food" on a cold winter's night, and homey meatballs are a welcome addition that can turn a starter into an entire meal. Hearty soups exist in every culture, and you'll find a wide range of recipes in this chapter. The meatballs included in the soups are all made small so that they fit on your soupspoon without cutting.

At the end of the chapter you'll find recipes for homemade stocks. Stocks are the "secret weapon" of why soups and sauces served in fine restaurants are frequently superior to those made at home with canned stocks. If you get into the habit of "stocking up" you will find that while you are gaining nutrients and flavor, you're also saving money. Think about those limp carrots and onion peels destined for the trash. Instead, they can be in your freezer and joined by some chicken bones or shrimp shells, and for pennies you can make a few quarts of stock.

So think about these hearty, healthful soups as a meal in a bowl, and enjoy all the emotional satisfaction that goes along with preparing—and eating—them.

Chicken Vegetable Soup with Matzo Balls

Makes 6 to 8 servings

Active time:
15 minutes

Start to finish:
1½ hours, including 30 minutes for dough to chill

Sometimes dubbed "Jewish Penicillin," a hearty bowl of chicken soup with light and fluffy dumplings made from eggs and ground matzo wafers doesn't need an excuse like a cold to enjoy. You'll find matzo meal in the international food aisle of most supermarkets.

Matzo balls:

4 large eggs

¼ cup chicken stock

¼ cup vegetable oil

1 cup matzo meal

Salt and freshly ground black
    pepper to taste

Soup:

8 cups Chicken Stock (page 100)
    or purchased stock

2 carrots, sliced

1 celery rib, sliced

1 small onion, diced

½ cup fresh peas or frozen peas,
    thawed

½ cup diced fresh string beans
    or frozen beans, thawed

Salt and freshly ground black
    pepper to taste

1. For matzo balls, place eggs in a mixing bowl, and whisk well with stock and oil. Stir in matzo meal, and season to taste with salt and pepper. Refrigerate mixture for at least 30 minutes.

2. Bring a large pot of salted water to a boil. Using wet hands, form matzo dough into 1-inch balls, and drop them into water. Cover the pot, reduce the heat to low, and simmer matzo balls for 35 minutes *without removing the cover from the pot.*

3. While matzo balls simmer, heat stock to a boil over medium-high heat. Add carrots, celery, and onion, reduce the heat to low, and cook vegetables, uncovered, for 10 to 12 minutes, or until carrots are tender. Add peas and string beans, and cook for an additional 5 minutes.

4. Remove matzo balls from the pan with a slotted spoon, and transfer them to soup. Season to taste with salt and pepper, and serve immediately.

Note: The soup can be made up to 2 days in advance and refrigerated, tightly covered. Reheat it over low heat, covered.

Matzo, also spelled matzah, is the traditional unleavened bread eaten by Jews for the week they celebrate Passover each year. The holiday commemorates the Jews' flight from Egypt, when they had no time for their bread to rise.

Spicy Thai Chicken Meatball Soup

Makes 4 to 6 servings

Active time: 20 minutes

Start to finish: 40 minutes

VARIATIONS

A combination of ground shrimp and cod for a lighter flavor.

To add more protein, add 1 cup diced extra-firm tofu to the broth.

Add sliced bok choy to the soup at the same time as the meatballs to increase the vegetable content without diluting the flavor.

Main course soups are part of every Asian cuisine, such as this one drawn from classic Thai cooking. The broth is laced with assertive flavors like ginger and chilies, and the delicate meatballs are cooked right in the soup.

Soup:

1 cup dried shiitake mushrooms

1 cup boiling water

1 (1-ounce) package cellophane noodles

1 cup firmly packed fresh cilantro leaves

1 tablespoon grated fresh ginger

3 garlic cloves, minced

1 jalapeño or serrano chile, seeds and ribs removed, and chopped

2 tablespoons fish sauce (nam pla)

1 tablespoon firmly packed light brown sugar

7 cups Chicken Stock (page 100) or purchased stock

Salt and freshly ground black pepper to taste

Meatballs:

3 tablespoons fish sauce (nam pla)

3 tablespoons cornstarch

1¼ pounds ground chicken

3 garlic cloves, pushed through a garlic press

1 tablespoon Asian sesame oil

For garnish:

Sliced scallions

Fresh cilantro leaves

1. Combine shiitake mushrooms and 1 cup boiling water, pushing them down into the water. Soak for 10 minutes, then drain mushrooms, reserving soaking liquid. Discard stems, and chop mushrooms. Set aside. Strain soaking liquid through a sieve lined with a paper coffee filter or paper towel. While mushrooms soak, follow package directions and soak cellophane

noodles. Drain, and cut into 2-inch lengths with sharp scissors.

2. While ingredients soak, make meatballs. Combine fish sauce and cornstarch in a mixing bowl, and stir well. Add chicken, garlic, and sesame oil, and mix well. Form mixture into ¾-inch balls, and set aside.

3. For soup, combine cilantro, ginger, garlic, chili, fish sauce, and brown sugar in a food processor fitted with a steel blade or in a blender. Puree until smooth. Scrape mixture into a 3-quart saucepan, and stir in chicken stock and reserved mushroom soaking liquid. Bring to a boil over medium-high heat, stirring occasionally.

4. Add meatballs, reduce the heat to low, and cook soup, uncovered, for 5 to 8 minutes, or until meatballs are cooked through and no longer pink. Add noodles and mushrooms, and simmer 2 minutes more. Season to taste with salt and pepper, ladle soup into bowls, and sprinkle each serving with scallions and cilantro.

Note: The soup can be made up to 2 days in advance and refrigerated, tightly covered. Reheat it over low heat, covered.

Fish sauce, also called nam pla, is a salty sauce with an extremely pungent odor made from fermented fish. It's used as a dipping sauce/condiment and seasoning ingredient throughout Southeast Asia. Nam pla is the Thai term; it's known as nuoc nam in Vietnam, and shottsuru in Japan.

Mexican Turkey Meatball Soup

Makes 4 to 6 servings

Active time:
20 minutes

Start to finish:
45 minutes

Crushed corn tortilla chips not only add their earthy flavor to this soup, they also provide some crunch; unlike breadcrumbs, the tortilla chips retain their texture. This is my version of tortilla soup, and the cornucopia of vegetables makes it a meal.

Meatballs:
1 large egg
¼ cup tomato juice
2 garlic cloves, minced
2 teaspoons ground cumin
1 teaspoon dried oregano
1¼ pounds ground turkey
½ cup crushed tortilla chips
Salt and freshly ground black
    pepper to taste
Vegetable oil spray

Soup:
¼ cup olive oil
1 large onion, diced
2 garlic cloves, minced
2 tablespoons chili powder
6 cups Chicken Stock (page 100)
    or purchased stock
2 (14.5-ounce) cans petite diced
    tomatoes, undrained
2 celery ribs, sliced
2 carrots, sliced
1 (15-ounce) can kidney beans,
    drained and rinsed
1 cup fresh corn kernels or frozen
    kernels, thawed
½ cup fresh peas or frozen peas,
    thawed

1. Preheat the oven to 450°F. Cover a rimmed baking sheet with heavy-duty aluminum foil, and spray the foil with vegetable oil spray.

2. Combine egg, tomato juice, garlic, cumin, and oregano in a medium mixing bowl, and whisk well. Add turkey and tortilla chips, season to taste with salt and pepper, and mix well. Make mixture into 1-inch meatballs, and arrange meatballs on the prepared pan. Spray tops of meatballs with vegetable oil spray. Bake meatballs for 12 to 15 minutes.

3. While meatballs bake, heat olive oil in a heavy 3-quart saucepan over medium-high heat. Add onion and garlic, and cook, stirring frequently, for 3 minutes, or until onion is translucent. Stir in chili powder, and cook for 1 minute, stirring constantly. Stir in chicken stock, tomatoes, celery, and carrots.

4. Bring to a boil and simmer soup, uncovered, for 20 minutes, or until vegetables are tender. Add meatballs, kidney beans, corn, and peas to soup, and simmer for 5 minutes. Season to taste with salt and pepper, and serve immediately.

Note: The soup can be made up to 2 days in advance and refrigerated, tightly covered. Reheat it over low heat, covered.

Be careful when adding salt to dishes that contain a salted food such as tortilla chips. Chances are the meatball mixture will need very little, if any, salt because the salt from the chips is part of the mixture.

Italian Wedding Soup with Turkey Meatballs

Makes 6 to 8 servings

**Active time:
20 minutes**

**Start to finish:
1 hour**

Substitute escarole for the curly endive.

Pork, or a combination of pork and veal, are equally delicious for the meatballs.

Wedding soup is actually an Italian-American creation, not a classic Italian dish. It is a mistranslation of *minestra maritata,* which has nothing to do with nuptials but is a reference to the fact that green vegetables and meats go well together. Tasty greens, swirls of egg, lots of heady Parmesan, and flavorful meatballs are what you'll find in this easy to prepare soup. Serve it with a loaf of garlic bread and your meal is complete.

Meatballs:
1 large egg
½ cup seasoned Italian breadcrumbs
¼ cup whole milk
1 small onion, grated
2 garlic cloves, minced
¼ cup chopped fresh Italian parsley
½ cup freshly grated Parmesan
1½ pounds ground turkey
Salt and freshly ground black
    pepper to taste

Soup:
8 cups Chicken Stock (page 100)
    or purchased stock
1 pound curly endive, rinsed, cored,
    and coarsely chopped
2 large eggs
½ cup freshly grated Parmesan,
    divided
Salt and freshly ground black
    pepper to taste

1. Combine egg, breadcrumbs, milk, onion, garlic, parsley, and Parmesan, and mix well. Add turkey, season to taste with salt and pepper, and mix well into a paste.

2. Combine chicken stock and endive in a 3-quart saucepan, and bring to a boil over medium-high heat. Reduce the heat to low, and simmer soup, uncovered, for 10 minutes.

3. Using wet hands, form meatball mixture into 1-inch balls, and drop them into simmering soup. Cook for 7 to 10 minutes, or until cooked through and no longer pink.

4. Whisk eggs with 2 tablespoons cheese. Stir soup and gradually add egg mixture to form thin strands. Season to taste with salt and pepper, and serve immediately, passing remaining cheese separately.

Note: The soup can be made up to 2 days in advance and refrigerated, tightly covered. Reheat it over low heat, covered.

Parmesan cheese is one of the distinctive and delectable ingredients in Italian cooking. Its flavor and aroma, however, dissipate quickly once the cheese is grated. That's why it's worth the effort to grate the real thing—Parmigiano-Reggiano—while cooking each recipe.

Red Lentil Soup with Turkey Meatballs

Makes 4 to 6 servings

Active time:
20 minutes

Start to finish:
50 minutes

Use green, brown, or yellow lentils in place of red ones.

Try dried cranberries or finely chopped dried apricots instead of dried currants.

Ground lamb, ground beef, or a combination of the two makes this a heartier soup.

While Americans are most familiar with brown lentils, ones with vibrant color are part of many of the world's cuisines, such as the red lentils in this thick and rich soup flavored with Middle Eastern spices.

Soup:

3 tablespoons olive oil

1 small onion, finely chopped

1 carrot, finely chopped

1 celery rib, finely chopped

3 garlic cloves, minced

1 tablespoon ground turmeric

2 teaspoons ground cumin

1 teaspoon ground coriander

6 cups Chicken Stock (page 100)
   or purchased stock

1 pound red lentils, rinsed

3 tablespoons chopped fresh parsley

Salt and freshly ground black
   pepper to taste

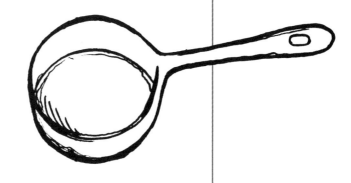

Meatballs:

2 tablespoons olive oil

1 medium onion, finely chopped

2 garlic cloves, minced

1 large egg

½ cup plain breadcrumbs

¼ cup milk

1¼ pounds ground turkey

⅓ cup dried currants

3 tablespoons chopped fresh parsley

Salt and freshly ground black
    pepper to taste

Vegetable oil spray

1. For soup, heat olive oil in a 3-quart saucepan over medium-high heat. Add onion, carrot, celery, and garlic, and cook, stirring frequently, for 3 minutes, or until onion is translucent. Add turmeric, cumin, and coriander, and cook for 1 minute, stirring constantly.

2. Stir in chicken stock, lentils, and parsley, and bring to a boil over medium-high heat, stirring occasionally. Reduce the heat to low, and simmer soup, uncovered, for 20 to 25 minutes, or until lentils are tender. Remove soup from the heat, and set aside.

3. While soup simmers, make meatballs. Preheat the oven to 450°F. Line a rimmed baking sheet with heavy-duty aluminum foil, and spray the foil with vegetable oil spray.

4. Heat oil in a small skillet over medium-high heat. Add onion and garlic, and cook, stirring frequently, for 3 minutes, or until onion is translucent. While vegetables cook, whisk egg in a mixing bowl, and add breadcrumbs and milk. Allow to sit for 5 minutes. Add turkey, dried currants, and parsley, and mix well.

5. Add onion mixture to the mixing bowl, season to taste with salt and pepper, and mix well. Make mixture into 1-inch meatballs, and arrange meatballs on the prepared pan. Spray tops of meatballs with vegetable oil spray.

6. Bake meatballs for 10 to 12 minutes, or until cooked through. Remove the pan from the oven, and set aside. While meatballs bake, carefully puree soup in a

food processor or in a blender; this should be done in batches. Return soup to the saucepan.

7. Add meatballs to soup, season to taste with salt and pepper, and serve immediately.

Note: The soup can be made up to 2 days in advance and refrigerated, tightly covered. Reheat it over low heat, covered.

"Whisk" is both a noun (the item itself) and a verb (what it does). The whisk is a cone made up of interlocking wires that converge in a handle. To whisk is to use the gadget. It should be rotated in a circular motion through the food in the mixing bowl.

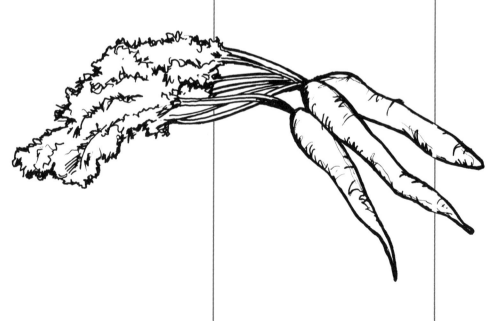

Classic Onion Soup with Gruyère-Beef Meatballs

Makes 6 to 8 servings

Active time:
25 minutes

Start to finish:
1¼ hours

VARIATIONS

Although not classicly French, red onions impart a sweeter flavor.

Instead of Gruyère, try Italian provolone or cheddar in the meatballs.

There's nothing like a steaming bowl of onion soup to warm your body on a winter night, and the addition of hearty meatballs made with Gruyère makes it a meal. The addition of red wine to the stock deepens the color of the soup as well as enhancing its flavor.

Soup:
3 tablespoons unsalted butter
1 tablespoon olive oil
3 pounds yellow onions, thinly sliced
1 teaspoon granulated sugar
3 tablespoons all-purpose flour
2 quarts Beef Stock (page 104) or purchased stock

¾ cup dry red wine
3 tablespoons chopped fresh parsley
1 tablespoon fresh thyme or 1 teaspoon dried
1 bay leaf
Salt and freshly ground black pepper to taste

Meatballs:
3 slices white bread
2 tablespoons whole milk
2 tablespoons unsalted butter
1 small onion, finely chopped
2 garlic cloves, minced
1 large egg
1½ pounds ground chuck
2 tablespoons chopped fresh parsley
¾ cup grated Gruyère
Salt and freshly ground black pepper to taste
Vegetable oil spray

1. For soup, heat butter and oil in a large saucepan over low heat. Add onions, toss to coat with fat, and cover the pan. Cook over low heat for 10 minutes, stirring occasionally. Uncover the pan, raise the heat to medium, and stir in sugar. Cook for 30 to 40 minutes, stirring frequently, until onions are dark brown.

2. Reduce the heat to low, stir in flour, and cook for 2 minutes, stirring constantly. Stir in stock, wine, parsley, thyme, and bay leaf. Bring soup to a boil and simmer, partially covered, for 40 minutes. Season to taste with salt and pepper; remove and discard bay leaf.

3. While soup simmers, prepare meatballs. Preheat the oven to 450°F. Line a rimmed baking sheet with heavy-duty aluminum foil, and spray the foil with vegetable oil spray. Tear bread into small pieces, and place in a bowl with milk; stir well.

4. Heat butter in a small skillet over medium-high heat. Add onion and garlic, and cook, stirring frequently, for 3 minutes, or until onion is translucent. While vegetables cook, whisk egg in a mixing bowl, and add bread mixture, beef, parsley, and cheese.

5. Add onion mixture to the mixing bowl, season to taste with salt and pepper, and mix well. Make mixture into 1-inch meatballs, and arrange meatballs on the prepared pan. Spray tops of meatballs with vegetable oil spray.

6. Bake meatballs for 8 to 10 minutes, or until cooked through. Remove the pan from the oven, and set aside. Add meatballs to soup, season to taste with salt and pepper, and serve immediately.

Note: The soup can be made up to 2 days in advance and refrigerated, tightly covered. Reheat it over low heat, covered.

Out of all the ways I've read to lessen the tear factor of slicing onions, the best one I know is to chill them well in advance. The volatile chemicals that cause all the tears do not escape as readily from a cold onion.

Italian Escarole and Meatball Soup

Makes 6 to 8 servings

Active time:
20 minutes

Start to finish:
45 minutes

VARIATIONS

For a more assertive flavor, make it with collard greens.

For a more delicate flavor and prettier color, use multi-colored Swiss chard.

Similar to Italian Wedding Soup with Turkey Meatballs (page 70), this soup combines meatballs with hearty greens. In this case, no eggs are added to the soup.

Meatballs:
3 tablespoons olive oil
1 large onion, chopped
2 garlic cloves, minced
1 large egg
½ cup seasoned Italian breadcrumbs
¼ cup whole milk
1½ pounds meatloaf mix
    (or ½ pound each of ground beef,
    ground pork, and ground veal)
½ cup freshly grated Parmesan
¼ cup chopped fresh parsley
Salt and freshly ground black
    pepper to taste
Vegetable oil spray

Soup:
1 (1-pound) head escarole
3 tablespoons olive oil
2 large onions, diced
2 garlic cloves, minced
8 cups Chicken Stock (page 100)
    or purchased stock
Salt and freshly ground black
    pepper to taste
For serving: ½ cup freshly grated
    Parmesan

1. Preheat the oven to 450°F. Line a rimmed baking sheet with heavy-duty aluminum foil, and spray the foil with vegetable oil spray.

2. Heat oil in a small skillet over medium-high heat. Add onion and garlic, and cook, stirring frequently, for 3 minutes, or until onion is translucent. While vegetables cook, whisk egg in a mixing bowl, and add breadcrumbs and milk. Stir well. Add meat, Parmesan, and parsley, and mix well.

3. Add onion mixture to mixing bowl, season to taste with salt and pepper, and mix well. Make mixture into 1-inch meatballs, and arrange meatballs on the prepared pan. Spray tops of meatballs with vegetable oil spray.

4. Bake meatballs for 8 to 10 minutes, or until cooked through. Remove the pan from the oven, and set aside.

5. While meatballs bake, prepare soup. Bring a large pot of salted water to a boil. Rinse escarole, discard core, and slice thinly. Blanch escarole for 5 minutes, then drain, and set aside.

6. Heat oil in a 3-quart saucepan over medium-high heat. Add onions and garlic and cook, stirring frequently, for 3 minutes, or until onions are translucent. Add escarole and stock, and bring to a boil over medium-high heat. Reduce the heat to low and simmer soup, uncovered, for 10 minutes. Add meatballs, season to taste with salt and pepper, and serve immediately, passing additional Parmesan separately.

Note: The soup can be made up to 2 days in advance and refrigerated, tightly covered. Reheat it over low heat, covered.

Blanching is a preliminary cooking of green vegetables and some fruits. The food is plunged into rapidly boiling salted water, and then quickly drained. For vegetables the process either removes bitterness or sets a dark green color. For fruits such as peaches and tomatoes, it makes the skins easy to slide off.

Two Mushroom, Barley, and Beef Meatball Soup

Makes 6 to 8 servings

Active time:
20 minutes

Start to finish:
1½ hours

VARIATIONS

The mushroom flavor will be more pronounced if you use chicken stock and make the meatballs from ground turkey rather than beef.

For the ultimate in mushroom flavor, substitute fresh portobello mushrooms for the white mushrooms.

While mushrooms grow everywhere, this thick, hearty soup is most closely identified with Eastern European countries such as Poland and Russia. The combination of aromatic and flavorful dried mushrooms with the delicate flavor and texture of fresh mushrooms makes it a winner.

Soup:

¼ cup dried porcini mushrooms

½ cup boiling water

2 tablespoons vegetable oil

1 large onion, diced

2 carrots, sliced

2 celery ribs, sliced

1 pound white mushrooms, stemmed and sliced

8 cups Beef Stock (page 104) or purchased stock

1 cup whole barley, rinsed well

3 tablespoons chopped fresh parsley

1 tablespoon fresh thyme or 1 teaspoon dried

Salt and freshly ground black pepper to taste

Meatballs:

4 slices white bread

⅓ cup milk

2 tablespoons vegetable oil

1 small onion, finely chopped

2 garlic cloves, minced

1 large egg

1½ pounds ground chuck

2 tablespoons chopped fresh parsley

Salt and freshly ground black
    pepper to taste

Vegetable oil spray

1. For soup, combine porcini mushrooms and ½ cup boiling water, pushing them down into the water. Soak for 10 minutes, then drain mushrooms, reserving soaking liquid, and chop mushrooms. Strain soaking liquid through a paper coffee filter or a paper towel. Set aside.

2. Heat oil in a 3-quart saucepan over medium-high heat. Add onion and cook, stirring frequently, for 3 minutes, or until onion is translucent. Add carrots, celery, mushrooms, stock, barley, parsley, thyme, chopped porcini, and reserved mushroom liquid, and bring to a boil over medium-high

heat. Reduce the heat to low, and simmer soup, covered, for 1 hour, or until vegetables and barley are tender. Season to taste with salt and pepper, and keep hot.

3. While soup simmers, prepare meatballs. Preheat the oven to 450°F. Line a rimmed baking sheet with heavy-duty aluminum foil, and spray the foil with vegetable oil spray. Tear bread into small pieces, and place in a bowl with milk; stir well.

4. Heat oil in a small skillet over medium-high heat. Add onion and garlic, and cook, stirring frequently, for 3 minutes, or until onion is translucent. While vegetables cook, whisk egg in a mixing bowl, and add bread mixture, beef, and parsley.

5. Add onion mixture to the mixing bowl, season to taste with salt and pepper, and mix well. Make mixture into 1-inch meatballs, and arrange meatballs on the prepared pan. Spray tops of meatballs with vegetable oil spray.

6. Bake meatballs for 10 to 12 minutes, or until cooked through. Remove the pan from the oven, and set aside. Add meatballs to soup, season to taste with salt and pepper, and serve immediately.

Note: The soup can be made up to 2 days in advance and refrigerated, tightly covered. Reheat it over low heat, covered.

Barley is one of the oldest grains known to man, dating back to the Stone Age. Even if you think you haven't eaten barley, there's a good chance you've enjoyed it in other forms. Barley is malted to make both beer and whiskey.

Chinese Hot and Sour Soup with Pork Meatballs

Unlike many dishes found on Chinese restaurant menus in North America, hot and sour soup is authentically Chinese; it comes from Szechwan province. The thick and hearty broth and flavorful meatballs are joined by healthful tofu in this satisfying dish.

Makes 4 to 6 servings

Active time:
20 minutes

Start to finish:
40 minutes

VARIATIONS

Make the balls from shrimp or a combination of shrimp and pork.

Add some fresh shiitake mushrooms or dried shiitake which have been rehydrated to the broth.

Meatballs:
½ cup dried shiitake mushrooms
1 cup boiling water
1 large egg
2 tablespoons soy sauce
4 scallions, white parts and
    3 inches of green tops, chopped
2 garlic cloves, minced
1¼ pounds ground pork

1 cup cooked white rice
Freshly ground black pepper to taste
Vegetable oil spray

Soup:
2 tablespoons vegetable oil
2 tablespoons Asian sesame oil
6 scallions, white parts and
    3 inches of green tops, sliced
3 garlic cloves, minced
6 cups Chicken Stock (page 100)
    or purchased
⅓ cup rice wine vinegar
¼ cup soy sauce
2 tablespoons dry sherry
½ to 1 teaspoon freshly ground
    black pepper
½ pound firm tofu, drained, rinsed,
    and cut into ½-inch cubes
2 tablespoons cornstarch
3 large eggs, lightly beaten
Salt and freshly ground black
    pepper to taste

1. Preheat the oven to 450°F. Line a rimmed baking sheet with heavy-duty aluminum foil, and spray the foil with vegetable oil spray.

2. Combine shiitake mushrooms and boiling water, pushing them down into the water. Soak for 10 minutes, then drain mushrooms, reserving soaking liquid. Discard stems, and chop mushrooms. Strain liquid through a sieve lined with a paper coffee filter or paper towel. Set aside.

3. Combine eggs, soy sauce, scallions, and garlic, and whisk well. Add pork, rice, and mushrooms, season to taste with salt, and mix well. Make mixture into 1-inch meatballs, and arrange meatballs on the prepared pan. Spray tops of meatballs with vegetable oil spray.

4. Bake meatballs for 8 to 10 minutes, or until well browned. Remove the pan from the oven, and set aside.

5. While meatballs bake, heat vegetable oil and sesame oil in a heavy 3-quart saucepan over medium-high heat. Add scallions and garlic and cook, stirring frequently, for 1 minute. Stir in chicken stock, rice vinegar, soy sauce, sherry, reserved mushroom soaking liquid, and pepper. Bring to a boil, and simmer soup, uncovered, for 10 minutes. Add tofu and meatballs, and simmer for an additional 10 minutes.

6. Combine cornstarch and 2 tablespoons cold water in a small bowl. Add to soup, and simmer for 2 minutes, or until lightly thickened. Slowly add egg while stirring. Simmer 1 minute, season to taste with salt and pepper, and serve immediately.

Note: The soup can be made up to 2 days in advance and refrigerated, tightly covered. Reheat it over low heat, covered.

Tofu, sometimes called bean curd, is a white custard-like food made in a manner similar to that of cheese. Soy milk, which is a great source of iron and other nutrients, is curdled and then the curds are pressed to extract the whey. The texture depends on how much whey is removed, and can range from very soft to hard.

Greek Lemon Egg Soup with Lamb Meatballs

Makes 4 to 6 servings

Active time:
20 minutes

Start to finish:
30 minutes

VARIATIONS

Not fond of lamb? Make the meatballs from beef or a combination of beef and veal.

Orzo, a rice-shaped pasta, can be used instead of rice, or any chopped cooked pasta works, too.

This soup, called *avgolemono*, is part of classic Greek cooking. It's thick while not too rich, and the key to its flavor is a good chicken stock. Floating in it are subtly seasoned meatballs made from lamb and rice.

Meatballs:

2 tablespoons olive oil

1 medium onion, finely chopped

1 garlic clove, minced

1 large egg

1¼ pounds ground lamb

1 cup cooked white rice

3 tablespoons chopped fresh parsley

1 tablespoon chopped fresh
    rosemary or 1 teaspoon dried

Salt and freshly ground black
    pepper to taste

Vegetable oil spray

Soup:

7 cups Chicken Stock (page 100)
    or purchased stock

4 large eggs

⅓ cup freshly squeezed lemon juice

½ teaspoon grated lemon zest

Salt and freshly ground black
    pepper to taste

1. Preheat the oven to 450°F. Line a rimmed baking sheet with heavy-duty aluminum foil, and spray the foil with vegetable oil spray.

2. For meatballs, heat oil in a small skillet over medium-high heat. Add onion and garlic, and cook, stirring frequently, for 3 minutes, or until onion is translucent. While vegetables cook, whisk eggs in a mixing bowl, and add lamb, rice, parsley, and rosemary.

3. Add onion mixture to mixing bowl, season to taste with salt and pepper, and mix well. Make mixture into 1-inch meatballs, and arrange meatballs on the prepared pan. Spray tops of meatballs with vegetable oil spray.

4. Bake meatballs for 10 to 12 minutes, or until cooked through. Remove the pan from the oven, and set aside.

5. While meatballs bake, bring stock to a boil over medium-high heat. While stock heats, whisk eggs well with lemon juice and lemon zest. Remove the pan from the heat, and stir for 45 seconds to cool soup. The liquid should not be bubbling or simmering at all. Stir in egg mixture, cover the pan, and let soup sit for 5 minutes to thicken.

6. Season soup to taste with salt and pepper, add meatballs, and serve immediately.

Note: The soup can be prepared 1 day in advance and refrigerated, tightly covered. Reheat it over very low heat, stirring frequently, and do not allow it to boil or the eggs will scramble.

Mexican Albondigas Soup with Chorizo Meatballs

Makes 6 to 8 servings

Active time: 25 minutes

Start to finish: 50 minutes

Filled with healthful vegetables and legumes, this soup is enriched by the flavor in the meatballs from the earthy and spicy chorizo sausage. Serve with some corn tortillas and a tomato salad.

Soup:

2 tablespoons olive oil

1 large onion, diced

2 garlic cloves, minced

1 jalapeño or serrano chile, seeds and ribs removed, and finely chopped

2 carrots, diced

2 celery ribs, sliced

8 cups Chicken Stock (page 100) or purchased stock

1 (14.5-ounce) can diced tomatoes, undrained

2 small zucchini, trimmed and diced

1 (15-ounce) can garbanzo beans, drained and rinsed

Salt and freshly ground black pepper to taste

Meatballs:

¼ cup olive oil

3 garlic cloves, peeled

1 cup firmly packed fresh cilantro leaves

1 pound ground pork

½ pound chorizo, removed from casings, if necessary

1 large egg, lightly beaten

½ cup plain breadcrumbs

Salt and freshly ground black pepper to taste

Vegetable oil spray

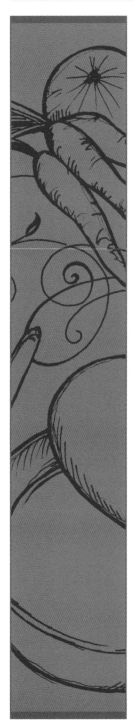

1. For soup, heat oil in a 3-quart saucepan over medium-high heat. Add onion, garlic, and chile, and cook, stirring frequently, for 3 minutes, or until onion is translucent. Add carrots, celery, stock, and tomatoes, and bring to a boil over medium-high heat. Reduce the heat to low, and simmer soup, covered, for 15 minutes. Add zucchini and garbanzo beans, and simmer for an additional 10 minutes, or until vegetables are tender. Keep soup hot.

2. While soup simmers, make meatballs. Preheat the oven to 450°F. Line a rimmed baking sheet with heavy-duty aluminum foil, and spray the foil with vegetable oil spray.

3. Combine oil, garlic, and cilantro in a blender or food processor, and puree until smooth. Combine puree, pork, chorizo, egg, and breadcrumbs in a mixing bowl, and mix well. Season to taste with salt and pepper. Make mixture into 1-inch meatballs, and arrange meatballs on the prepared pan. Spray tops of meatballs with vegetable oil spray.

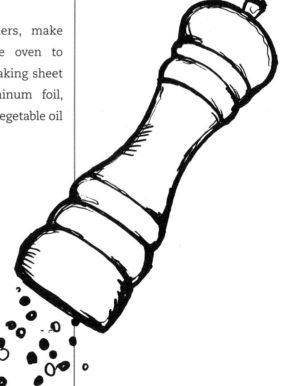

4. Bake meatballs for 8 to 10 minutes, or until cooked through. Add meatballs to soup, season to taste with salt and pepper, and serve immediately.

Note: The soup can be made up to 2 days in advance and refrigerated, tightly covered. Reheat it over low heat, covered.

Chorizo is a highly-seasoned pork sausage flavored with garlic, chili powder, and other spices. It's used in both Mexican and Spanish cooking, and if you can't find it look for its cousin from the Iberian Peninsula, linguiça.

Chinese Vegetable Soup with Shrimp and Pork Meatballs

Makes 6 to 8 servings

Active time:
25 minutes

Start to finish:
55 minutes

VARIATIONS

Some rehydrated shiitake mushrooms can be added.

Add some fresh spinach leaves to the broth to up the nutrient content without changing the flavor.

Use ground turkey instead of the pork and shrimp as the protein in the meatballs.

This is one of my favorite meals to eat when I'm dieting; it contains very few calories, the vegetables are crunchy so there is textural variation to the eating experience, and the broth makes it very filling—as well as delicious.

Meatballs:
2 tablespoons soy sauce
2 tablespoons cornstarch
3 large egg whites
1 tablespoon Asian sesame oil
3 scallions, white parts and
    3 inches of green tops, chopped
3 tablespoons chopped fresh cilantro
1 tablespoon grated fresh ginger
2 garlic cloves, minced
1 pound ground pork
½ pound finely chopped shrimp
½ cup finely chopped water
    chestnuts
Salt and freshly ground black
    pepper to taste

Soup:

7 cups Chicken Stock (page 100)
    or purchased stock

6 scallions, white parts and
    2 inches of green tops, chopped

2 garlic cloves, minced

1 tablespoon grated fresh ginger

2 tablespoons soy sauce

1 large carrot, cut into a fine
    julienne

2 cups chopped bok choy or
    Napa cabbage

1 cup thinly sliced snow peas

Salt and freshly ground black
    pepper to taste

Garnish:

Additional chopped scallions

1. For meatballs, mix soy sauce with cornstarch. Combine egg whites, soy sauce mixture, sesame oil, scallions, cilantro, ginger, and garlic in a mixing bowl, and whisk well. Add pork, shrimp, and water chestnuts, season to taste with salt and pepper, and mix well into a paste. Chill mixture for 30 minutes.

2. For soup, combine chicken stock, scallions, garlic, ginger, soy sauce, and carrot in a 3-quart saucepan, and bring to a boil over medium-high heat. Reduce the heat to low, and simmer soup, uncovered, for 10 minutes.

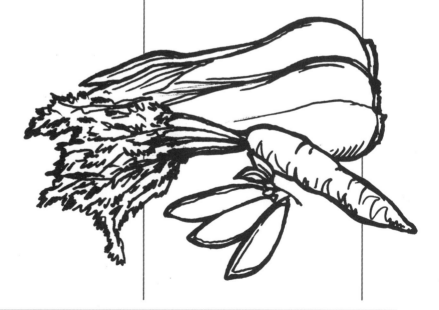

3. Using wet hands, form meatball mixture into 1-inch balls, and drop them into simmering soup. Cook for 7 to 10 minutes, or until cooked through and no longer pink. Add bok choy and snow peas, and simmer for 2 minutes. Season to taste with salt and pepper, and serve immediately, garnished with additional scallions.

Note: The soup can be made up to 2 days in advance and refrigerated, tightly covered. Reheat it over low heat, covered.

Julienne is a long, rectangular cut used for vegetables. For hard vegetables like carrots or potatoes, trim them so that the sides are straight, which will make it easier to make even cuts. Slice the vegetable length-wise, using parallel cuts of the proper thickness. Stack the slices, aligning the edges, and make parallel cuts of the same thickness through the stack.

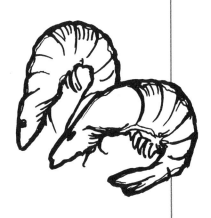

New England Chowder with Clam Fritters

Makes 4 to 6 servings

Active time:
25 minutes

Start to finish:
50 minutes

Early chowder recipes call for everything from beer to ketchup, but not milk. What we know as New England chowder dates from the mid-nineteenth century. One of the greatest convenience foods on the market is shucked and pre-minced quahog or cherrystone clams; you'll find them in the seafood department.

Soup:
1 pint fresh chopped clams
4 tablespoons (½ stick) unsalted butter, divided
2 medium onions, diced
2 celery ribs, sliced
1 (8-ounce) bottle clam juice
2 medium red potatoes, cut into ½-inch dice
2 tablespoons chopped fresh parsley
1 bay leaf
1 tablespoon fresh thyme or 1 teaspoon dried
Salt and freshly ground black pepper to taste
3 tablespoons all-purpose flour
2 cups whole milk
1 cup heavy cream or half-and-half

Fritters:
1 large egg
¾ cup whole milk
1½ cups all-purpose flour
1½ teaspoons baking powder
2 scallions, white parts only, finely chopped
Salt and freshly ground black pepper to taste
3 cups vegetable oil for frying

VARIATIONS

Fry ½ pound bacon, cut into 1-inch lengths in a skillet until crisp. Remove bacon from the pan with a slotted spoon, and discard all but 4 tablespoons bacon fat. Cook vegetables in bacon fat rather than butter, crumble cooked bacon, and add it to soup along with clam fritters.

Add ½ cup cooked corn kernels to the soup, along with ¼ cup sautéed chopped red bell pepper.

1. For soup, drain clams in a sieve over a bowl, reserving juice in the bowl. Press down with the back of a spoon to extract as much liquid as possible from clams. Refrigerate clams until ready to use.

2. Melt 2 tablespoons butter in a large saucepan over medium heat. Add onions and celery, and cook, stirring frequently, for 3 minutes, or until onions are translucent. Add bottled clam juice and reserved clam juice to the pan, along with potatoes, parsley, bay leaf, and thyme. Bring to a boil, reduce the heat to low, and simmer, covered, for 12 minutes, or until potatoes are tender.

3. While mixture simmers, melt remaining 2 tablespoons butter in a small saucepan over low heat. Stir in flour and cook, stirring constantly, for 2 minutes. Raise the heat to medium and whisk in milk. Bring to a boil, whisking frequently, and simmer for 2 minutes. Stir thickened milk into the pot with vegetables, and add cream. Bring to a boil, reduce the heat to low, and simmer, uncovered, for 3 minutes. Remove and discard bay leaf, season to taste with salt and pepper, and keep hot.

4. While vegetables simmer, make clam fritters. Combine egg and milk in a mixing bowl, and whisk well. Add flour and baking powder, and whisk well. Stir in reserved clams and scallions, and season to taste with salt and pepper.

5. Preheat the oven to 150°F. Line a baking sheet with paper towels. Heat oil in a deep-sided saucepan over medium-high heat to a temperature of 375°F. Drop fritter batter by 1-tablespoon amounts into hot oil, and fry for 2 to 3 minutes, or until golden brown, turning as necessary with a slotted spoon. Remove fritters, and drain on paper towel–lined baking sheet. Place fritters in the oven, and repeat until all batter is fried.

6. To serve, ladle soup into bowls, and top each serving with fritters.

Note: The soup can be made up to 2 days in advance and refrigerated, tightly covered. Reheat it over low heat, covered. Do not make fritters until just before serving.

In Melville's *Moby Dick*, Ishmael and Queequeg land on Nantucket and are sent to Hosea Hussey's Try Pots; the name comes from the black iron cauldron used aboard whale ships for melting blubber to liquid oil. Melville writes that "fishiest of all fishy places was the Try Pots. Chowder for breakfast, and chowder for dinner, and chowder for supper."

Manhattan Chowder with Clam Fritters

Makes 4 to 6 servings

Active time:
30 minutes

Start to finish:
45 minutes

Adding tomatoes and other vegetables to chowder is considered heresy in New England, but this version is popular from the Mid-Atlantic states and further south. While named for New York, legend has it that the chowder was actually developed by the Portuguese settlers in Rhode Island in the late eighteenth century.

Soup:
2 tablespoons olive oil
1 medium onion, diced
½ green or red bell pepper, seeds
    and ribs removed, and chopped
2 celery ribs, sliced

2 medium red potatoes, cut into
    ⅓-inch dice
1 pint fresh minced clams, drained,
    with juice reserved
2 (8-ounce) bottles clam juice
1 (14.5-ounce) can diced tomatoes,
    preferably petite diced, undrained
3 tablespoons chopped fresh parsley
1 tablespoon fresh thyme or
    1 teaspoon dried
Salt and freshly ground black
    pepper to taste

Fritters:
1 large egg
¾ cup whole milk
1½ cups all-purpose flour
1½ teaspoons baking powder
2 scallions, white parts only,
    finely chopped
Salt and freshly ground black
    pepper to taste
3 cups vegetable oil for frying

VARIATIONS

For some Southwestern flavor add 2 tablespoons chili powder and 1 tablespoon ground cumin to the sautéed vegetables. Cook over low heat, stirring constantly, for 1 minute. Then add ½ cup corn kernels to the soup.

For an Italian-style soup, add ¼ cup chopped fresh basil with the other herbs.

1. For soup, drain clams in a sieve over a bowl, reserving juice in the bowl. Press down with the back of a spoon to extract as much liquid as possible from clams. Refrigerate clams until ready to use.

2. Heat oil in a heavy 2-quart saucepan over medium-high heat. Add onion, bell pepper, and celery. Cook, stirring frequently, for 3 minutes, or until onion is translucent. Add potatoes, juice from fresh clams, bottled clam juice, tomatoes, parsley, and thyme to the pan. Bring to a boil, reduce the heat to low, and simmer for 10 minutes, stirring occasionally, or until potatoes are tender. Season to taste with salt and pepper, and keep hot.

3. While vegetables simmer, make clam fritters. Combine egg and milk in a mixing bowl, and whisk well. Add flour and baking powder, and whisk well. Stir in reserved clams and scallions, and season to taste with salt and pepper.

4. Preheat the oven to 150°F. Line a baking sheet with paper towels.

Heat oil in a deep-sided saucepan over medium-high heat to a temperature of 375°F. Drop fritter batter by 1–tablespoon amounts into hot oil, and fry for 2 to 3 minutes, or until golden brown, turning as necessary with a slotted spoon. Remove fritters, and drain on paper towel-lined baking sheet. Place fritters in the oven, and repeat until all batter is fried.

5. To serve, ladle soup into bowls, and top each serving with fritters.

Note: The soup can be made up to 2 days in advance and refrigerated, tightly covered. Reheat it over low heat, covered. Do not make fritters until just before serving.

Clementine Paddleford was a flowery New York restaurant critic in the early twentieth century. She once wrote that "chowder breathes reassurance. It steams consolation."

Chicken Stock

Makes 3 quarts

Active time:
10 minutes

Start to finish:
3½ hours

Richly flavored, homemade chicken stock is as important as good olive oil in my kitchen, and it's as easy to make as boiling water. I never buy chicken to make stock, since there are always scraps left over from cooking chicken. Keep a plastic bag in your freezer for the skin and other tidbits that are trimmed off chicken before it's cooked. When the bag is full, it's time to make stock.

5 pounds chicken bones, skin, and trimmings

4 celery ribs, cut into thick slices

2 onions, quartered

2 carrots, cut into thick slices

2 tablespoons whole black peppercorns

6 garlic cloves, peeled

4 sprigs parsley

4 sprigs thyme or 1 teaspoon dried

2 bay leaves

1. Place 6 quarts water and chicken in a large stockpot, and bring to a boil over high heat. Reduce the heat to low, and skim off foam that rises during the first 10 to 15 minutes of simmering. Simmer stock, uncovered, for 1 hour, then add celery, onions, carrots, peppercorns, garlic, parsley, thyme, and bay leaves. Simmer for 2½ hours.

2. Strain stock through a fine-meshed sieve, pushing with the back of a spoon to extract as much liquid as possible. Discard solids, divide stock among small plastic containers, and refrigerate. Remove and discard fat from surface of stock.

Note: The stock can be refrigerated and used within 3 days, or it can be frozen up to 6 months.

Quick Chicken Stock

Makes 2 quarts

Active time:
10 minutes

Start to finish:
30 minutes

It's happened to me, too. I go to the freezer for a quart of chicken stock and discover that the larder is bare. Here's a way to make a reasonable facsimile of stock in just a few minutes.

2 quarts canned low-sodium
    chicken stock
4 celery ribs, finely chopped
1 onion, diced
2 carrots, finely chopped
2 tablespoons whole black
    peppercorns
6 garlic cloves, peeled
4 sprigs parsley
4 sprigs thyme or 1 teaspoon dried
2 bay leaves

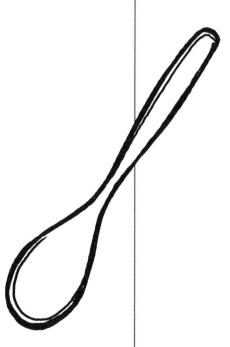

1. Combine stock, celery, onion, carrots, peppercorns, garlic, parsley, thyme, and bay leaves in a large stockpot, and bring to a boil over high heat. Reduce the heat to low, cover the pan, and simmer 20 minutes.

2. Strain stock through a fine-meshed sieve, pressing with the back of a spoon to extract as much liquid as possible. Divide stock into small plastic containers, and refrigerate when cool.

Note: The stock can be refrigerated and used within 3 days, or it can be frozen up to 6 months.

If you've got some limp carrots or celery ribs in the refrigerator, they're still good for making stock. Add them to the bag with your chicken scraps. Using onion skins in a stock imparts a rich brown color.

Beef Stock

Makes 2 quarts

Active time:
15 minutes

Start to finish:
3½ hours

Browning the meat adds a rich brown color and slightly caramelized flavor to this stock, which is the backbone of so many meat-based recipes. When cutting up a chuck roast to make stew, or trim fat off of beef before broiling it, save those scraps to add to your stock.

2 pounds beef shank
    (or 1 pound beef stew meat
    or chuck roast)
1 carrot, cut into thick slices
1 medium onion, sliced
1 celery rib, sliced
1 tablespoon whole black
    peppercorns
3 sprigs fresh parsley
3 sprigs fresh thyme or
    1 teaspoon dried
2 garlic cloves, peeled
1 bay leaf

1. Preheat the oven broiler. Line a broiler pan with heavy-duty aluminum foil. Broil beef for 3 minutes per side, or until browned. Transfer beef to a large stockpot, and add 2 quarts water. Bring to a boil over high heat. Reduce the heat to low, and skim off foam that rises during the first 10 to 15 minutes of simmering. Simmer for 1 hour, uncovered, then add carrot, onion, celery, peppercorns, parsley, thyme, garlic, and bay leaf. Simmer for 3 hours.

2. Strain stock through a fine-meshed sieve, pushing with the back of a spoon to extract as much liquid as possible. Discard solids, divide stock among small plastic containers, and refrigerate. Before using, remove and discard fat from surface of stock.

Note: The stock can be refrigerated and used within 3 days, or it can be frozen up to 6 months.

Vegetable Stock

Makes 2 quarts

Active time:
10 minutes

Start to finish:
1¼ hours

Agood vegetable stock creates a depth of flavor not found when cooking with water. Feel free to add different vegetables to the stock; parsnips, lettuce cores, or zucchini can enhance the flavor. Don't, however, include any members of the cabbage family, such as broccoli and Brussels sprouts; they will dominate the taste.

2 carrots, thinly sliced

2 celery ribs, sliced

2 leeks, white parts only,
    thinly sliced

1 small onion, thinly sliced

1 tablespoon whole black
    peppercorns

3 sprigs fresh parsley

3 sprigs fresh thyme or
    1 teaspoon dried

2 garlic cloves, peeled

1 bay leaf

1. Pour 3 quarts water into a stockpot, and add carrots, celery, leeks, onion, peppercorns, parsley, thyme, garlic, and bay leaf. Bring to a boil over high heat, then reduce the heat to low and simmer stock, uncovered, for 1 hour.

2. Strain stock through a fine-meshed sieve, pushing with the back of a spoon to extract as much liquid as possible. Discard solids, divide stock among small plastic containers, and refrigerate.

Note: The stock can be refrigerated and used within 3 days, or it can be frozen up to 6 months.

Seafood Stock

Makes 2 quarts

Active time:
15 minutes

Start to finish:
1¾ hours

If your fish market sells cooked lobster meat or shrimp, chances are they will give you any leftover shells necessary for making homemade seafood stock either for free or at a very reasonable cost.

3 lobster bodies (whole lobsters
    from which the tail and claw
    meat has been removed) or
    2 lobster bodies and the shells
    from 2 pounds raw shrimp
1 cup dry white wine
1 carrot, cut into 1-inch chunks
1 medium onion, sliced
1 celery stalk, sliced
1 tablespoon whole black
    peppercorns
3 sprigs fresh parsley
3 sprigs fresh thyme or
    1 teaspoon dried
2 garlic cloves, peeled
1 bay leaf

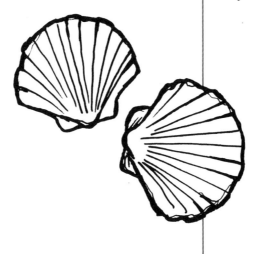

1. Pull top shell off a lobster body. Scrape off and discard feathery gills, then break body into small pieces. Place pieces into a 3-quart saucepan, and repeat with remaining lobster bodies. Add shrimp shells, if used.

2. Pour 2 quarts water and wine into the saucepan, and add carrots, onion, celery, peppercorns, parsley, thyme, garlic, and bay leaf. Bring to a boil over high heat, then reduce the heat to low and simmer stock, uncovered, for 1½ hours.

3. Strain stock through a fine-meshed sieve, pushing with the back of a spoon to extract as much liquid as possible. Discard solids, divide stock among small plastic containers, and refrigerate.

Note: The stock can be refrigerated and used within 3 days, or it can be frozen up to 6 months.

Seafood stock is perhaps the hardest to make if you don't live near the coast. A good substitute is bottled clam juice. Use it in place of the water, and simmer it with vegetables and wine, as in the Quick Chicken Stock (page 100), to intensify its flavor.

Now That's a Meatball:

International

Beef Meatballs

Meatballs from ground beef are an essential part of every American cook's repertoire; a meatball recipe was probably the first dish many learned to cook. During my childhood beef was the only ground meat found in the supermarket except for sausage, so occasionally those two would be combined. While that is hardly the case today, and later chapters feature recipes for everything from pork and veal to lamb and poultry, the stars of the recipes in this chapter is beef.

In today's economy enjoying beef in its ground form is one of the most economical ways to serve it. While chuck roasts and other cuts for pot roasts and stews cost about the same as ground chuck, they take far longer to cook. Almost all of the recipes in this chapter can be on the table in less than one hour; that's about one-third the time it takes to produce a stew or braised dish.

Again, returning to the memories of my childhood, ground beef was pretty much the only option. Today's meat case is filled with a dizzying array of packages with various fat contents and ground from various parts of the cow. My choice is always ground chuck, which is used in these recipes because it has the best beefy flavor and is reasonably priced. While you can spend far more on ground sirloin, I don't think it has the inherent taste of ground chuck.

Blue Cheese Beef Meatballs

Makes 4 to 6 servings

Active time:
15 minutes

Start to finish:
30 minutes

Blue cheese is a natural pairing with hearty beef. The meatballs are dipped in a light blue cheese sauce to add moisture and reinforce the sharp cheesy flavor.

3 slices white bread

⅓ cup whole milk

2 tablespoons unsalted butter

1 small onion, finely chopped

2 garlic cloves, minced

1 large egg

2 tablespoons chopped fresh parsley

¾ cup crumbled blue cheese

1 tablespoon fresh thyme
     or 1 teaspoon dried

1¼ pounds ground chuck

Salt and freshly ground black
     pepper to taste

Vegetable oil spray

For dipping:

1 cup Blue Cheese Sauce (page 41)
     or purchased blue cheese
     dressing

VARIATIONS

Ground turkey can be substituted for the beef. Cook turkey to an internal temperature of 160°F on an instant-read thermometer or until cooked through and no longer pink.

Also, any blue-veined cheese —from Italian Gorgonzola to English stilton —works well in this recipe.

1. Preheat the oven to 450°F. Line a rimmed baking sheet with heavy-duty aluminum foil, and spray the foil with vegetable oil spray. Tear bread into small pieces, and place bread in a bowl with milk; stir well.

2. Heat butter in a small skillet over medium-high heat. Add onion and garlic, and cook, stirring frequently, for 3 minutes, or until onion is translucent. While vegetables cook, whisk egg in a mixing bowl, and add bread mixture, parsley, cheese, and thyme, and mix well.

3. Add onion mixture and beef to the mixing bowl, season to taste with salt and pepper, and mix well again. Make mixture into 1½-inch meatballs, and arrange meatballs on the prepared pan. Spray tops of meatballs with vegetable oil spray.

4. Bake meatballs for 12 to 15 minutes, or until cooked through. Remove the pan from the oven, and serve immediately, accompanied by a bowl of Blue Cheese Sauce for dipping.

Note: The beef mixture can be prepared up to 1 day in advance and refrigerated, tightly covered. Also, the meatballs can be baked up to 2 days in advance and refrigerated, tightly covered. Reheat them in a 350°F oven, covered, for 10 to 12 minutes, or until hot.

The blue veins that appear in blue cheese are actually a mold that is a member of the penicillin family. In some cases the fresh cheese is injected with the mold spores, while in other cases the mold is mixed right into the curds.

Beef Meatball Stroganoff

Makes 4 to 6 servings

Active time:
20 minutes

Start to finish:
45 minutes

VARIATIONS

Make the meatballs from ground turkey or ground veal, and then substitute chicken stock for the beef stock.

Add ½ pound sautéed mushrooms to the sauce.

Beef Stroganoff, supposedly named for a European prince, was the epitome of elegant dinner party fare back in the 1960s when I learned to cook. It, like quiche, got a bad rap as a cliché, but it's really delicious; serve it over buttered egg noodles.

2 tablespoons olive oil
2 large onions, chopped
3 garlic cloves, minced
1 large egg
2 tablespoons whole milk
½ cup plain breadcrumbs
1¼ pounds ground chuck
Salt and freshly ground black
    pepper to taste
2 tablespoons unsalted butter
3 tablespoons all-purpose flour
1½ cups beef stock
2 tablespoons tomato paste
1 tablespoon Dijon mustard
½ cup sour cream
2 tablespoons chopped fresh parsley
Vegetable oil spray

1. Preheat the oven broiler. Line a rimmed baking sheet with heavy-duty aluminum foil, and spray the foil with vegetable oil spray.

2. Heat oil in a skillet over medium-high heat. Add onion and garlic and cook, stirring frequently, for 3 minutes, or until onion is translucent. While vegetables cook,

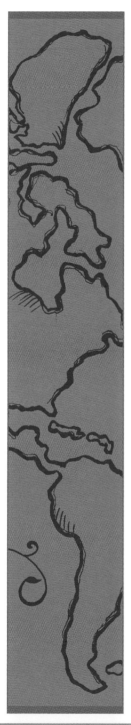

combine egg and milk in a mixing bowl, and whisk until smooth. Add breadcrumbs to the mixing bowl, and mix well.

3. Add ½ of onion mixture and beef, season to taste with salt and pepper, and mix well again. Make mixture into 2-inch meatballs, and arrange meatballs on the prepared pan. Spray tops of meatballs with vegetable oil spray.

4. Broil meatballs 6 inches from the broiler element, turning them with tongs to brown all sides. While meatballs brown, add butter to the skillet containing remaining onions and garlic. Add flour, and cook over low heat for 2 minutes, stirring constantly. Add stock in a slow stream, whisking constantly, and bring to a boil. Whisk in tomato paste and mustard. Reduce the heat and simmer, whisking occasionally, for 3 minutes.

5. Remove meatballs from the baking pan with a slotted spoon, and add meatballs to sauce. Bring to a boil, and simmer meatballs, covered, over low heat, turning occasionally with a slotted spoon, for 15 minutes. Stir in sour cream and parsley, and serve immediately. *Do not allow sauce to boil.*

Note: The meatball mixture can be prepared up to 1 day in advance and refrigerated, tightly covered. Also, the dish can be cooked up to 2 days in advance and refrigerated, tightly covered. Reheat in a 350°F oven, covered, for 15 to 20 minutes, or until hot.

A sauce made with sour cream can't be allowed to boil, or else the sour cream will curdle and separate in the sauce. If you worry about reheating a dish such as this one, try making the sauce with crème fraîche instead; it has almost a similar flavor but won't curdle.

Peppery Mustard Beef Meatballs

Makes 4 to 6 servings

Active time:
15 minutes

Start to finish:
30 minutes

Use lamb in place of the beef; omit the capers and add 2 tablespoons chopped fresh rosemary (or 2 teaspoons dried rosemary) to the meat mixture.

A touch of heady red wine, some herbs, and piquant capers flavor these hearty beef meatballs that are similar in flavor to the classic French steak au poivre. Just put them out with additional Dijon mustard for dipping.

1 large egg
¼ cup dry red wine
½ cup plain breadcrumbs, divided
2 tablespoons grainy Dijon mustard
2 shallots, finely chopped
2 garlic cloves, minced
2 tablespoons small capers, drained,
    rinsed, and chopped
1 tablespoon fresh thyme or
    1 teaspoon dried
1¼ pounds ground chuck
Salt to taste
3 tablespoons coarsely ground
    mixed peppercorns
Vegetable oil spray

For dipping:
½ cup Dijon mustard

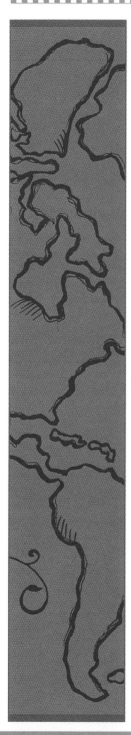

1. Preheat the oven to 450°F. Line a rimmed baking sheet with heavy-duty aluminum foil, and spray the foil with vegetable oil spray.

2. Combine egg and wine in a mixing bowl, and whisk well. Add ¼ cup breadcrumbs, mustard, shallots, garlic, capers, and thyme, and mix well. Add beef, season to taste with salt, and mix well again.

3. Combine remaining ¼ cup breadcrumbs and pepper in a small bowl. Form meat mixture into 1½-inch meatballs, and roll meatballs in pepper mixture. Arrange meatballs on the prepared pan, and spray tops of meatballs with vegetable oil spray.

4. Bake meatballs for 12 to 15 minutes, or until cooked through. Serve immediately accompanied by a bowl of additional Dijon mustard for dipping.

Note: The beef mixture can be prepared up to 1 day in advance and refrigerated, tightly covered. Also, the meatballs can be baked up to 2 days in advance and refrigerated, tightly covered. Reheat them in a 350°F oven, covered, for 10 to 12 minutes or until hot.

Shepherd's Pie with Meatballs and Cheddar-Mashed Potato Topping

Makes 6 to 8 servings

Active time: 25 minutes

Start to finish: 1¼ hours

Shepherd's pie is a classic served at pubs throughout Great Britain since the eighteenth century. It was originally created as an economical way to use up the leftovers from the traditional "Sunday joint," which was a leg of lamb served with potatoes and vegetables. Here, flavorful meatballs in a rich brown gravy with vegetables are then crowned with a layer of cheddar-flavored mashed potatoes for this all-in-one dinner, perfect for a chilly fall or winter night. A tossed green salad is all you need.

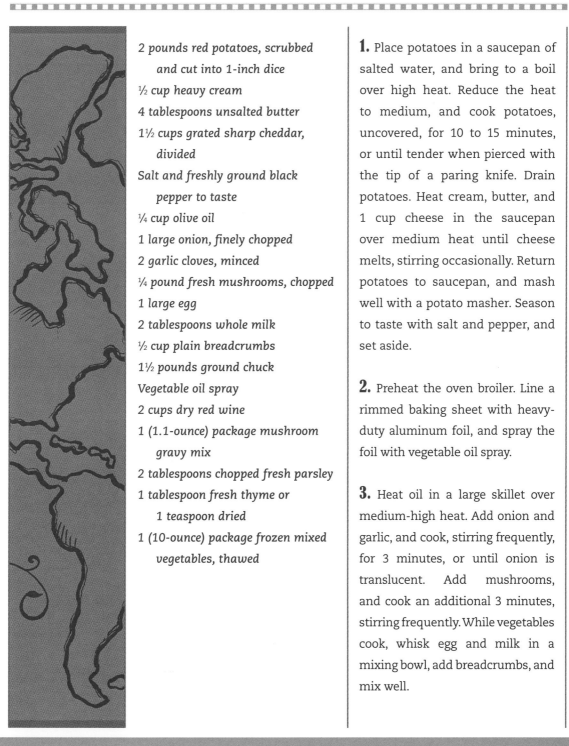

2 pounds red potatoes, scrubbed
	and cut into 1-inch dice
½ cup heavy cream
4 tablespoons unsalted butter
1½ cups grated sharp cheddar,
	divided
Salt and freshly ground black
	pepper to taste
¼ cup olive oil
1 large onion, finely chopped
2 garlic cloves, minced
¼ pound fresh mushrooms, chopped
1 large egg
2 tablespoons whole milk
½ cup plain breadcrumbs
1½ pounds ground chuck
Vegetable oil spray
2 cups dry red wine
1 (1.1-ounce) package mushroom
	gravy mix
2 tablespoons chopped fresh parsley
1 tablespoon fresh thyme or
	1 teaspoon dried
1 (10-ounce) package frozen mixed
	vegetables, thawed

1. Place potatoes in a saucepan of salted water, and bring to a boil over high heat. Reduce the heat to medium, and cook potatoes, uncovered, for 10 to 15 minutes, or until tender when pierced with the tip of a paring knife. Drain potatoes. Heat cream, butter, and 1 cup cheese in the saucepan over medium heat until cheese melts, stirring occasionally. Return potatoes to saucepan, and mash well with a potato masher. Season to taste with salt and pepper, and set aside.

2. Preheat the oven broiler. Line a rimmed baking sheet with heavy-duty aluminum foil, and spray the foil with vegetable oil spray.

3. Heat oil in a large skillet over medium-high heat. Add onion and garlic, and cook, stirring frequently, for 3 minutes, or until onion is translucent. Add mushrooms, and cook an additional 3 minutes, stirring frequently. While vegetables cook, whisk egg and milk in a mixing bowl, add breadcrumbs, and mix well.

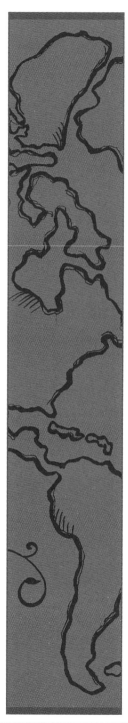

4. Add onion mixture and beef to the mixing bowl, season to taste with salt and pepper, and mix well again. Make mixture into 1½-inch meatballs, and arrange meatballs on the prepared pan. Spray tops of meatballs with vegetable oil spray.

5. Broil meatballs 6 inches from the broiler element, turning them with tongs to brown all sides. Remove meatballs from baking pan with a slotted spoon, and set aside.

6. Combine wine, gravy mix, parsley, and thyme in a saucepan, and whisk well. Bring to a boil over medium-high heat, whisking frequently, and simmer over low heat for 2 minutes.

7. Preheat the oven to 400°F, and grease a 9 x 13-inch baking pan. Arrange meatballs in the pan, and pour sauce over them. Cover the pan with heavy-duty aluminum foil, and bake for 15 minutes. Stir in the mixed vegetables, and bake an additional 10 minutes.

8. Increase the oven temperature to 450°F. Spread potato mixture on top of meatballs, and sprinkle with remaining ½ cup cheese. Bake for 15 minutes, or until top is golden. Serve immediately.

Note: The meatball mixture can be prepared up to 1 day in advance and refrigerated, tightly covered. Also, the dish can be cooked up to 2 days in advance and refrigerated, tightly covered. Reheat in a 350°F oven, covered, for 15 to 20 minutes, or until hot.

Provençal Beef Meatballs with Red Wine Sauce

Makes 4 to 6 servings

Active time:
20 minutes

Start to finish:
1¼ hours

VARIATIONS

Add ½ pound sautéed sliced mushrooms to the sauce.

Cut red potatoes into 1-inch cubes, and bake them in the dish along with the meatballs and sauce.

Think of this dish as a meatball version of the classic French boeuf bourguignon; the meatballs are cooked in a mixture of red wine and herbs. Serve the meatballs over buttered egg noodles or mashed potatoes and accompanied with a Burgundy wine. In a dish such as this one in which the meatballs are merely browned but not cooked through initially, the dish must be cooked to completion before refrigerating. The partially cooked meatballs contain raw egg, and can cause illness.

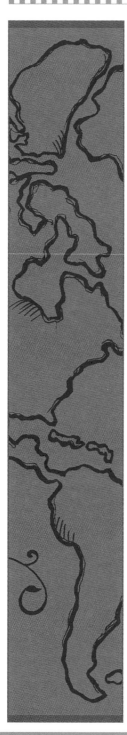

3 tablespoons unsalted butter

1 medium onion, chopped

2 garlic cloves, minced

1 large egg

¼ cup whole milk

½ cup plain breadcrumbs

3 tablespoons chopped fresh parsley

1 tablespoon fresh thyme or
    1 teaspoon dried

1¼ pounds ground chuck

Salt and freshly ground black
    pepper to taste

Vegetable oil spray

1¼ cups dry red wine

1 cup beef stock

3 tablespoons tomato paste

1 tablespoon herbes de Provence

1 cup grated Gruyère

1. Preheat the oven broiler. Line a rimmed baking sheet with heavy-duty aluminum foil, and spray the foil with vegetable oil spray.

2. Heat butter in a small skillet over medium-high heat. Add onion and garlic and cook, stirring frequently, for 3 minutes, or until onion is translucent. While vegetables cook, combine egg and milk in a mixing bowl, and whisk until smooth. Add breadcrumbs, parsley, and thyme, and mix well.

3. Add onion mixture and beef, season to taste with salt and pepper, and mix well again. Make mixture into 2-inch meatballs, and arrange meatballs on the prepared pan. Spray tops of meatballs with vegetable oil spray.

4. Broil meatballs 6 inches from the broiler element, turning them with tongs to brown all sides. Remove meatballs from the broiler, and transfer to a 9 x 13-inch pan. Preheat the oven to 375°F.

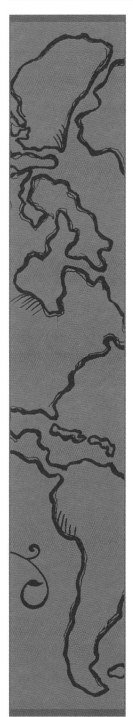

5. Whisk wine, stock, tomato paste, and herbes de Provence in a mixing bowl, and season to taste with salt and pepper. Pour mixture over meatballs. Cover the pan with aluminum foil, and bake for 30 minutes. Remove the pan from the oven, sprinkle cheese on top, and bake for an additional 15 minutes, or until cheese is melted and bubbly. Serve immediately.

Note: The meatball mixture can be prepared up to 1 day in advance and refrigerated, tightly covered. Also, the dish can be cooked up to 2 days in advance and refrigerated, tightly covered. Reheat in a 350°F oven, covered, for 15 to 20 minutes, or until hot.

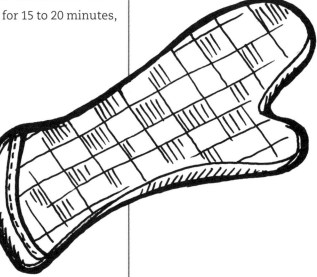

Wild Mushroom and Caramelized Onion Beef Meatballs

Makes 4 to 6 servings

Active time:
30 minutes

Start to finish:
45 minutes

VARIATION

Ground lamb can be substituted for the beef.

Between the sweet brown onions, the woodsy mushrooms, and the heady cheese there is so much flavor in these meatballs that they need no additional sauce for dipping or topping. Serve them with mashed potatoes and a green salad.

3 tablespoons olive oil
2 tablespoons (¼ stick) unsalted
   butter
2 large onions, diced
Salt and freshly ground black
   pepper to taste
2 teaspoons granulated sugar
½ pound fresh shiitake mushrooms
2 garlic cloves, minced
1 large egg
½ cup plain breadcrumbs
3 tablespoons whole milk
½ cup grated Gruyère
2 teaspoons fresh thyme or
   1 teaspoon dried
1¼ pounds ground chuck
Vegetable oil spray

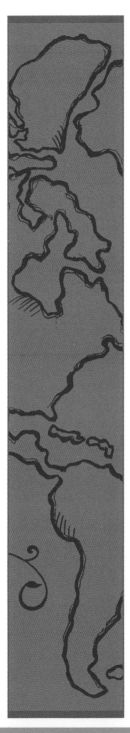

1. Heat oil and butter in a large skillet over medium heat. Add onions, and toss to coat. Cover the pan, and cook onions for 10 minutes, stirring occasionally. Sprinkle onions with salt, pepper, and sugar, and raise the heat to medium-high. Cook onions for 10 to 15 minutes, or until brown.

2. While onions cook, wipe mushrooms with a damp paper towel, discard stems, and chop finely. Preheat the oven to 450°F. Line a rimmed baking sheet with heavy-duty aluminum foil, and spray the foil with vegetable oil spray.

3. Add mushrooms and garlic to the skillet, and cook, stirring frequently, for 5 to 7 minutes or until mushrooms are soft.

4. Combine egg, breadcrumbs, milk, cheese, and thyme in a mixing bowl, and mix well. Add beef and vegetables, season to taste with salt and pepper, and mix well again. Make mixture into 1½-inch meatballs, and arrange meatballs on the prepared pan. Spray tops of meatballs with vegetable oil spray.

5. Bake meatballs for 12 to 15 minutes, or until cooked through. Remove the pan from the oven, and serve immediately.

Note: The beef mixture can be prepared up to 1 day in advance and refrigerated, tightly covered. Also, the meatballs can be baked up to 2 days in advance and refrigerated, tightly covered. Reheat them in a 350°F oven, covered, for 10 to 12 minutes, or until hot.

> The process of cooking vegetables covered over low heat is called "sweating," although it has nothing to do with exercise. The purpose of this initial covered cooking is to soften the vegetables without letting them brown; this facilitates the browning later on.

Mustard-Dill Beef Meatballs

Makes 4 to 6 servings

Active time:
15 minutes

Start to finish:
30 minutes

VARIATIONS

For a lighter dish, replace the beef with ground turkey or ground pork.

Many Scandinavian dishes feature aromatic dill. The freshness of the dill is a nice balance with the sharpness of the mustard.

2 tablespoons unsalted butter
1 small onion, chopped
2 garlic cloves, minced
½ cup beef stock
1 large egg
2 tablespoons Dijon mustard
3 slices seeded rye bread
¼ cup chopped fresh dill
1¼ pounds ground chuck
Salt and freshly ground black
*   pepper to taste*
Vegetable oil spray

For dipping:
1 cup Dill and Scallion Sauce
*   (page 42)*

1. Preheat the oven to 450°F. Line a rimmed baking sheet with heavy-duty aluminum foil, and spray the foil with vegetable oil spray.

2. Heat butter in a small skillet over medium-high heat. Add onion and garlic and cook, stirring frequently, for 3 minutes, or until onion is translucent. While vegetables cook, combine stock, egg, and mustard in a mixing bowl, and whisk until smooth. Tear bread into small pieces, and add to the bowl, along with dill, and mix well.

3. Add shallot mixture and beef, season to taste with salt and pepper, and mix well again. Make mixture into 1½-inch meatballs, and arrange meatballs on the prepared pan. Spray tops of meatballs with vegetable oil spray.

4. Bake meatballs for 12 to 15 minutes, or until cooked through. Remove the pan from the oven, and serve immediately, accompanied by a bowl of Dill and Scallion Sauce for dipping.

Note: The beef mixture can be prepared up to 1 day in advance and refrigerated, tightly covered. Also, the meatballs can be baked up to 2 days in advance and refrigerated, tightly covered. Reheat them in a 350°F oven, covered, for 10 to 12 minutes, or until hot.

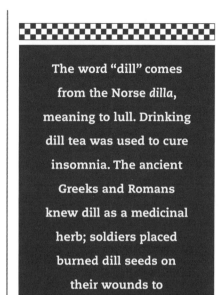

The word "dill" comes from the Norse *dilla*, meaning to lull. Drinking dill tea was used to cure insomnia. The ancient Greeks and Romans knew dill as a medicinal herb; soldiers placed burned dill seeds on their wounds to promote healing.

Beef Meatballs with Mustard and Dried Apricots

Makes 4 to 6 servings

Active time: 15 minutes

Start to finish: 30 minutes

VARIATION

Make these meatballs with ground pork or ground turkey.

These are one of my favorite hors d'oeuvre to serve at a cocktail party; the combination of the dried apricots with the sharp mustard makes each morsel a flavorful bite.

3 tablespoons olive oil

2 large shallots, chopped

2 garlic cloves, minced

1 large egg

⅓ cup Dijon mustard, divided

3 tablespoons whole milk

¾ cup panko breadcrumbs

½ cup finely chopped dried apricots

2 tablespoons chopped fresh sage
   or 2 teaspoons dried

2 tablespoons chopped fresh cilantro

1¼ pounds ground chuck

Salt and freshly ground black
   pepper to taste

½ cup apricot preserves

½ teaspoon hot red pepper sauce

Vegetable oil spray

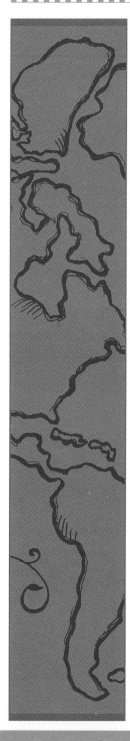

1. Preheat the oven to 450°F. Line a rimmed baking sheet with heavy-duty aluminum foil, and spray the foil with vegetable oil spray.

2. Heat oil in a small skillet over medium-high heat. Add shallots and garlic and cook, stirring frequently, for 5 minutes, or until shallots are soft. While vegetables cook, combine egg, ¼ cup mustard, and milk in a mixing bowl, and whisk until smooth. Add breadcrumbs, dried apricots, sage, and cilantro, and mix well.

3. Add shallot mixture and beef, season to taste with salt and pepper, and mix well again. Make mixture into 1½-inch meatballs, and arrange meatballs on the prepared pan. Spray tops of meatballs with vegetable oil spray.

4. Bake meatballs for 12 to 15 minutes, or until cooked through. While meatballs bake, combine remaining mustard, apricot preserves, and hot red pepper sauce in a small mixing bowl, and whisk well.

5. Remove the pan from the oven, and serve immediately accompanied by the bowl of apricot mustard sauce.

Note: The beef mixture can be prepared up to 1 day in advance and refrigerated, tightly covered. Also, the meatballs can be baked up to 2 days in advance and refrigerated, tightly covered. Reheat them in a 350°F oven, covered, for 10 to 12 minutes, or until hot.

Since Japanese panko breadcrumbs are fluffier than Western breadcrumbs, they produce a lighter and more tender meatball. Substitute them for plain breadcrumbs in any recipe in this book.

Scandinavian Beef Meatballs in Sour-Cherry Sauce

Makes 4 to 6 servings

- - - - - - - - - - - - - - - - -

Active time:
25 minutes

- - - - - - - - - - - - - - - - -

Start to finish:
50 minutes

VARIATION

Make the meatballs from a combination of ground pork and ground beef; it will be lighter and the fruit flavor will seem more intense.

Northern European cuisines, such as those from the Scandinavian countries as well as Germany and Austria, frequently use fruit in savory dishes, like the dried cherries here. Serve these meatballs over buttered egg noodles and with a carrot or parsnip puree.

If you have trouble finding dried sour cherries, use dried sweet cherries or dried cranberries. Add two tablespoons of freshly squeezed lemon juice to the sauce to compensate.

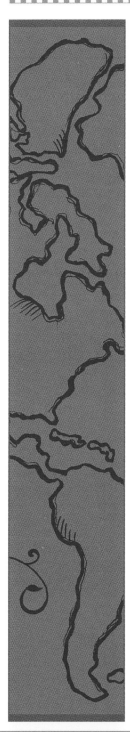

1½ cups dried sour cherries

2 cups beef stock, divided

¼ cup olive oil

2 medium onions, chopped

1 small carrot, chopped

1 large egg

½ cup plain breadcrumbs

2 garlic cloves, minced

¾ teaspoon ground cinnamon

½ teaspoon ground ginger

Pinch of ground allspice

1¼ pounds ground chuck

Salt and freshly ground black
    pepper to taste

1 tablespoon cornstarch

1 tablespoon kirsch

Vegetable oil spray

1. Combine dried cherries and 1¾ cups beef stock in a saucepan, and bring to a boil over medium-high heat. Remove the pan from the heat, and allow cherries to soak. Heat oil in a large skillet over medium-high heat, add onions and carrot, and cook, stirring frequently, for 3 minutes, or until onions are translucent. Add cherries and stock, bring to a boil, and simmer sauce, covered, for 15 minutes.

2. While sauce simmers, preheat the oven broiler. Line a rimmed baking sheet with heavy-duty aluminum foil, and spray the foil with vegetable oil spray.

3. Combine egg and remaining ¼ cup stock in a mixing bowl, and whisk until smooth. Add breadcrumbs, garlic, cinnamon, ginger, and allspice, and mix well. Add beef, season to taste with salt and pepper, and mix well again. Make mixture into 1½-inch meatballs, and arrange meatballs on the prepared pan. Spray tops of meatballs with vegetable oil spray.

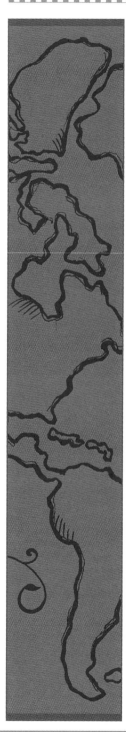

4. Broil meatballs 6 inches from the broiler element, turning them with tongs to brown all sides. Remove meatballs from baking pan with a slotted spoon, and add meatballs to sauce. Bring to a boil, and simmer meatballs, covered, over low heat, turning occasionally with a slotted spoon, for 15 minutes.

5. Combine cornstarch and kirsch in a small bowl, and stir well. Add mixture to sauce, and simmer, uncovered, for 2 minutes, or until slightly thickened. Serve immediately.

Note: The meatball mixture can be prepared up to 1 day in advance and refrigerated, tightly covered. Also, the dish can be cooked up to 2 days in advance and refrigerated, tightly covered. Reheat in a 350°F oven, covered, for 15 to 20 minutes, or until hot.

Beef Meatballs with Apples and Raisins

Makes 4 to 6 servings

Active time: 25 minutes

Start to finish: 1½ hours

VARIATIONS

Instead of raisins, use chopped dried apricots, dried cranberries, or some combination of dried fruit.

Instead of beef, make the dish with ground turkey, ground veal, or some combination of the two.

This is one of my favorite all-time dishes, and both my sister and I remember it from childhood as the filling for blanched cabbage leaves. I dispensed with the cabbage wrappers many years ago, and just revel in the sweet and sour flavors of the sauce.

1¼ pounds ground chuck
1 cup cooked white rice
1 small onion, grated
2 garlic cloves, minced
Salt and freshly ground black pepper to taste
3 Golden Delicious apples, peeled, cored, and diced
¾ cup raisins
1 (15-ounce) can tomato sauce
¾ cup cider vinegar
¾ cup firmly packed dark brown sugar
Vegetable oil spray

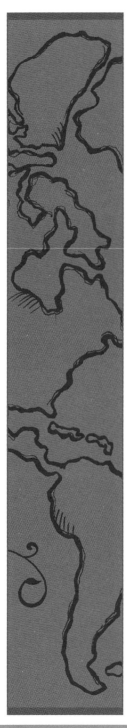

1. Preheat the oven broiler. Line a rimmed baking sheet with heavy-duty aluminum foil, and spray the foil with vegetable oil spray.

2. Combine beef, rice, onion, garlic, salt, and pepper in a mixing bowl, and mix well. Make mixture into 2-inch meatballs, and arrange meatballs on the prepared pan. Spray tops of meatballs with vegetable oil spray.

3. Broil meatballs 6 inches from the broiler element, turning them with tongs to brown all sides. Remove the pan from the oven, and set aside. Preheat the oven to 375°F, and grease a 9 x 13-inch pan.

4. Place apples and raisins on the bottom of the prepared pan, and place meatballs on top. Combine tomato sauce, vinegar, and brown sugar in a mixing bowl, and whisk well. Pour mixture over meatballs.

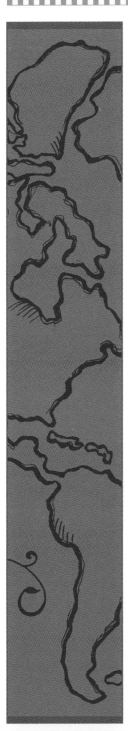

5. Cover the pan with foil, and bake for 30 minutes. Remove the foil, and bake for an additional 30 minutes, or until apples are soft. Serve immediately.

Note: The meatball mixture can be prepared up to 1 day in advance and refrigerated, tightly covered. Also, the dish can be cooked up to 2 days in advance and refrigerated, tightly covered. Reheat in a 350°F oven, covered, for 15 to 20 minutes, or until hot.

The German language has a few terms for meatball. They are sometimes called *frikadellen*, primarily in the northern part of the country, or *hackbällchen* in other areas, such as those adjoining Austria.

Beef Meatball Hungarian Goulash

Makes 4 to 6 servings

Active time: 25 minutes

Start to finish: 45 minutes

VARIATION

Make the meatballs from ground turkey or ground pork.

Goulash is the native stew of Hungary, and almost all meats end up cooked this flavorful way. Serve these meatballs over some buttered egg noodles with a steamed green vegetable for a contrasting color and flavor.

2 tablespoons olive oil

2 large onions, chopped

3 garlic cloves, minced

1 large egg

2 tablespoons whole milk

2 slices seeded rye bread

1¼ pounds ground chuck

Salt and freshly ground black pepper to taste

5 tablespoons paprika, preferably Hungarian

2 tablespoons tomato paste

2 cups beef stock

2 teaspoons crushed caraway seeds

¾ cup sour cream

Vegetable oil spray

1. Preheat the oven broiler. Line a rimmed baking sheet with heavy-duty aluminum foil, and spray the foil with vegetable oil spray.

2. Heat oil in a skillet over medium-high heat. Add onion and garlic and cook, stirring frequently, for 3 minutes, or until onion is translucent. While vegetables cook, combine egg and milk in a mixing

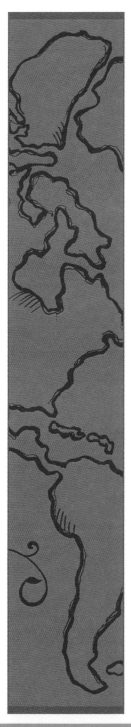

bowl, and whisk until smooth. Break bread into tiny pieces and add to mixing bowl, and mix well.

3. Add ½ of onion mixture and beef, season to taste with salt and pepper, and mix well again. Make mixture into 2-inch meatballs, and arrange meatballs on the prepared pan. Spray tops of meatballs with vegetable oil spray.

4. Broil meatballs 6 inches from the broiler element, turning them with tongs to brown all sides. While meatballs brown, add paprika to the skillet containing remaining onions and garlic. Cook over low heat for 1 minute, stirring constantly. Add tomato paste, stock, and caraway seeds, and whisk well. Bring to a boil over medium-high heat, stirring occasionally.

5. Remove meatballs from the baking pan with a slotted spoon, and add meatballs to sauce. Bring to a boil, and simmer the meatballs, covered, over low heat, turning occasionally with a slotted spoon, for 15 minutes. Stir in sour cream,

and serve immediately. *Do not allow sauce to boil.*

Note: The meatball mixture can be prepared up to 1 day in advance and refrigerated, tightly covered. Also, the dish can be cooked up to 2 days in advance and refrigerated, tightly covered. Reheat in a 350°F oven, covered, for 15 to 20 minutes, or until hot.

Paprika is a powder made by grinding aromatic sweet red pepper pods several times. The color can vary from deep red to bright orange, and the flavor ranges from mild to pungent and hot. Hungarian cuisine is characterized by paprika as a flavoring, and Hungarian paprika is considered the best.

Herbed Italian Beef Meatballs

Makes 4 to 6 servings

Active time:
20 minutes

Start to finish:
35 minutes

VARIATIONS

Make the meatballs with a combination of ground beef, ground pork, and Italian sausage.

Make the meatballs with ground turkey.

A combination of different herbs, various vegetables, and two cheeses give these easy meatballs tremendous flavor. They make a great hors d'oeuvre, or you can keep them in the freezer to use on pizza or to top spaghetti.

3 slices white bread
3 tablespoons whole milk
3 tablespoons olive oil
1 small onion, finely chopped
2 garlic cloves, minced
1 small carrot, grated
1 large egg
3 tablespoons chopped fresh parsley
2 tablespoons chopped fresh basil
    or 2 teaspoons dried
1 tablespoon chopped fresh oregano
    or 1 teaspoon dried
½ cup grated whole milk mozzarella
¼ cup freshly grated Parmesan
1¼ pounds ground chuck
Salt and freshly ground black
    pepper to taste
Vegetable oil spray

For dipping:
1 cup Herbed Tomato Sauce
    (page 38) or any purchased
    marinara sauce, heated

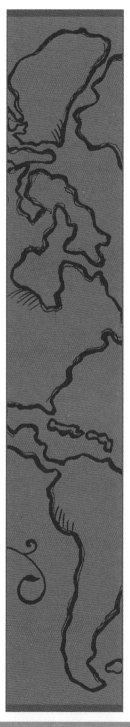

1. Preheat the oven to 450°F. Line a rimmed baking sheet with heavy-duty aluminum foil, and spray the foil with vegetable oil spray. Tear bread into small pieces, and place bread in a bowl with milk; stir well.

2. Heat oil in a small skillet over medium-high heat. Add onion, garlic, and carrot, and cook, stirring frequently, for 3 minutes, or until onion is translucent. While vegetables cook, whisk egg in a mixing bowl, and add bread mixture, parsley, basil, oregano, mozzarella, and Parmesan, and mix well.

3. Add onion mixture and beef to the mixing bowl, season to taste with salt and pepper, and mix well again. Make mixture into 1½-inch meatballs, and arrange meatballs on the prepared pan. Spray tops of meatballs with vegetable oil spray.

4. Bake meatballs for 12 to 15 minutes, or until cooked through. Remove the pan from the oven, and serve immediately, accompanied by a bowl of Herbed Tomato Sauce for dipping.

Note: The beef mixture can be prepared up to 1 day in advance and refrigerated, tightly covered. Also, the meatballs can be baked up to 2 days in advance and refrigerated, tightly covered. Reheat them in a 350°F oven, covered, for 10 to 12 minutes, or until hot.

A great way to grate cheese, especially hard cheeses like Parmesan, is in a food processor. If grating cheese by hand with a box grater, spray some vegetable oil spray on the blades and the cheese will be easier to grate.

Southwestern Barbecued Beef Meatballs

Makes 4 to 6 servings

Active time:
20 minutes

Start to finish:
35 minutes

These easy-to-make meatballs contain a wide range of popular Southwestern flavors —from fiery chiles to creamy cheese and lots of herbs and spices. Serve them with a basket of warm flour tortillas for making burritos.

1 large egg

2 chipotle chiles in adobo sauce

2 tablespoons whole milk

½ cup plain breadcrumbs

½ cup grated jalapeño Jack cheese

3 tablespoons chopped fresh cilantro

3 tablespoons diced canned mild green chiles, drained

4 garlic cloves, minced

1 tablespoon dried oregano

1 tablespoon Spanish smoked paprika

2 teaspoons ground cumin

1¼ pounds ground chuck

Salt and freshly ground black pepper to taste

Vegetable oil spray

For dipping:
1 cup Southwestern Barbecue Sauce (page 39) or bottled salsa, heated

VARIATIONS

Make lighter meatballs by using ground turkey in place of the beef.

Adjust the spiciness by using plain Monterey Jack cheese rather than the jalapeño version and serving with a mild barbecue sauce, such as the Southern Barbecue Sauce (page 00).

1. Preheat the oven to 450°F. Line a rimmed baking sheet with heavy-duty aluminum foil, and spray the foil with vegetable oil spray.

2. Combine egg, chipotle chiles, milk, and breadcrumbs in a food processor or in a blender, and puree until smooth. Scrape mixture into a mixing bowl. Add cheese, cilantro, green chiles, garlic, oregano, paprika, and cumin, and mix well.

3. Add beef, season to taste with salt and pepper, and mix well again. Make mixture into 1½-inch meatballs, and arrange meatballs on the prepared pan. Spray tops of meatballs with vegetable oil spray.

4. Bake meatballs for 12 to 15 minutes, or until cooked through. Remove the pan from the oven, and serve immediately accompanied by a bowl of Southwestern Barbecue Sauce for dipping.

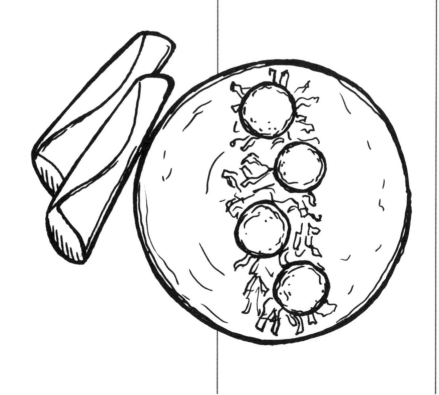

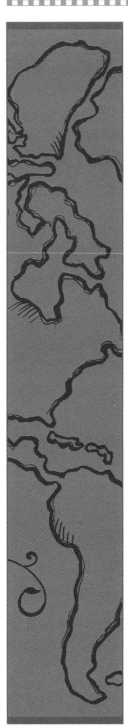

Note: The meatball mixture can be prepared up to 1 day in advance and refrigerated, tightly covered. Also, the dish can be cooked up to 2 days in advance and refrigerated, tightly covered. Reheat in a 350°F oven, covered, for 15 to 20 minutes, or until hot.

Those small cans of chiles can look a lot alike, especially when you're in a hurry. Make sure you buy is the mild green chiles, not diced jalapeño peppers. You'd be in for a surprise.

Spicy Mexican Smoked Cheddar-Beef Meatballs

Makes 4 to 6 servings

Active time:
25 minutes

Start to finish:
40 minutes

The bacon adds a smoky nuance to these spicy meatballs, which are delicious served with Mexican rice or saffron rice and some sautéed zucchini. And beer is the best beverage to accompany them.

¼ pound bacon, cut into thin slivers
1 medium onion, chopped
3 garlic cloves, minced
2 large jalapeño or serrano chiles, seeds and ribs removed, and finely chopped
1 large egg
¼ cup whole milk
½ cup plain breadcrumbs
½ cup grated smoked cheddar
2 tablespoons chopped fresh cilantro
1 tablespoon dried oregano
2 teaspoons ground cumin
1¼ pounds ground chuck
Salt and freshly ground black pepper to taste
Vegetable oil spray

For dipping:
1 cup Mexican Tomato Sauce (page 48), heated

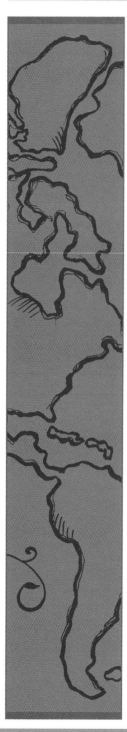

1. Preheat the oven to 450°F. Line a rimmed baking sheet with heavy-duty aluminum foil, and spray the foil with vegetable oil spray.

2. Place bacon in a large skillet over medium-high heat. Cook, stirring occasionally, until bacon is crisp. Remove bacon from the pan with a slotted spoon, and set aside. Discard all but 2 tablespoons bacon fat from the skillet.

3. Add onion, garlic, and chiles to the skillet and cook, stirring frequently, for 3 minutes, or until onion is translucent. While vegetables cook, combine egg and milk in a mixing bowl, and whisk until smooth. Add breadcrumbs, cheddar, cilantro, oregano, and cumin, and mix well.

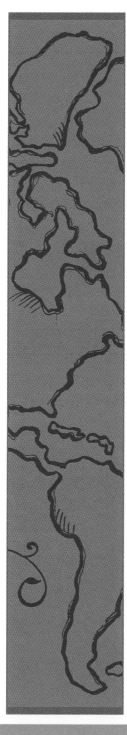

4. Add onion mixture, bacon, and beef, season to taste with salt and pepper, and mix well again. Make mixture into 1½-inch meatballs, and arrange meatballs on the prepared pan. Spray tops of meatballs with vegetable oil spray.

5. Bake meatballs for 12 to 15 minutes, or until cooked through. Remove the pan from the oven, and serve immediately accompanied by a bowl of Mexican Tomato Sauce for dipping.

Note: The beef mixture can be prepared up to 1 day in advance and refrigerated, tightly covered. Also, the meatballs can be baked up to 2 days in advance and refrigerated, tightly covered. Reheat them in a 350°F oven, covered, for 10 to 12 minutes, or until hot.

As a general rule, the smaller the chile pepper, the hotter the chile pepper. That's why an equal number is given for tiny serrano and much larger jalapeño peppers. And another generality is that most of the "heat" is in the seeds and ribs, which is why you are most often instructed to remove them.

Moroccan Beef Meatballs with Tomato Sauce

Makes 4 to 6 servings

Active time: 20 minutes

Start to finish: 45 minutes

VARIATION

Use ground lamb in place of the beef for the meatballs.

Aromatic cinnamon and earthy cumin are the dominant flavors in these Moroccan-inspired meatballs. Serve them over couscous to enjoy every drop of sauce.

¼ cup olive oil

2 large onions, chopped

4 garlic cloves, minced

1 large egg

2 tablespoons whole milk

½ cup panko breadcrumbs

⅔ cup chopped fresh parsley, divided

1 tablespoon chili powder

½ teaspoon ground cinnamon

1¼ pounds ground chuck

Salt and cayenne to taste

2 (8-ounce) cans tomato sauce

2 teaspoons ground cumin

Vegetable oil spray

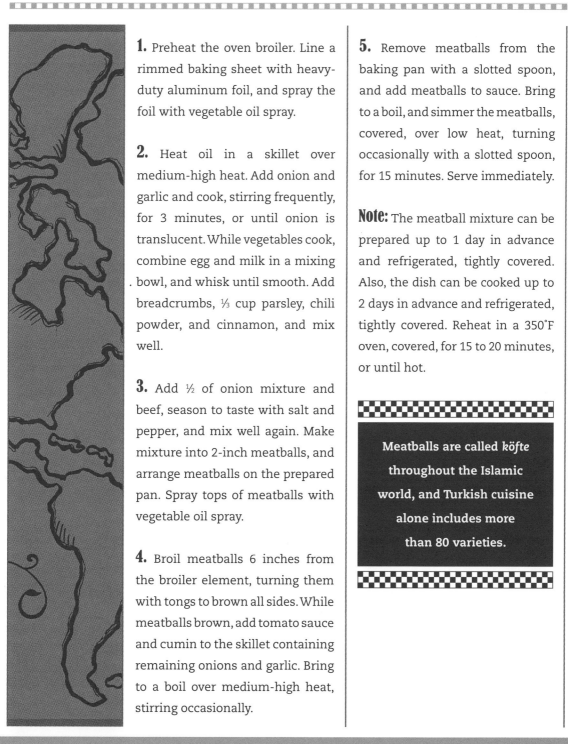

1. Preheat the oven broiler. Line a rimmed baking sheet with heavy-duty aluminum foil, and spray the foil with vegetable oil spray.

2. Heat oil in a skillet over medium-high heat. Add onion and garlic and cook, stirring frequently, for 3 minutes, or until onion is translucent. While vegetables cook, combine egg and milk in a mixing bowl, and whisk until smooth. Add breadcrumbs, ⅓ cup parsley, chili powder, and cinnamon, and mix well.

3. Add ½ of onion mixture and beef, season to taste with salt and pepper, and mix well again. Make mixture into 2-inch meatballs, and arrange meatballs on the prepared pan. Spray tops of meatballs with vegetable oil spray.

4. Broil meatballs 6 inches from the broiler element, turning them with tongs to brown all sides. While meatballs brown, add tomato sauce and cumin to the skillet containing remaining onions and garlic. Bring to a boil over medium-high heat, stirring occasionally.

5. Remove meatballs from the baking pan with a slotted spoon, and add meatballs to sauce. Bring to a boil, and simmer the meatballs, covered, over low heat, turning occasionally with a slotted spoon, for 15 minutes. Serve immediately.

Note: The meatball mixture can be prepared up to 1 day in advance and refrigerated, tightly covered. Also, the dish can be cooked up to 2 days in advance and refrigerated, tightly covered. Reheat in a 350°F oven, covered, for 15 to 20 minutes, or until hot.

Meatballs are called *köfte* throughout the Islamic world, and Turkish cuisine alone includes more than 80 varieties.

Grilled Middle Eastern Beef Meatballs

Makes 4 to 6 servings

Active time:
15 minutes

Start to finish:
30 minutes

Grilling ground meat on skewers is ubiquitous in Middle Eastern cooking, and because these kebabs contain no egg, they can be seared on the outside and enjoyed rare on the inside.

8 to 12 (8-inch) bamboo skewers
1¼ pounds ground chuck
4 garlic cloves, minced
¼ cup grated red onion
¼ cup chopped fresh parsley
1 tablespoon ground coriander
2 teaspoons ground cumin
½ teaspoon ground cinnamon
Salt and freshly ground black
    pepper to taste

For dipping:
1 cup Middle Eastern Yogurt Sauce
    (page 51) or purchased hummus

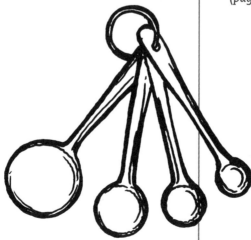

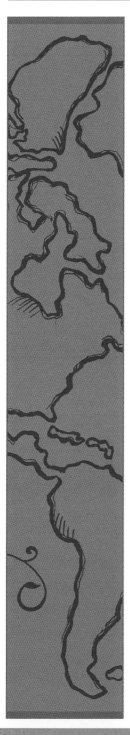

1. Soak the bamboo skewers in cold water to cover. Prepare a medium-hot charcoal or gas grill, or preheat the oven broiler.

2. Combine beef, garlic onion, parsley, coriander, cumin, cinnamon, salt, and pepper in a mixing bowl, and mix well.

3. Divide mixture into 8 to 12 portions, and form each portion into a sausage shape. Insert a skewer into each sausage so that the tip of the skewer is almost at the top of the meat.

4. Grill skewers for a total of 6 minutes, uncovered if using a charcoal grill, turning them gently with tongs to cook all sides. Serve immediately, accompanied by a bowl of Middle Eastern Yogurt Sauce for dipping.

Note: The beef mixture can be prepared up to 1 day in advance and refrigerated, tightly covered. Also, the skewers can be grilled up to 2 days in advance and refrigerated, tightly covered. Reheat them in a 350°F oven, covered, for 10 to 12 minutes, or until hot.

To add additional flavor to grilled skewered dishes, use large rosemary branches as skewers. Soak them in water as you would bamboo skewers. Once heated, they add aroma to the fire and the food.

Caribbean Beef Meatballs in Spiced Rum Sauce

Makes 4 to 6 servings

Active time:
20 minutes

Start to finish:
55 minutes

VARIATIONS

Make the meatballs from chopped fish such as cod, and then cook them directly in the sauce without broiling.

Make the meatballs with ground chicken or turkey.

The foods of the Caribbean often include ingredients associated with both Asian cooking (ginger and lime) and Western cooking (olives and tomatoes) because the islands were instrumental in the trade routes. Spices went in both directions. Heady rum adds its own special flavor to this spicy sauce.

1¼ pounds ground chuck
1 cup cooked rice
1 small onion, grated
2 garlic cloves, minced
Salt and freshly ground black
    pepper to taste

2 tablespoons vegetable oil
1 small red onion, chopped
4 garlic cloves, minced
1 green bell pepper, seeds and ribs
    removed, and chopped
1 large jalapeño or serrano chile,
    seeds and ribs removed, and
    finely chopped
2 cups beef stock
¼ cup dark rum
¼ cup sliced pimiento-stuffed olives
3 medium tomatoes, cored, seeded,
    and chopped
2 tablespoons grated fresh ginger
2 tablespoons tomato paste
2 tablespoons molasses
2 tablespoons freshly squeezed
    lime juice
¼ cup chopped fresh cilantro
1 tablespoon cornstarch
Vegetable oil spray

For garnish: ½ cup coarsely chopped
    salted peanuts

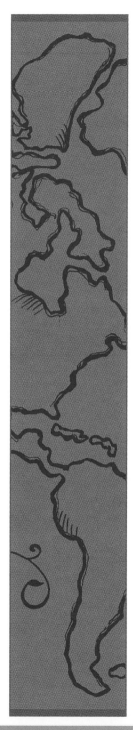

1. Preheat the oven broiler. Line a rimmed baking sheet with heavy-duty aluminum foil, and spray the foil with vegetable oil spray.

2. Combine beef, rice, onion, garlic, salt, and pepper in a mixing bowl, and mix well. Make mixture into 2-inch meatballs, and arrange meatballs on the prepared pan. Spray tops of meatballs with vegetable oil spray.

3. Broil meatballs 6 inches from the broiler element, turning them with tongs to brown all sides. Remove the pan from the oven, and set aside.

4. Heat oil in a large skillet over medium-high heat. Add red onion, garlic, bell pepper, and chile pepper, and cook, stirring frequently, for 3 minutes, or until onion is translucent. Stir in stock, rum, olives, tomatoes, ginger, tomato paste, molasses, and lime juice, and bring to a boil, stirring frequently. Reduce the heat to low, and simmer sauce for 10 minutes.

5. Add meatballs and cilantro to sauce. Bring to a boil, and simmer meatballs, covered, over low heat, turning occasionally with a slotted spoon, for 15 minutes. Combine cornstarch and 1

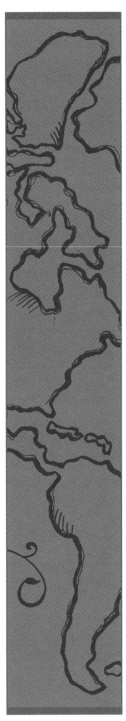

tablespoon cold water in a small cup, and stir well. Add mixture to the skillet and simmer for 2 minutes, or until lightly thickened. Serve immediately, sprinkled with peanuts.

Note: The meatball mixture can be prepared up to 1 day in advance and refrigerated, tightly covered. Also, the dish can be cooked up to 2 days in advance and refrigerated, tightly covered. Reheat in a 350°F oven, covered, for 15 to 20 minutes, or until hot.

Green peppers are always available and most always cheaper than colored peppers. They are merely immature peppers picked before they turn color. They are less expensive because they are not as perishable in this young condition, and they are easier to transport. Their flavor, however, is not as sweet as yellow and red ones.

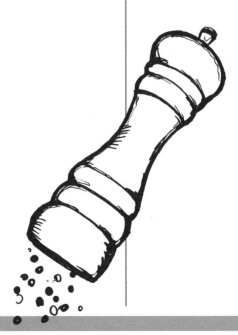

Chinese Beef Meatballs with Peppers and Onions

Makes 4 to 6 servings

Active time:
25 minutes

Start to finish:
50 minutes

VARIATION

Substitute pork or chicken in place of the beef, and use chicken stock instead of beef stock.

This hearty dish is a variation on pepper steak, traditionally popular in Chinese-American restaurants. The rice is included in the meatballs, so the dinner is complete.

1¼ pounds ground chuck
1 cup cooked white rice
4 scallions, white parts and
    3 inches of green tops, chopped
4 garlic cloves, minced and divided
¼ cup soy sauce, divided
2 tablespoons dry sherry
2 tablespoons Asian sesame oil
Freshly ground black pepper to taste
1½ cups beef stock
3 tablespoons Chinese fermented
    black beans, finely chopped
2 tablespoons cornstarch
2 teaspoons granulated sugar
3 tablespoons vegetable oil
2 tablespoons grated fresh ginger
½ teaspoon red pepper flakes
    or to taste
1 large red onion, halved lengthwise
    and thinly sliced
2 bell peppers of any color, seeds
    and ribs removed, and thinly
    sliced
3 tablespoons chopped fresh cilantro
Vegetable oil spray

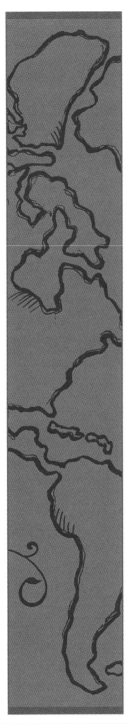

1. Preheat the oven to 450°F. Line a rimmed baking sheet with heavy-duty aluminum foil, and spray the foil with vegetable oil spray.

2. Combine beef, rice, scallions, 2 garlic cloves, 2 tablespoons soy sauce, sherry, sesame oil, and pepper in a mixing bowl, and mix well. Make mixture into 1½-inch meatballs, and arrange meatballs on the prepared pan. Spray tops of meatballs with vegetable oil spray. Combine stock, black beans, remaining soy sauce, cornstarch, and sugar in a bowl, and stir well to dissolve sugar. Set aside.

3. Bake meatballs for 12 to 15 minutes, or until cooked through. Remove the pan from the oven, and set aside. While meatballs bake, heat oil in a large skillet over high heat, swirling to coat. Add remaining 2 garlic cloves, ginger, and red pepper flakes, and stir-fry for 15 seconds, or until fragrant. Add onion and bell peppers and stir-fry for 2 minutes. Add sauce, and stir-fry for 2 minutes or until slightly thickened.

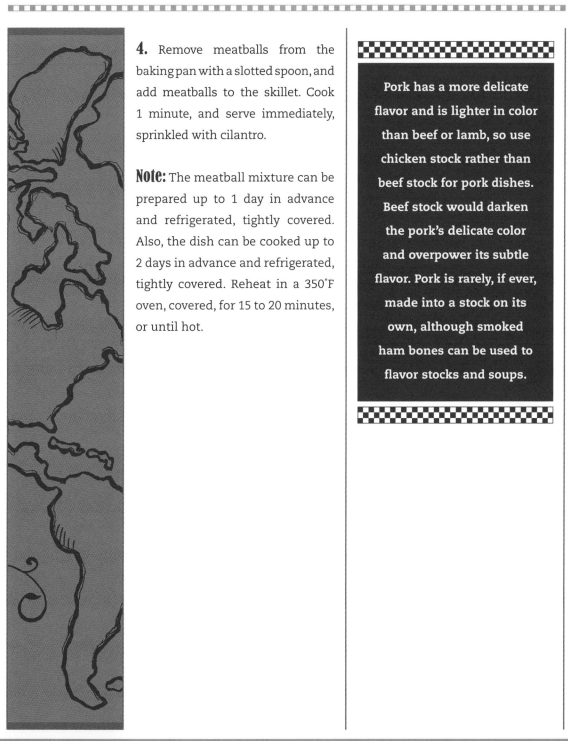

4. Remove meatballs from the baking pan with a slotted spoon, and add meatballs to the skillet. Cook 1 minute, and serve immediately, sprinkled with cilantro.

Note: The meatball mixture can be prepared up to 1 day in advance and refrigerated, tightly covered. Also, the dish can be cooked up to 2 days in advance and refrigerated, tightly covered. Reheat in a 350°F oven, covered, for 15 to 20 minutes, or until hot.

Pork has a more delicate flavor and is lighter in color than beef or lamb, so use chicken stock rather than beef stock for pork dishes. Beef stock would darken the pork's delicate color and overpower its subtle flavor. Pork is rarely, if ever, made into a stock on its own, although smoked ham bones can be used to flavor stocks and soups.

Caribbean Chutney Beef Meatballs

Makes 4 to 6 servings

**Active time:
15 minutes**

**Start to finish:
30 minutes**

VARIATION

Make the meatballs from ground turkey or ground chicken.

These meatballs include the fiery flavors of traditional Jamaican jerk seasoning, but their heat is tempered by the addition of sweet chutney.

1 large egg
½ cup jarred mango chutney,
    such as Major Grey's
2 tablespoons whole milk
½ cup plain breadcrumbs
2 tablespoons chopped fresh cilantro
4 garlic cloves, minced
1 tablespoon freshly squeezed
    lime juice
1 tablespoon curry powder
2 teaspoons ground cumin
¼ teaspoon ground allspice
3 to 5 dashes hot red pepper sauce
1¼ pounds ground chuck
Salt and freshly ground black
    pepper to taste
Vegetable oil spray

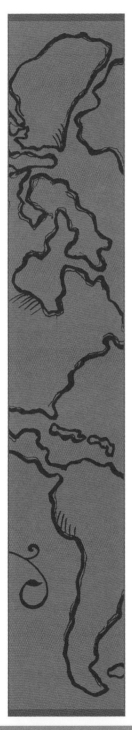

1. Preheat the oven to 450°F. Line a rimmed baking sheet with heavy-duty aluminum foil, and spray the foil with vegetable oil spray.

2. Combine egg, chutney, milk, and breadcrumbs in a food processor or in a blender, and puree until smooth. Scrape mixture into a mixing bowl, and add cilantro, garlic, lime juice, curry powder, cumin, allspice, and hot red pepper sauce.

3. Add beef, season to taste with salt and pepper, and mix well again. Make mixture into 1½-inch meatballs, and arrange meatballs on the prepared pan. Spray tops of meatballs with vegetable oil spray.

4. Bake meatballs for 12 to 15 minutes, or until cooked through. Remove the pan from the oven, and serve immediately.

Note: The beef mixture can be prepared up to 1 day in advance and refrigerated, tightly covered. Also, the meatballs can be baked up to 2 days in advance and refrigerated, tightly covered. Reheat them in a 350°F oven, covered, for 10 to 12 minutes or until hot.

The easiest way to break apart a whole head of garlic is to slam the root end onto the countertop. The cloves will easily come apart.

Japanese Scallion Beef Meatballs

Makes 4 to 6 servings

Active time:

15 minutes

Start to finish:

30 minutes

VARIATION

Make the meatballs from ground pork, and serve with Asian Dipping Sauce (page 54) rather than the more assertive mustard-based sauce.

Negimaki, which is thin slices of beef rolled around scallions and then grilled, are a Japanese classic. These meatballs include all the same flavors, and are perfect as hors d'oeuvre.

1¼ pounds ground chuck

1 cup cooked white rice

1 bunch scallions, white parts and
  3 inches of green tops, chopped

3 garlic cloves, minced

¼ cup soy sauce

2 tablespoons Asian sesame oil

1 tablespoon grated fresh ginger

¼ teaspoon Chinese five-spice
  powder

Freshly ground black pepper to taste

Vegetable oil spray

For dipping:

1 cup Sesame Honey Mustard Sauce
  (page 53)

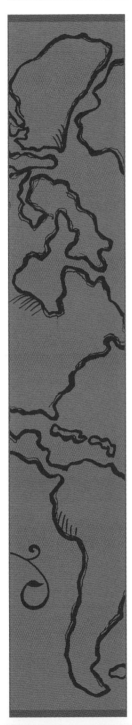

1. Preheat the oven to 450°F. Line a rimmed baking sheet with heavy-duty aluminum foil, and spray the foil with vegetable oil spray.

2. Combine beef, rice, scallions, garlic, soy sauce, sesame oil, ginger, five-spice powder, and pepper in a mixing bowl, and mix well. Make mixture into 1½-inch meatballs, and arrange meatballs on the prepared pan. Spray tops of meatballs with vegetable oil spray.

3. Bake meatballs for 12 to 15 minutes, or until cooked through. Remove the pan from the oven, and serve immediately accompanied by a bowl of Sesame Honey Mustard Sauce for dipping.

Note: The beef mixture can be prepared up to 1 day in advance and refrigerated, tightly covered. Also, the meatballs can be baked up to 2 days in advance and refrigerated, tightly covered. Reheat them in a 350°F oven, covered, for 10 to 12 minutes, or until hot.

These meatballs are also good candidates for the grill because they don't contain a raw egg. Look at the recipe for Grilled Middle Eastern Beef Meatballs (page 150) for the procedure.

PORCINE PLEASURES:

MEATBALLS WITH PORK, SAUSAGE, AND HAM

I'm constantly amazed at the versatility of pork. Because of pork's naturally subtle, delicate flavor, and buttery texture, it is somewhat similar to chicken. Pork can be flavored so many ways to achieve a variety of truly delicious results.

Perhaps it's these qualities that has made pork the meat of choice to sausage-makers around the world who flavor the pork with everything from herbs and chiles to nuts and fruits. And remember, pork can also be smoked and/or cured to become ham, enjoyed as much in Parma as in Pasadena.

During the past few decades American pork has been bred to be lower in fat, thus the ad campaign about "the other white meat." Another advantage to cooking with pork is that it is relatively inexpensive; even the prized tenderloins sell for a fraction of the price of beef tenderloins or racks of lamb.

The recipes in this chapter run the gamut for ways to enjoy pork from many of the world's cuisines. You'll find recipes that are quick and casual because much of the seasoning is in the sausage itself, and you'll find dishes that are easy but also elegant enough to serve to guests.

Crunchy Pork Meatballs in Bourbon Barbecue Sauce

Makes 4 to 6 servings

Active time: 20 minutes

Start to finish: 45 minutes

VARIATION

Use ground turkey in place of ground pork.

Water chestnuts were one of the first Asian ingredients adopted by American cooks because they give food a crunchy texture; even fifty years ago they were being included in non-Asian dishes. This recipe is an updated version of the classic meatballs in barbecue sauce; it's laced with bourbon and mustard.

2 tablespoons vegetable oil

1 large onion, chopped

4 garlic cloves, minced

1 large egg

2 tablespoons whole milk

3 pieces whole wheat bread

1 (8-ounce) can water chestnuts, drained, rinsed, and chopped

2 tablespoons chopped fresh parsley

2 tablespoons chopped fresh sage or 1 tablespoon dried

1¼ pounds ground pork

Salt and freshly ground black pepper to taste

1 cup Southern Barbecue Sauce (page 39) or purchased barbecue sauce

¾ cup chicken stock

½ cup bourbon

¼ cup firmly packed light brown sugar

2 tablespoons grainy Dijon mustard

2 teaspoons cornstarch

Vegetable oil spray

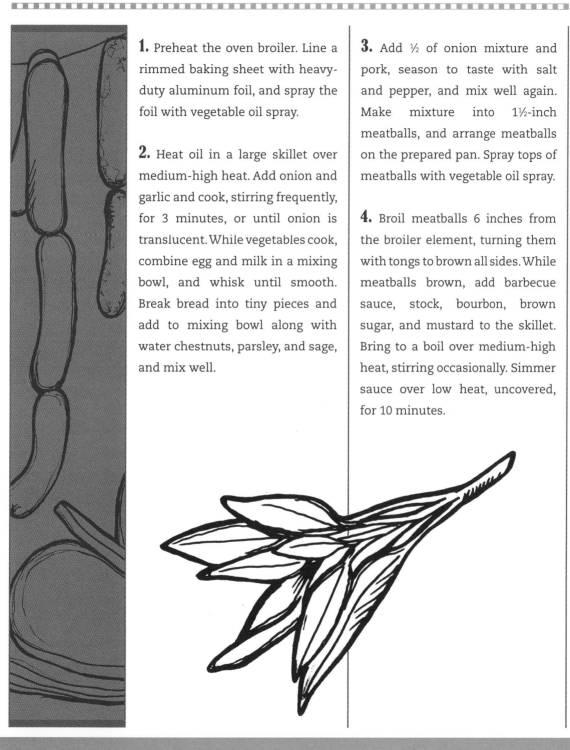

1. Preheat the oven broiler. Line a rimmed baking sheet with heavy-duty aluminum foil, and spray the foil with vegetable oil spray.

2. Heat oil in a large skillet over medium-high heat. Add onion and garlic and cook, stirring frequently, for 3 minutes, or until onion is translucent. While vegetables cook, combine egg and milk in a mixing bowl, and whisk until smooth. Break bread into tiny pieces and add to mixing bowl along with water chestnuts, parsley, and sage, and mix well.

3. Add ½ of onion mixture and pork, season to taste with salt and pepper, and mix well again. Make mixture into 1½-inch meatballs, and arrange meatballs on the prepared pan. Spray tops of meatballs with vegetable oil spray.

4. Broil meatballs 6 inches from the broiler element, turning them with tongs to brown all sides. While meatballs brown, add barbecue sauce, stock, bourbon, brown sugar, and mustard to the skillet. Bring to a boil over medium-high heat, stirring occasionally. Simmer sauce over low heat, uncovered, for 10 minutes.

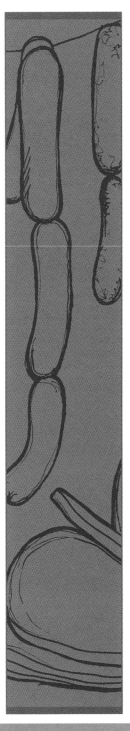

5. Remove meatballs from the baking pan with a slotted spoon, and add meatballs to sauce. Bring to a boil, and simmer the meatballs, covered, over low heat, turning occasionally with a slotted spoon, for 15 minutes. Mix cornstarch with 1 tablespoon cold water in a small bowl, and add to sauce. Cook for 1 minute, or until slightly thickened. Season to taste with salt and pepper, and serve immediately.

Note: The pork mixture can be prepared up to 1 day in advance and refrigerated, tightly covered. Also, the dish can be cooked up to 2 days in advance and refrigerated, tightly covered. Reheat it in a 350°F oven, covered, for 15 to 20 minutes, or until hot.

Our word barbecue, which appears in American dictionaries before the Revolutionary War, comes from the Spanish *barbacoa*, which refers to the framework of sticks over which food was cooked. We now use barbecue both as a noun and a verb.

Ham Meatballs in Apple-Madeira Sauce

Makes 4 to 6 servings

Active time: 20 minutes

Start to finish: 50 minutes

VARIATION

Instead of the raisins use a combination of chopped dried apricots and dried cranberries.

The mellow flavor of baked ham is bound with fresh pork for these meatballs and then cooked in a sauce made with heady Madeira wine and fruits. Serve for a Sunday brunch, and it's a great way to use up leftover ham.

2 tablespoons unsalted butter

1 large onion, chopped

1 large carrot, chopped

3 garlic cloves, minced

1 Granny Smith apple, peeled, cored, and chopped

1 cup apple cider, divided

¾ cup Madeira or medium-dry sherry

½ cup raisins

2 tablespoons chopped fresh parsley

2 teaspoons fresh thyme or ½ teaspoon dried

½ teaspoon ground cinnamon

1 large egg

½ cup plain breadcrumbs

1 pound cooked ham, finely chopped

½ pound ground pork

Salt and freshly ground black pepper to taste

1 tablespoon cornstarch

Vegetable oil spray

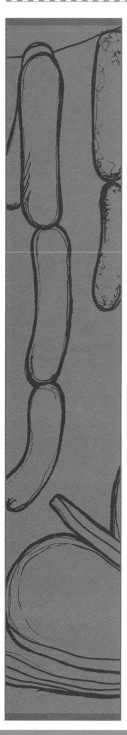

1. Heat butter in a large skillet over medium-high heat. Add onion, carrot, and garlic, and cook, stirring frequently, for 3 minutes, or until onion is translucent. Remove ½ of vegetable mixture, and set aside. Add apple, ¾ cup cider, Madeira, raisins, parsley, thyme, and cinnamon to the skillet, and bring to a boil over medium-high heat, stirring occasionally. Simmer sauce over low heat, uncovered, for 15 minutes.

2. While sauce simmers, preheat the oven broiler. Line a rimmed baking sheet with heavy-duty aluminum foil, and spray the foil with vegetable oil spray.

3. Combine egg, remaining ¼ cup cider, and breadcrumbs in a mixing bowl, and whisk until smooth. Add reserved vegetable mixture, ham, and pork, season to taste with salt and pepper, and mix well again. Make mixture into 1½-inch meatballs, and arrange meatballs on the prepared pan. Spray tops of meatballs with vegetable oil spray.

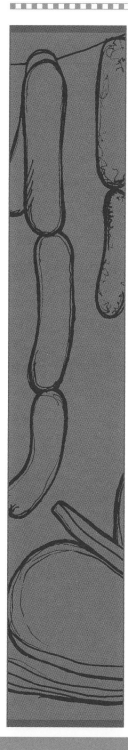

4. Broil meatballs 6 inches from the broiler element, turning them with tongs to brown all sides. Remove meatballs from the baking pan with a slotted spoon, and add meatballs to sauce. Bring to a boil, and simmer meatballs over low heat, covered, turning occasionally with a slotted spoon, for 15 minutes. Mix cornstarch with 1 tablespoon cold water in a small bowl, and add to sauce. Cook for 1 minute, or until slightly thickened. Season sauce to taste with salt and pepper, and serve immediately.

Note: The pork mixture can be prepared up to 1 day in advance and refrigerated, tightly covered. Also, the dish can be made up to 2 days in advance and refrigerated, tightly covered. Reheat it in a 350°F oven, covered, for 15 to 20 minutes, or until hot.

Some time-honored methods of cutting fruits and vegetables make sense in high-end restaurant kitchens where chefs have assistants prepping for them, but these techniques don't make sense in our busy lives. If it matters how the apples in the dish look, then peeling, coring, and then slicing each half or quarter is still the best method. But if the apples are going to be hidden, as in this dish, there's a faster way: Peel the apple and keep turning it in your hand as you cut off slices. Soon all you'll be left with is the core, which you can discard. It's much faster.

Crunchy Southwestern Pork Meatballs

Makes 4 to 6 servings

Active time:
20 minutes

Start to finish:
35 minutes

VARIATION

Make the meatballs from ground chicken or turkey.

The assertive flavors of traditional Southwestern cooking remain popular in the pantheon of American regional cuisines, and this easy recipe includes many of them. The crushed tortilla chips add texture to the meatballs, too.

2 slices white bread
2 tablespoons whole milk
2 tablespoons olive oil
½ small red onion, finely chopped
2 garlic cloves, minced
1 tablespoon chili powder
1 teaspoon ground cumin
½ teaspoon dried oregano
1 large egg
½ cup tortilla chips (crushed in heavy-duty plastic bag)
3 tablespoons chopped fresh cilantro
1¼ pounds ground pork
Salt and freshly ground black pepper to taste
Vegetable oil spray

For dipping:
1 cup Mexican Tomato Sauce (page 48) or bottled salsa, heated

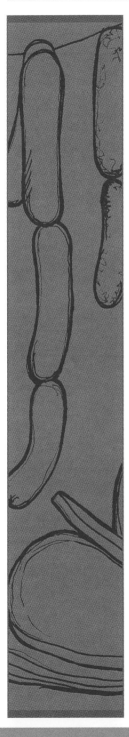

1. Preheat the oven to 450°F. Line a rimmed baking sheet with heavy-duty aluminum foil, and spray the foil with vegetable oil spray. Tear bread into small pieces, and place bread in a bowl with milk; stir well.

2. Heat oil in a small skillet over medium-high heat. Add onion and garlic, and cook, stirring frequently, for 3 minutes, or until onion is translucent. Add chili powder, cumin, and oregano, and cook, stirring constantly, for 1 minute. While vegetables cook, whisk egg in a mixing bowl, and add bread mixture, crushed tortilla chips, and cilantro, and mix well.

3. Add onion mixture and pork to the mixing bowl, season to taste with salt and pepper, and mix well again. Make mixture into 1½-inch meatballs, and arrange meatballs on the prepared pan. Spray tops of meatballs with vegetable oil spray.

4. Bake meatballs for 12 to 15 minutes, or until cooked through. Remove the pan from the oven, and serve immediately, accompanied by a bowl of Mexican Tomato Sauce for dipping.

Note: The pork mixture can be prepared up to 1 day in advance and refrigerated, tightly covered. Also, the meatballs can be baked up to 2 days in advance and refrigerated, tightly covered. Reheat them in a 350°F oven, covered, for 10 to 12 minutes, or until hot.

Heat and light are the two enemies of dried herbs and spices, so a pretty display rack over the stove is about the worst place to store them. Keep them in a cool, dark place to preserve their potency. The best test for freshness and potency is to smell the contents. If you don't smell them, buy a new bottle.

Sausage, Cheddar, and Red Pepper Meatballs

Makes 4 to 6 servings

Active time:
20 minutes

Start to finish:
35 minutes

VARIATION

Substitute ground pork, veal, or turkey for the sausage if you want a dish with milder flavor.

The combination of cheddar and sausage is quintessentially American, and I like the addition of lots of sweet red bell peppers. These are always a hit when served as a hors d'oeuvre, or at brunch along with scrambled eggs.

2 tablespoons olive oil
1 large red bell pepper, seeds and ribs removed, and chopped
3 scallions, white parts only, chopped
2 garlic cloves, minced
1 large egg
2 tablespoons whole milk
1 cup seasoned Italian breadcrumbs, divided
¾ cup grated cheddar cheese
3 tablespoons chopped fresh parsley
2 teaspoons fresh thyme or ½ teaspoon dried
1¼ pounds bulk breakfast sausage
Salt and freshly ground black pepper to taste
Vegetable oil spray

For dipping:
1 cup Herbed Tomato Sauce (page 38) or purchased marinara sauce, heated

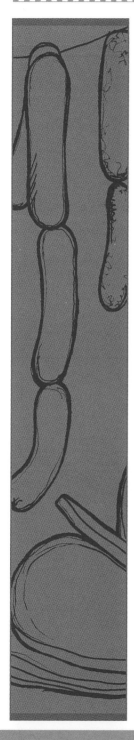

1. Preheat the oven to 450°F. Line a rimmed baking sheet with heavy-duty aluminum foil, and spray the foil with vegetable oil spray.

2. Heat oil in a skillet over medium-high heat. Add red peppers, scallions, and garlic, and cook, stirring frequently, for 5 minutes, or until peppers are soft. While vegetables cook, whisk egg and milk in a mixing bowl, add ½ cup breadcrumbs, cheddar, parsley, and thyme, and mix well.

3. Add vegetable mixture and sausage to the mixing bowl, season to taste with salt and pepper, and mix well again. Make mixture into 1½-inch meatballs, and roll meatballs in remaining breadcrumbs. Arrange meatballs on the prepared pan, and spray tops of meatballs with vegetable oil spray.

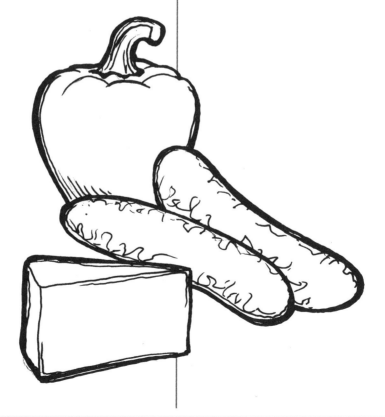

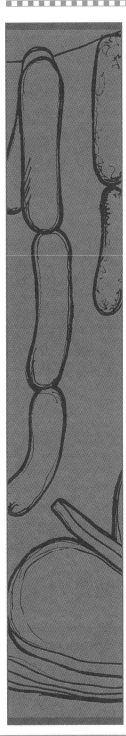

4. Bake meatballs for 12 to 15 minutes, or until cooked through. Remove the pan from the oven, and serve immediately accompanied by a bowl of Herbed Tomato Sauce for dipping.

Note: The sausage mixture can be prepared up to 1 day in advance and refrigerated, tightly covered. Also, the meatballs can be baked up to 2 days in advance and refrigerated, tightly covered. Reheat them in a 350°F oven, covered, for 10 to 12 minutes, or until hot.

Bell peppers are hard to deal with because they don't sit flat on the cutting board. It's easier to slice and dice bell peppers from the inside out. Once the seeds and ribs have been removed, place the shiny, slippery skin on a cutting board; it's easier to control your knife and cut the size pieces you desire.

Sausage Meatballs with Plums and Wine Sauce

Makes 4 to 6 servings

Active time:

20 minutes

Start to finish:

1 hour

VARIATIONS

If you find fresh kielbasa sausage, it's great in this recipe.

Use bulk maple-flavored pork sausage.

Cooking sausages with fruit is common in German and other Northern European cuisines, and using flavorful and spicy Italian sausage balances the sweetness of the fruit. Serve these on top of buttered egg noodles with a green salad on the side.

¾ cup granulated sugar

¾ cup red wine vinegar

½ cup dry red wine

1 (3-inch) cinnamon stick

4 whole cloves

6 ripe purple plums

1 large egg

2 tablespoons chicken stock or water

½ cup plain breadcrumbs

2 tablespoons chopped fresh parsley

1¼ pounds bulk sweet Italian sausage

Salt and freshly ground black pepper to taste

2 teaspoons cornstarch

Vegetable oil spray

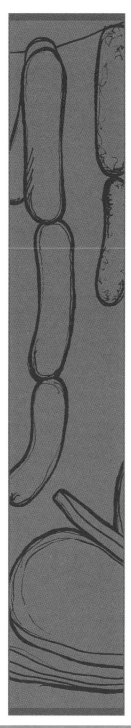

1. Combine sugar, vinegar, wine, cinnamon stick, and cloves in a non-reactive saucepan, and bring to a boil over medium-high heat, stirring occasionally. Simmer 5 minutes, then add plums, cover the pan, and simmer plums for 10 minutes over low heat. Remove plums from the pan with a slotted spoon, reserving poaching liquid. When cool enough to handle, remove and discard stones and slice fruit. Set aside.

2. While plums poach, preheat the oven broiler. Line a rimmed baking sheet with heavy-duty aluminum foil, and spray the foil with vegetable oil spray.

3. Combine egg, stock, breadcrumbs, and parsley in a mixing bowl, and mix well. Add sausage, season to taste with salt and pepper, and mix well again. Make mixture into 1½-inch meatballs, and arrange meatballs on the prepared pan. Spray tops of meatballs with vegetable oil spray.

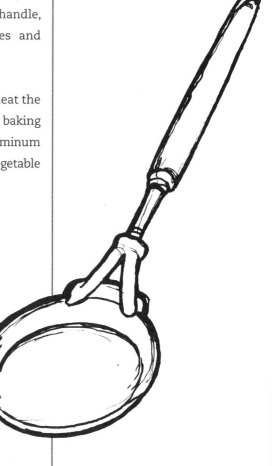

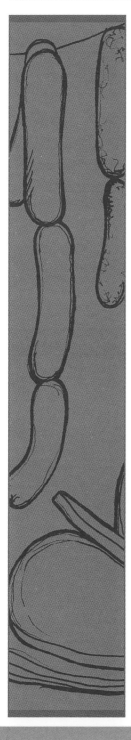

4. Broil meatballs 6 inches from the broiler element, turning them with tongs to brown all sides.

5. Remove meatballs from the baking pan with a slotted spoon, and add meatballs to reserved poaching liquid. Bring to a boil, and simmer meatballs, covered, over low heat, turning occasionally with a slotted spoon, for 15 minutes. Remove meatballs from the pan with a slotted spoon, and add to plum slices.

6. Cook poaching liquid over medium-high heat until reduced by ½. Mix cornstarch with 1 tablespoon cold water in a small bowl, and add to sauce. Cook for 1 minute, or until slightly thickened. Return meatballs and plums to sauce to reheat, and serve immediately.

Note: The pork mixture can be prepared up to 1 day in advance and refrigerated, tightly covered. Also, the dish can be cooked up to 2 days in advance and refrigerated, tightly covered. Reheat it in a 350°F oven, covered, for 15 to 20 minutes,

There's rarely much leftover red wine in my house; my friends and I drink it. If you don't want to drink it, here's what to do: Boil it down in a saucepan until it's reduced by half, then freeze it in ice cube trays. When you're making a dish in the future that calls for red wine, just pull out a few cubes.

English Pork Meatballs in Onion Sauce

Makes 4 to 6 servings

Active time:
20 minutes

Start to finish:
1 hour

VARIATION

Substitute ground turkey for the pork.

In traditional English cooking these meatballs are called "faggots," and they are traditionally served with mashed potatoes and peas. While authentic recipes call for using pork innards, I've adapted the recipe to use ground pork.

2 tablespoons vegetable oil
2 tablespoons unsalted butter
4 large onions, thinly sliced
Salt and freshly ground black
    pepper to taste
2 teaspoons granulated sugar
½ cup dry white wine
2 cups chicken stock
2 tablespoons chopped fresh parsley
2 teaspoons fresh thyme or
    ½ teaspoon dried
1 large egg
2 tablespoons whole milk
½ cup plain breadcrumbs
¼ teaspoon ground nutmeg
1¼ pounds ground pork
Salt and freshly ground black
    pepper to taste
2 teaspoons cornstarch
Vegetable oil spray

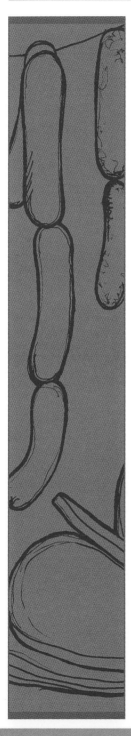

1. Heat oil and butter in a large skillet over medium heat. Add onions, and toss to coat. Cover the pan, and cook onions for 10 minutes, stirring occasionally. Sprinkle onions with salt, pepper, and sugar, and raise the heat to medium-high. Cook onions for 15 to 20 minutes, stirring occasionally, or until brown. Add wine, and cook over high heat for 1 minute, stirring constantly. Add stock, parsley, and thyme, and bring to a boil over medium-high heat. Reduce the heat to low, and simmer sauce, uncovered, for 5 minutes.

2. While onions cook, preheat the oven broiler. Line a rimmed baking sheet with heavy-duty aluminum foil, and spray the foil with vegetable oil spray. Combine egg and milk in a mixing bowl, and whisk until smooth. Add breadcrumbs and nutmeg to the mixing bowl, and mix well. Add pork, season to taste with salt and pepper, and mix well.

3. Make mixture into 2-inch meatballs, and arrange meatballs on the prepared pan. Spray tops of meatballs with vegetable oil spray. Broil meatballs 6 inches from the

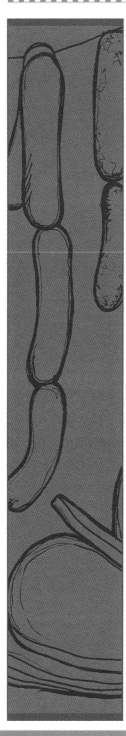

broiler element, turning them with tongs to brown all sides. Remove the pan from the oven, and set aside.

4. Add meatballs to sauce, bring to a boil, and simmer meatballs, covered, over low heat, turning occasionally with a slotted spoon, for 15 minutes. Combine cornstarch and 1 tablespoon cold water in a small bowl, and stir well. Add mixture to sauce, and cook for an additional 2 minutes, or until slightly thickened. Season sauce to taste with salt and pepper, and serve immediately.

Note: The pork mixture can be prepared up to 1 day in advance and refrigerated, tightly covered. Also, the dish can be cooked up to 2 days in advance and refrigerated, tightly covered. Reheat it in a 350°F oven, covered, for 15 to 20 minutes, or until hot.

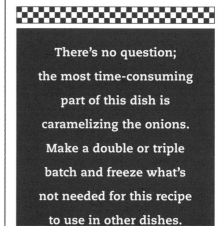

There's no question; the most time-consuming part of this dish is caramelizing the onions. Make a double or triple batch and freeze what's not needed for this recipe to use in other dishes.

Pork Meatballs in Apple Cream Sauce

Makes 4 to 6 servings

Active time:
20 minutes

Start to finish:
55 minutes

VARIATIONS

Add ⅔ cup chopped dried apples for a more assertive apple flavor in place of the fresh apples.

Ground veal and either ground chicken or turkey can be used in place of the pork.

The cuisine of the Normandy region of France is characterized by the use of apples, a special brandy called Calvados, and cream. This recipe is based on that ingredients trinity. Serve with a steamed green vegetable and some rice or pasta.

2 tablespoons unsalted butter

1 large onion, chopped

2 garlic cloves, minced

1 large egg

2 tablespoons whole milk

½ cup plain breadcrumbs

1¼ pounds ground pork

Salt and freshly ground black pepper to taste

2 Granny Smith apples, peeled, cored, and chopped

1 cup apple cider, divided

1 cup chicken stock

¼ cup applejack brandy

2 tablespoons Dijon mustard

½ cup heavy cream

1 tablespoon cornstarch

Vegetable oil spray

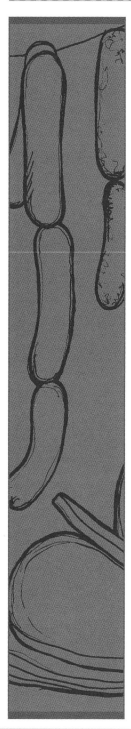

1. Preheat the oven broiler. Line a rimmed baking sheet with heavy-duty aluminum foil, and spray the foil with vegetable oil spray.

2. Heat butter in a large skillet over medium-high heat. Add onion and garlic and cook, stirring frequently, for 3 minutes, or until onion is translucent. While vegetables cook, combine egg and milk in a mixing bowl, and whisk until smooth. Add breadcrumbs to the mixing bowl, and mix well.

3. Add ½ of onion mixture and pork, season to taste with salt and pepper, and mix well again. Make mixture into 2-inch meatballs, and arrange meatballs on the prepared pan. Spray tops of meatballs with vegetable oil spray.

4. Broil meatballs 6 inches from the broiler element, turning them with tongs to brown all sides. Remove the pan from the oven, and set aside.

5. Add apples, ¾ cup cider, chicken stock, brandy, and mustard to the skillet, and bring to a boil over medium-high heat, stirring occasionally. Simmer sauce, uncovered, for 10 minutes, or until volume is reduced by ⅓. Add meatballs and cream to sauce, bring to a boil, and simmer meatballs, covered, over low heat, turning occasionally with a slotted spoon, for 15 minutes.

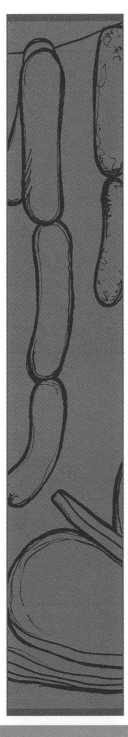

6. Combine cornstarch and remaining ¼ cup cider in a small bowl, and stir well. Add mixture to sauce, and cook for an additional 2 minutes, or until lightly thickened. Season sauce to taste with salt and pepper, and serve immediately.

Note: The pork mixture can be prepared up to 1 day in advance and refrigerated, tightly covered. Also, the dish can be cooked up to 2 days in advance and refrigerated, tightly covered. Reheat it in a 350°F oven, covered, for 15 to 20 minutes, or until hot.

There isn't really a Jolly Green Giant, but there certainly was a Johnny Appleseed. Named John Chapman, he was born in Massachusetts in 1774. Unlike the artistic depictions of him propagating apples by tossing seeds out of his backpack, Chapman actually started nurseries for European species of apple brought from England as seedlings in the Allegheny Valley in 1800. By the time of his death in 1845, he had pushed as far west as Indiana, establishing thousands of apple tree groves.

Ham Meatballs with Italian Vegetable Sauce

Makes 4 to 6 servings

Active time:
20 minutes

Start to finish:
40 minutes

The saltiness of ham complements the robust tomato and vegetable sauce in which these meatballs are finished. Serve them on pasta accompanied by a green salad.

¼ cup olive oil

3 medium onions, halved and
   thinly sliced

1 green bell pepper, seeds and ribs
   removed, and thinly sliced

1 red bell pepper, seeds and ribs
   removed, and thinly sliced

3 garlic cloves, minced

1 (14.5-ounce) can crushed
   tomatoes, undrained

1 (8-ounce) can tomato sauce

½ cup dry white wine, divided

2 tablespoons chopped fresh parsley

1 tablespoon Italian seasoning

1 bay leaf

1 large egg

½ cup seasoned Italian breadcrumbs

1 pound cooked ham, finely chopped

½ pound ground pork

Salt and freshly ground black
   pepper to taste

Vegetable oil spray

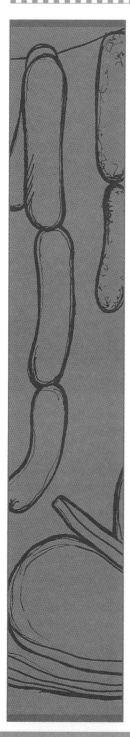

1. Heat oil in a large skillet over medium-high heat. Add onions, green pepper, red pepper, and garlic, and cook, stirring frequently, for 3 minutes, or until onions are translucent. Add tomatoes, tomato sauce, ¼ cup wine, parsley, Italian seasoning, and bay leaf. Bring to a boil over medium-high heat, stirring occasionally. Reduce the heat to low and simmer sauce, uncovered, for 15 minutes.

2. While sauce simmers, preheat the oven broiler. Line a rimmed baking sheet with heavy-duty aluminum foil, and spray the foil with vegetable oil spray.

3. Combine egg, remaining ¼ cup wine, and breadcrumbs in a mixing bowl, and whisk until smooth. Add ham and pork, season to taste with salt and pepper, and mix well again. Make mixture into 1½-inch meatballs, and arrange meatballs on the prepared pan. Spray tops of meatballs with vegetable oil spray.

4. Broil meatballs 6 inches from the broiler element, turning them with tongs to brown all sides.

Remove meatballs from the baking pan with a slotted spoon, and add meatballs to sauce. Bring to a boil, and simmer meatballs, covered, over low heat, turning occasionally with a slotted spoon, for 15 minutes. Remove and discard bay leaf, season to taste with salt and pepper, and serve immediately.

Note: The pork mixture can be prepared up to 1 day in advance and refrigerated, tightly covered. Also, the dish can be cooked up to 2 days in advance and refrigerated, tightly covered. Reheat it in a 350°F oven, covered, for 15 to 20 minutes, or until hot.

Italian seasoning, a mixture of basil, oregano, rosemary, and thyme, is used frequently in Mediterranean cooking. Any one of those component herbs can be used alone in the same quantity as the Italian seasoning in a recipe.

Italian Lemon and Rosemary Pork Meatballs

Makes 4 to 6 servings

Active time: 20 minutes

Start to finish: 35 minutes

When traveling in Umbria a few years ago I fell in love with porchetta, slowly roasted pork shoulder or loin stuffed with rosemary and garlic and drizzled with lemon. All those flavors appear in this quick and easy meatball version.

3 slices white bread
¼ cup whole milk
2 tablespoons olive oil
2 shallots, chopped
6 garlic cloves, minced
1 large egg
Zest and juice of 2 lemons
¼ cup freshly grated Parmesan
3 tablespoons chopped fresh
    rosemary or 1 tablespoon dried
2 tablespoons chopped fresh parsley
1¼ pounds ground pork
Salt and freshly ground black
    pepper to taste
Vegetable oil spray

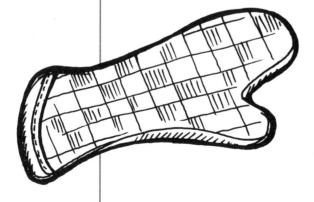

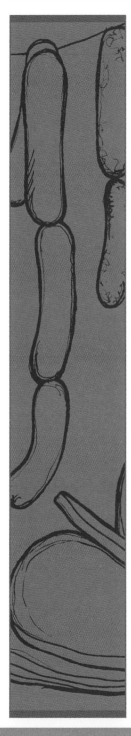

1. Preheat the oven to 450°F. Line a rimmed baking sheet with heavy-duty aluminum foil, and spray the foil with vegetable oil spray. Tear bread into small pieces, and place bread in a bowl with milk; stir well.

2. Heat oil in a small skillet over medium-high heat. Add shallots and garlic, and cook, stirring frequently, for 3 minutes, or until translucent. While vegetables cook, whisk egg in a mixing bowl, and add bread mixture, lemon zest, Parmesan, rosemary, and parsley, and mix well.

3. Add shallot mixture and pork to the mixing bowl, season to taste with salt and pepper, and mix well again. Make mixture into 1½-inch meatballs, and arrange meatballs on the prepared pan. Spray tops of meatballs with vegetable oil spray.

4. Bake meatballs for 12 to 15 minutes, or until cooked through. Remove the pan from the oven, drizzle lemon juice over meatballs, and serve immediately.

Note: The pork mixture can be prepared up to 1 day in advance and refrigerated, tightly covered. Also, the meatballs can be baked up to 2 days in advance and refrigerated, tightly covered. Reheat them in a 350°F oven, covered, for 10 to 12 minutes, or until hot.

Zest really does have something to do with zesty; it's the thin, colored outer portion of citrus skin that contains all the aromatic oils. The white pith just beneath it is bitter, so take pains to separate the zest from the fruit without also taking any pith with it. Remove the zest using a special citrus zester, a vegetable peeler, or a paring knife. You can also grate it using the fine holes of a box grater.

Mexican Pork Meatballs in Chipotle Sauce

Makes 4 to 6 servings

Active time:
25 minutes

Start to finish:
40 minutes

VARIATION

Make the meatballs from ground chicken or turkey.

This is not a dish for delicate palates; it's both aromatic and spicy and contains many of the essential ingredients of Mexican cooking. Serve it with some Mexican rice or saffron rice and cold beer.

¼ cup olive oil

2 large onions, chopped

4 garlic cloves, minced

1 large egg

2 tablespoons whole milk

½ cup plain breadcrumbs

⅔ cup chopped fresh cilantro, divided

1 tablespoon chili powder

1 tablespoon dried oregano

1¼ pounds ground pork

Salt and cayenne to taste

1 (15-ounce) can tomato sauce

2 teaspoons ground cumin

2 chipotle chiles in adobo sauce, drained and finely chopped

Freshly ground black pepper to taste

Vegetable oil spray

1. Preheat the oven broiler. Line a rimmed baking sheet with heavy-duty aluminum foil, and spray the foil with vegetable oil spray.

2. Heat oil in a skillet over medium-high heat. Add onions and garlic

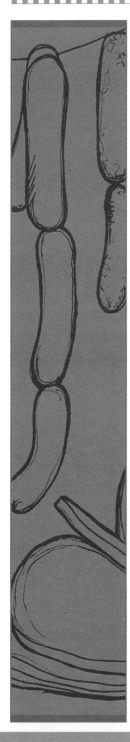

and cook, stirring frequently, for 3 minutes, or until onions are translucent. While vegetables cook, combine egg and milk in a mixing bowl, and whisk until smooth. Add breadcrumbs, ⅓ cup cilantro, chili powder, and oregano, and mix well.

3. Add ½ of onion mixture and pork, season to taste with salt and cayenne, and mix well again. Make mixture into 2-inch meatballs, and arrange meatballs on the prepared pan. Spray tops of meatballs with vegetable oil spray.

4. Broil meatballs 6 inches from the broiler element, turning them with tongs to brown all sides. While meatballs brown, add tomato sauce, cumin, and chipotle to the skillet containing remaining onions and garlic. Bring to a boil over medium-high heat, stirring occasionally.

5. Remove meatballs from the baking pan with a slotted spoon, and add meatballs to sauce. Bring to a boil, and simmer the meatballs, covered, over low heat,

turning occasionally with a slotted spoon, for 15 minutes. Season to taste with pepper, and serve immediately.

Note: The pork mixture can be prepared up to 1 day in advance and refrigerated, tightly covered. Also, the dish can be cooked up to 2 days in advance and refrigerated, tightly covered. Reheat it in a 350°F oven, covered, for 15 to 20 minutes, or until hot.

Chipotle chiles in adobo sauce is a canned Mexican product, and both the peppers, which are smoked jalapeños and the rich, dark red sauce, are used to flavor dishes. The sauce also contains herbs and vinegar, so it's similar to a hot red pepper sauce but with a more complex, richer flavor.

Mexican Pork and Zucchini Meatballs

Makes 4 to 6 servings

Active time: 20 minutes

Start to finish: 45 minutes

VARIATION

Make the meatballs from ground chicken or turkey.

Zucchini adds both subtle flavor and texture to this zesty Mexican dish. Serve it with some saffron rice, and top it with guacamole and salsa, if you wish.

3 tablespoons olive oil
1 medium onion, chopped
1 small zucchini, finely chopped
3 garlic cloves, minced
1 large egg
2 tablespoons whole milk
½ cup plain breadcrumbs
1 tablespoon dried oregano
1 teaspoon ground cumin
1¼ pounds ground pork
Salt and freshly ground black pepper to taste
1 (28-ounce) can crushed tomatoes in tomato puree
1 or 2 chipotle chiles in adobo sauce, drained
¼ cup chopped fresh cilantro
Vegetable oil spray

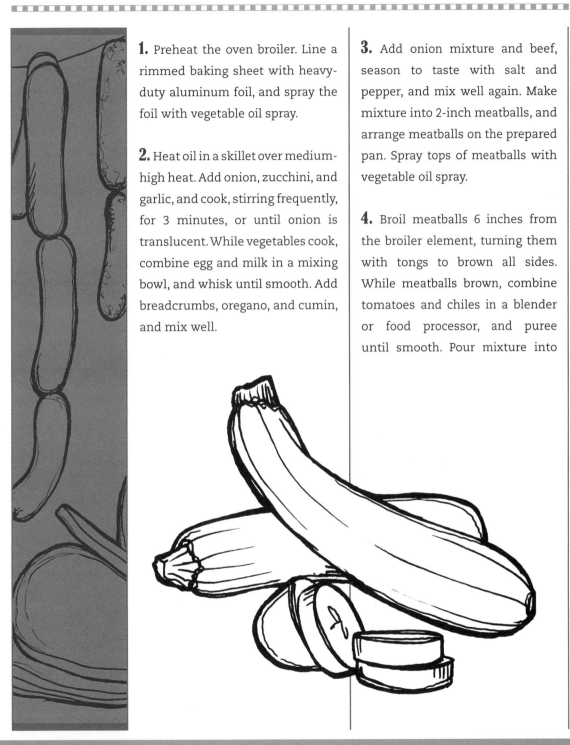

1. Preheat the oven broiler. Line a rimmed baking sheet with heavy-duty aluminum foil, and spray the foil with vegetable oil spray.

2. Heat oil in a skillet over medium-high heat. Add onion, zucchini, and garlic, and cook, stirring frequently, for 3 minutes, or until onion is translucent. While vegetables cook, combine egg and milk in a mixing bowl, and whisk until smooth. Add breadcrumbs, oregano, and cumin, and mix well.

3. Add onion mixture and beef, season to taste with salt and pepper, and mix well again. Make mixture into 2-inch meatballs, and arrange meatballs on the prepared pan. Spray tops of meatballs with vegetable oil spray.

4. Broil meatballs 6 inches from the broiler element, turning them with tongs to brown all sides. While meatballs brown, combine tomatoes and chiles in a blender or food processor, and puree until smooth. Pour mixture into

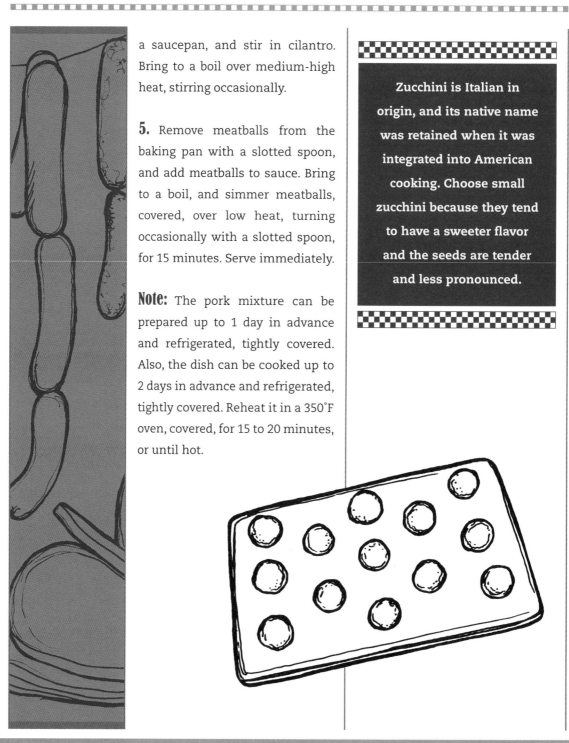

a saucepan, and stir in cilantro. Bring to a boil over medium-high heat, stirring occasionally.

5. Remove meatballs from the baking pan with a slotted spoon, and add meatballs to sauce. Bring to a boil, and simmer meatballs, covered, over low heat, turning occasionally with a slotted spoon, for 15 minutes. Serve immediately.

Note: The pork mixture can be prepared up to 1 day in advance and refrigerated, tightly covered. Also, the dish can be cooked up to 2 days in advance and refrigerated, tightly covered. Reheat it in a 350°F oven, covered, for 15 to 20 minutes, or until hot.

Zucchini is Italian in origin, and its native name was retained when it was integrated into American cooking. Choose small zucchini because they tend to have a sweeter flavor and the seeds are tender and less pronounced.

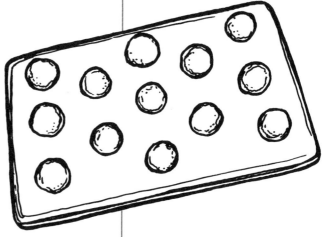

Caribbean Pork Meatballs with Mango

Makes 4 to 6 servings

Active time:
25 minutes

Start to finish:
1 hour

VARIATIONS

Instead of mango, make with chopped papaya or pineapple.

Substitute ground veal or ground turkey for the pork.

While curry powder is most often associated with Indian food, it's also very much at home in the West Indies. These meatballs have a hot and sweet flavor from the fresh fruit as well as chutney in the sauce; serve them over rice.

3 tablespoons vegetable oil

1 large onion, chopped

3 garlic cloves, minced

1 large egg

2 tablespoons whole milk

3 slices white bread

½ teaspoon ground ginger

¼ teaspoon ground nutmeg

1¼ pounds ground pork

Salt and freshly ground black pepper to taste

1 tablespoon curry powder

1 cup pineapple juice

1 cup chicken stock

⅓ cup jarred mango chutney, such as Major Grey's, chopped

2 cups diced fresh mango

1 (10-ounce) package frozen peas, thawed

1 tablespoon cornstarch

Vegetable oil spray

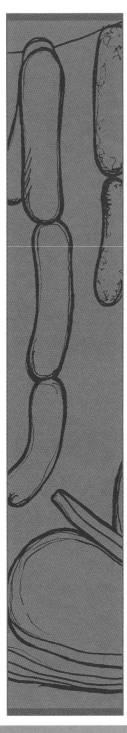

1. Preheat the oven broiler. Line a rimmed baking sheet with heavy-duty aluminum foil, and spray the foil with vegetable oil spray.

2. Heat oil in a large skillet over medium-high heat. Add onion and garlic and cook, stirring frequently, for 3 minutes, or until onion is translucent. While vegetables cook, combine egg and milk in a mixing bowl, and whisk until smooth. Break bread into tiny pieces and add to the mixing bowl along with ginger and nutmeg, and mix well.

3. Add ½ of onion mixture and pork, season to taste with salt and pepper, and mix well again. Make mixture into 1½-inch meatballs, and arrange meatballs on the prepared pan. Spray tops of meatballs with vegetable oil spray.

4. Broil meatballs 6 inches from the broiler element, turning them with tongs to brown all sides. While meatballs brown, add curry powder to vegetables remaining in the skillet, and cook over low heat for 1 minute, stirring constantly.

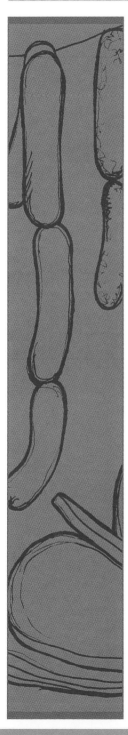

Add pineapple juice, chicken stock, and chutney to the skillet. Bring to a boil over medium-high heat, stirring occasionally. Simmer sauce over medium heat, uncovered, for 10 minutes.

5. Remove meatballs from the baking pan with a slotted spoon, and add meatballs to sauce, along with mango and peas. Bring to a boil, and simmer meatballs, covered, over low heat, turning occasionally with a slotted spoon, for 15 minutes. Mix cornstarch with 1 tablespoon cold water. Add mixture to sauce, and cook for an additional 2 minutes, or until lightly thickened. Season to taste with salt and pepper, and serve immediately.

Note: The pork mixture can be prepared up to 1 day in advance and refrigerated, tightly covered. Also, the dish can be cooked up to 2 days in advance and refrigerated, tightly covered. Reheat it in a 350°F oven, covered, for 15 to 20 minutes, or until hot.

If you find it difficult to peel a mango, try peeling it from the other direction. Mangoes have an easy and hard way to peel, and it can vary from fruit to fruit.

Chinese Sweet and Sour Pork Meatballs

Makes 4 to 6 servings

Active time:
25 minutes

Start to finish:
50 minutes

VARIATIONS

Make the meatballs from beef, chicken, or veal.

Instead of pineapple, try mango or papaya as the fruit.

Before traditional Chinese food became popular in this country, Chinese-American dishes often paired sweet and sour flavors. I remember making these meatballs for my sister and her college roommate in the 1960s. Guess what? It's still good. The rice is in the meatballs so the meal is complete.

1¼ pounds ground pork

1 cup cooked white rice

4 scallions, white parts and
    3 inches of green tops, chopped

4 garlic cloves, minced, divided

¼ cup soy sauce, divided

2 tablespoons Asian sesame oil

Freshly ground black pepper to taste

¾ cup pineapple juice

½ cup ketchup

⅓ cup firmly packed light
    brown sugar

¼ cup cider vinegar

¼ cup water

1 tablespoon cornstarch

2 tablespoons grated fresh ginger

½ teaspoon crushed red pepper
    flakes or to taste

2 tablespoons peanut or
    vegetable oil

1 sweet onion, like Vidalia or
    Bermuda, sliced lengthwise

1 red bell pepper, seeds and ribs
    removed, and sliced

2 cups diced fresh pineapple

Vegetable oil spray

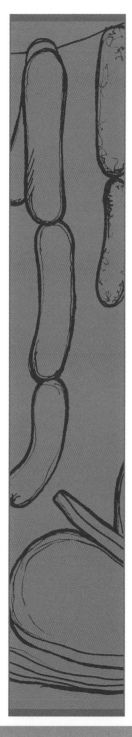

1. Preheat the oven to 450°F. Line a rimmed baking sheet with heavy-duty aluminum foil, and spray the foil with vegetable oil spray.

2. Combine pork, rice, scallions, 2 garlic cloves, 2 tablespoons soy sauce, sesame oil, and pepper in a mixing bowl, and mix well. Make mixture into 1½-inch meatballs, and arrange meatballs on the prepared pan. Spray tops of meatballs with vegetable oil spray.

3. Bake meatballs for 12 to 15 minutes, or until cooked through. Remove the pan from the oven, and set aside. Combine pineapple juice, ketchup, brown sugar, vinegar, ¼ cup water, and cornstarch in a bowl, and stir well to dissolve sugar. Set aside.

4. While meatballs bake, heat oil in a large skillet over high heat, swirling to coat. Add remaining garlic, ginger, and red pepper flakes, and stir-fry for 15 seconds, or until fragrant. Add onion and bell pepper and stir-fry for 1 minute. Add sauce and pineapple, and cook, stirring frequently, for 2 minutes, or until slightly thickened.

5. Remove meatballs from the baking pan with a slotted spoon, and add meatballs to the skillet. Cook 1 minute, and serve immediately.

Note: The pork mixture can be prepared up to 1 day in advance and refrigerated, tightly covered. Also, the dish can be cooked up to 2 days in advance and refrigerated, tightly covered. Reheat it in a 350°F oven, covered, for 15 to 20 minutes, or until hot.

The English word *pineapple* evolved because of the fruit's resemblance to a pine cone rather than anything to do with its flavor or color. The Tupi, an indigenous tribe in Brazil, called the fruit *was anana*, which means "excellent fruit." Hummingbirds, which are native to the tropics, are the natural pollinators for pineapple.

Steamed Chinese Pork Meatballs

Makes 4 to 6 servings

Active time:
20 minutes

Start to finish:
5 hours, including 4 hours to soak rice

Rice-coated steamed meatballs are one of my favorite dim sum treats. I never realized how easy they are to make at home until I began developing this recipe. Serve with some fried rice or lo mein and some stir-fried vegetables.

2 cups glutinous rice
½ cup dried shiitake mushrooms
1 cup boiling water
1 large egg
2 tablespoons soy sauce
1½ tablespoons cornstarch
2 teaspoons granulated sugar
½ cup finely chopped water
    chestnuts
½ cup panko breadcrumbs
3 tablespoons chopped fresh cilantro
2 garlic cloves, minced
2 scallions, white parts and
    2 inches of green tops, rinsed,
    trimmed, and chopped
1 tablespoon grated fresh ginger
1¼ pounds ground pork
Vegetable oil spray

For dipping:
1 cup Sweet and Sour Sauce (page
    56) or purchased sauce, heated

1. Soak rice covered with cold water in a mixing bowl for 4 hours, or preferably overnight. Once soaked, drain rice well, and place it on a lint-free cloth.

2. Combine shiitake mushrooms and 1 cup boiling water in a bowl, pushing them down into the water. Soak for 10 minutes, then drain mushrooms and reserve soaking liquid. Discard stems, and chop mushrooms. Set aside.

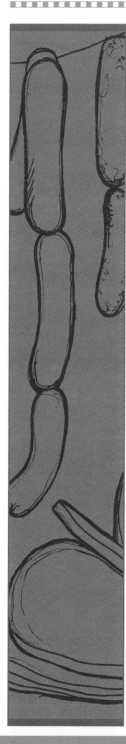

3. Combine egg, 2 tablespoons mushroom soaking liquid, soy sauce, cornstarch, and sugar in a mixing bowl, and whisk until smooth. Add mushrooms, water chestnuts, breadcrumbs, cilantro, garlic, scallion, ginger, and pork, and mix well.

4. Make mixture into 1½-inch balls, and roll balls in rice, pressing it in. Spray bamboo steamer baskets with vegetable oil spray, and arrange meatballs in baskets.

5. Steam meatballs for 30 to 35 minutes, and serve immediately, accompanied by a bowl of Sweet and Sour Sauce for dipping.

Note: The pork mixture can be prepared up to 1 day in advance and refrigerated, tightly covered. Also, the meatballs can be steamed up to 2 days in advance and refrigerated, tightly covered. Reheat them in the steamer for 5 to 10 minutes, or until hot.

Although fresh shiitake mushrooms are relative newcomers to the American produce section, they are the granddaddy of all cultivated mushrooms. The Japanese have been cultivating them for more than 2,000 years. The ancient Greeks and Romans did not cultivate mushrooms; they merely encouraged wild ones to grow. It was not until the eighteenth century, when Olivier de Serres was agronomist to French King Louis XIV, that mushroom cultivation began in Europe.

Beijing Pork Meatballs

Makes 4 to 6 servings

Active time:
20 minutes

Start to finish:
35 minutes

VARIATION

Substitute ground chicken or ground turkey for the pork.

I made this recipe up one day to entice a friend's young child into eating more vegetables. It was so delicious it became part of my repertoire.

2 tablespoons Asian sesame oil

1 tablespoon vegetable oil

3 scallions, white parts and
    2 inches of green tops, chopped

3 garlic cloves, minced

1 tablespoon grated fresh ginger

1 tablespoon fermented black beans,
    chopped

1 carrot, finely chopped

1 celery rib, finely chopped

1 large egg

3 tablespoon hoisin sauce

1 tablespoon soy sauce

1 tablespoon Chinese chili paste
    with garlic

½ cup cooked white rice

1¼ pounds ground pork

Vegetable oil spray

For dipping:

1 cup Sesame Honey
    Mustard Sauce (page 53)

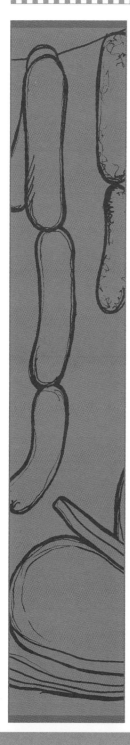

1. Preheat the oven to 450°F. Line a rimmed baking sheet with heavy-duty aluminum foil, and spray the foil with vegetable oil spray.

2. Heat sesame oil and vegetable oil in a skillet over medium-high heat. Add scallions, garlic, ginger, and black beans, and cook, stirring frequently, for 1 minute. Add carrot and celery, and cook, stirring frequently, for 3 minutes. While vegetables cook, whisk egg, hoisin sauce, soy sauce, and chili paste in a mixing bowl. Add rice, and mix well.

3. Add vegetable mixture and pork to the mixing bowl, and mix well again. Make mixture into 1½-inch meatballs, and arrange meatballs on the prepared pan. Spray tops of meatballs with vegetable oil spray.

4. Bake meatballs for 12 to 15 minutes, or until cooked through. Remove the pan from the oven, and serve immediately accompanied by a bowl of Sesame Honey Mustard Sauce for dipping.

Note: The pork mixture can be prepared up to 1 day in advance and refrigerated, tightly covered. Also, the meatballs can be baked up to 2 days in advance and refrigerated, tightly covered. Reheat them in a 350°F oven, covered, for 10 to 12 minutes, or until hot.

Fermented black beans are tiny black soybeans preserved in salt, so they have a very pungent flavor. They should be chopped to release their flavor prior to cooking. Because they are preserved with salt, they last up to 2 years if refrigerated once opened.

Grilled Thai Pork Meatballs

Makes 4 to 6 servings

Active time: 20 minutes

Start to finish: 30 minutes

VARIATION

Ground turkey or ground veal are equally good as the basis for the meatballs.

The luscious aroma from grilling kebabs permeates the air at Thai street food markets. The flavors of fish sauce, garlic, and cilantro are present in these grilled meatballs.

8 to 12 (8-inch) bamboo skewers

2 tablespoons Asian sesame oil

4 shallots, diced

4 garlic cloves, minced

3 tablespoons fish sauce (nam pla)

3 tablespoons dry sherry

½ cup panko breadcrumbs

2 tablespoons chopped fresh cilantro

1 tablespoon granulated sugar

2 tablespoons cornstarch

1¼ pounds ground pork

Salt and freshly ground black
    pepper to taste

For dipping:

1 cup Thai Sweet and Spicy Dipping
    Sauce (page 58)

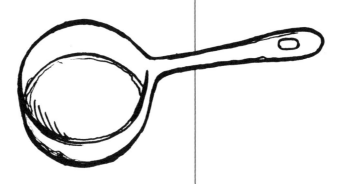

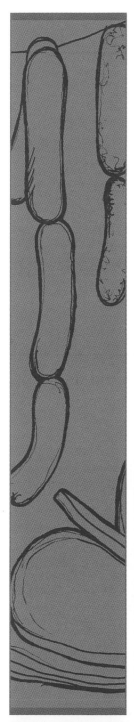

1. Soak the bamboo skewers in cold water to cover. Prepare a medium charcoal or gas grill, or preheat the oven broiler.

2. Heat sesame oil in a small skillet over medium-high heat. Add shallot and garlic, and cook, stirring frequently, for 3 minutes, or until shallots are translucent.

It's a shame to waste much of a bunch of an herb like parsley, cilantro, and dill, when you need but a few tablespoons for a recipe. Trim off the stems, and then wrap small bundles in plastic wrap, and freeze them. When you need some, you can "chop" the herb with the blunt side of a knife. Herbs chop easily when frozen, and this method results in better flavors than using dried herbs.

While vegetables cook, combine fish sauce, sherry, breadcrumbs, cilantro, sugar, and cornstarch in a mixing bowl, and mix well.

3. Add vegetable mixture and pork to the mixing bowl, season to taste with salt and pepper, and mix well again.

4. Divide mixture into 8 to 12 portions, and form each portion into a sausage shape. Insert a skewer into each sausage so that the tip of the skewer is almost at the top of the meat.

5. Grill skewers for a total of 10 minutes, covered, turning them gently with tongs to cook all sides. Serve immediately accompanied by a bowl of Thai Sweet and Spicy Dipping Sauce.

Note: The pork mixture can be prepared up to 1 day in advance and refrigerated, tightly covered. Also, the skewers can be grilled up to 2 days in advance and refrigerated, tightly covered. Reheat them in a 350°F oven, covered, for 10 to 12 minutes, or until hot.

MEATING THE CHALLENGE:

MEATBALLS MADE FROM LAMB AND VEAL

While ground beef, ground pork, and sausage have been fixtures in the meat case for generations, grinding lamb and delicate veal is a recent phenomenon. This is truly a shame, because the ground form is the most affordable for enjoying the flavor of these luxury meats.

More veal is eaten per capita in Italy than in any other country, which is why so many of the recipes in this chapter are Italian inspired. Veal is also eaten in some northern European cuisines, but rarely beyond.

The same is not true for lamb; it's a world traveler. It is popular in countries bordering the Mediterranean, as well as in the Middle East. It has long been the favorite meat in Greek cooking and plays an important role in Spain's culinary heart, too. Lamb is also very well represented in Persian and Indian dishes.

Veal Meatballs Parmigiana

Makes 4 to 6 servings

Active time: 25 minutes

Start to finish: 1 hour

Veal parmigiana is an Italian-American invention. You'd be hard pressed to find it on a menu in Italy. But we love it. This meatball version is easy to make and ideal to serve at a buffet dinner. All you need is a tossed salad and some crusty garlic bread.

3 tablespoons olive oil

1 medium onion, chopped

3 garlic cloves, minced

1 large egg

2 tablespoons whole milk

3 pieces white sandwich bread

2 tablespoons chopped fresh parsley

1¼ pounds ground veal

Salt and freshly ground black
    pepper to taste

2 cups Herbed Tomato Sauce
    (page 38) or purchased
    marinara sauce

2 cups grated whole milk mozzarella

¼ cup freshly grated Parmesan

Vegetable oil spray

1. Preheat the oven broiler. Line a rimmed baking sheet with heavy-duty aluminum foil, and spray the foil with vegetable oil spray.

2. Heat oil in a large skillet over medium-high heat. Add onion and garlic and cook, stirring frequently, for 3 minutes, or until onion is translucent. While vegetables cook,

combine egg and milk in a mixing bowl, and whisk until smooth. Break bread into tiny pieces and add to mixing bowl along with parsley, and mix well.

3. Add onion mixture and veal, season to taste with salt and pepper, and mix well again. Make mixture into 1½-inch meatballs, and arrange meatballs on the prepared pan. Spray tops of meatballs with vegetable oil spray.

4. Broil meatballs 6 inches from the broiler element, turning them with tongs to brown all sides. While meatballs brown, heat Herbed Tomato Sauce in a large skillet over medium-high heat, stirring occasionally.

5. Remove meatballs from the baking pan with a slotted spoon, and add meatballs to sauce. Bring to a boil, and simmer meatballs, covered, over low heat, turning occasionally with a slotted spoon, for 15 minutes. Season to taste with salt and pepper, and reheat the oven broiler.

6. Transfer meatballs and sauce to a 9 x 13-inch baking pan, and sprinkle mozzarella and Parmesan over meatballs. Broil 6 inches from the broiler element for 2 minutes, or until cheese is bubbly and browned. Serve immediately.

Note: The veal mixture can be prepared up to 1 day in advance and refrigerated, tightly covered. Also, the dish can be cooked up to 2 days in advance and refrigerated, tightly covered. Reheat in a 350°F oven, covered, for 15 to 20 minutes, or until hot.

Meatballs played a role in a famous ad campaign in the 1960s when the phrase "Mamma Mia! That's a some spicy meatball!" entered the vernacular as an ad for Alka Seltzer.

Veal Meatballs Marsala

Makes 4 to 6
servings

Active time:
25 minutes

Start to finish:
50 minutes

VARIATION

· *Substitute ground
chicken or turkey
for the veal.*

Veal, like chicken and pork, is mildly flavored and takes to a wide variety of seasonings and sauces. The heady Marsala wine, mushrooms, and herbs create a delicious mélange for the meatballs; serve this over small pasta, such as orzo.

3 tablespoons olive oil

1 medium onion, chopped

6 garlic cloves, minced

1 large egg

2 tablespoons whole milk

3 pieces white sandwich bread

⅓ cup chopped fresh parsley, divided

1¼ pounds ground veal

Salt and freshly ground black
    pepper to taste

3 tablespoons unsalted butter

½ pound mushrooms, wiped with
    a damp paper towel, stemmed,
    and diced

3 tablespoons all-purpose flour

1 tablespoon chopped fresh oregano
    or 1 teaspoon dried

2 teaspoons fresh thyme or
    ½ teaspoon dried

1 cup chicken stock

⅔ cup sweet Marsala wine

Vegetable oil spray

1. Preheat the oven broiler. Line a rimmed baking sheet with heavy-duty aluminum foil, and spray the foil with vegetable oil spray.

2. Heat oil in a large skillet over medium-high heat. Add onion and garlic and cook, stirring frequently, for 3 minutes, or until onion is translucent. While vegetables cook, combine egg and milk in a mixing bowl, and whisk until smooth. Break bread into tiny pieces and add to mixing bowl along with 2 tablespoons parsley, and mix well.

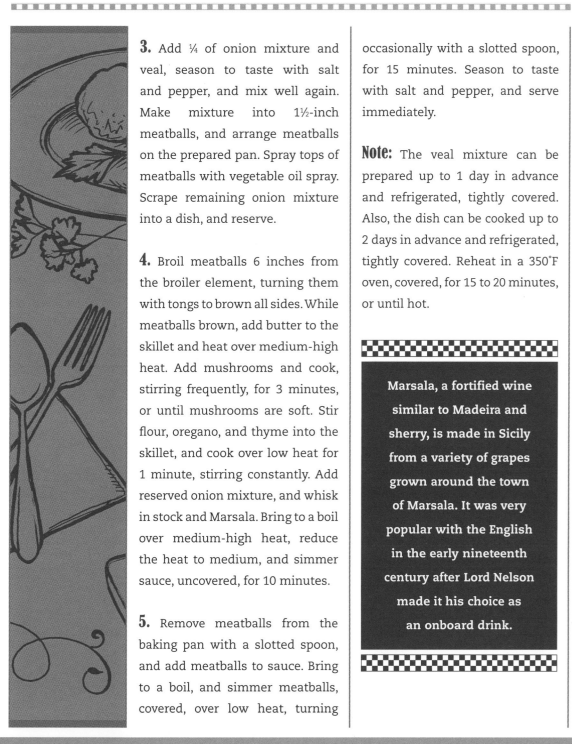

3. Add ¼ of onion mixture and veal, season to taste with salt and pepper, and mix well again. Make mixture into 1½-inch meatballs, and arrange meatballs on the prepared pan. Spray tops of meatballs with vegetable oil spray. Scrape remaining onion mixture into a dish, and reserve.

4. Broil meatballs 6 inches from the broiler element, turning them with tongs to brown all sides. While meatballs brown, add butter to the skillet and heat over medium-high heat. Add mushrooms and cook, stirring frequently, for 3 minutes, or until mushrooms are soft. Stir flour, oregano, and thyme into the skillet, and cook over low heat for 1 minute, stirring constantly. Add reserved onion mixture, and whisk in stock and Marsala. Bring to a boil over medium-high heat, reduce the heat to medium, and simmer sauce, uncovered, for 10 minutes.

5. Remove meatballs from the baking pan with a slotted spoon, and add meatballs to sauce. Bring to a boil, and simmer meatballs, covered, over low heat, turning occasionally with a slotted spoon, for 15 minutes. Season to taste with salt and pepper, and serve immediately.

Note: The veal mixture can be prepared up to 1 day in advance and refrigerated, tightly covered. Also, the dish can be cooked up to 2 days in advance and refrigerated, tightly covered. Reheat in a 350°F oven, covered, for 15 to 20 minutes, or until hot.

Marsala, a fortified wine similar to Madeira and sherry, is made in Sicily from a variety of grapes grown around the town of Marsala. It was very popular with the English in the early nineteenth century after Lord Nelson made it his choice as an onboard drink.

Veal Meatballs with Leeks and Blue Cheese

Makes 4 to 6 servings

Active time:
25 minutes

Start to finish:
40 minutes

VARIATION

Substitute ground chicken or turkey for the veal.

This is a meatball version of veal cordon bleu, except that the sharp and pungent blue cheese is mixed right in with the veal. Sweet leeks balance the flavor. These are always a hit when served as an hors d'oeuvre.

3 large leeks
3 tablespoons unsalted butter
2 garlic cloves, minced
½ cup chicken stock
1 large egg
½ cup plain breadcrumbs
½ cup crumbled blue cheese
2 tablespoons chopped fresh parsley
1 tablespoon fresh thyme or
    1 teaspoon dried
1¼ pounds ground veal
Salt and freshly ground black
    pepper to taste
Vegetable oil spray

For dipping:
1 cup Blue Cheese Sauce (page 41)
    or purchased blue cheese
    dressing

1. Preheat the oven to 450°F. Line a rimmed baking sheet with heavy-duty aluminum foil, and spray the foil with vegetable oil spray. Rinse leeks, trim root end, and discard all but white and light green portions. Chop leeks, and rinse them well in a colander, rubbing to dislodge any grit. Drain well, and set aside.

2. Heat butter in a skillet over medium-high heat. Add leeks and garlic, and cook, stirring frequently, for 5 minutes, or until leeks are soft. Add chicken stock to the skillet, and continue to cook, stirring frequently, for 5 minutes, or until only 3 tablespoons liquid remain. Set aside to cool.

3. While vegetables cook, whisk eggs in a mixing bowl and add breadcrumbs, blue cheese, parsley, and thyme, and mix well.

4. Add vegetable mixture and veal to the mixing bowl, season to taste with salt and pepper, and mix well again. Make mixture into 1½-inch meatballs, and arrange meatballs on the prepared pan. Spray tops of meatballs with vegetable oil spray.

5. Bake meatballs for 12 to 15 minutes, or until cooked through. Remove the pan from the oven, and serve immediately, accompanied by a bowl of Blue Cheese Sauce for dipping.

Note: The veal mixture can be prepared up to 1 day in advance and refrigerated, tightly covered. Also, the meatballs can be baked up to 2 days in advance and refrigerated, tightly covered. Reheat them in a 350°F oven, covered, for 10 to 12 minutes, or until hot.

Cheeses with blue veining caused by mold have been savored for centuries in Europe, but it was only in the twentieth century that they were successfully cultured in North America. At first, the blue cheeses were made with goat's milk, but now cow's milk is used.

Spinach and Gruyère Veal Meatballs

Makes 4 to 6 servings

Active time: 25 minutes

Start to finish: 40 minutes

VARIATION

Substitute ground pork, chicken, or turkey for the veal.

Fresh-tasting spinach and mellow Gruyère are delicious flavors to add to the delicate veal, and these can be served either plain or with a sauce. There's a lot of flavor in the meatballs themselves.

2 tablespoons unsalted butter
2 shallots, chopped
2 cups firmly packed baby spinach
    leaves, rinsed and dried
1 large egg
2 tablespoons dry vermouth or
    dry white wine
½ cup panko breadcrumbs
1 cup grated Gruyère
2 tablespoons chopped fresh parsley
1¼ pounds ground veal
Salt and freshly ground black
    pepper to taste
Vegetable oil spray

For dipping:
1 cup Herbed Tomato Sauce
    (page 38) or purchased
    marinara sauce, heated

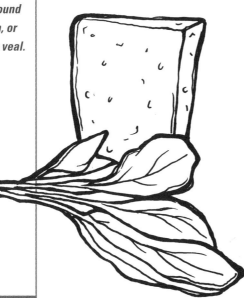

1. Preheat the oven to 450°F. Line a rimmed baking sheet with heavy-duty aluminum foil, and spray the foil with vegetable oil spray.

2. Heat butter in a small skillet over medium-high heat. Add shallots, and cook, stirring frequently, for 3 minutes, or until shallots are translucent. Add spinach to the skillet, and continue to cook, stirring frequently, for 2 minutes, or until spinach is wilted.

3. While vegetables cook, whisk egg and vermouth in a mixing bowl, and add breadcrumbs, cheese, and parsley, and mix well.

4. Add vegetable mixture and veal to the mixing bowl, season to taste with salt and pepper, and mix well again. Make mixture into 1½-inch meatballs, and arrange meatballs on the prepared pan. Spray tops of meatballs with vegetable oil spray.

5. Bake meatballs for 12 to 15 minutes, or until cooked through. Remove the pan from the oven, and serve immediately, accompanied by a bowl of Herbed Tomato Sauce for dipping.

Note: The veal mixture can be prepared up to 1 day in advance and refrigerated, tightly covered. Also, the meatballs can be baked up to 2 days in advance and refrigerated, tightly covered. Reheat them in a 350°F oven, covered, for 10 to 12 minutes, or until hot.

In the film *The Wedding Singer* the title character, played by Adam Sandler, gives singing lessons to an old Italian woman in exchange for plates of her famous meatballs.

Veal Meatballs with Olives and Sun-Dried Tomatoes

Makes 4 to 6 servings

Active time:
25 minutes

Start to finish:
40 minutes

VARIATIONS

Substitute ground pork, chicken, or turkey for the veal.

For a heartier dish, substitute ½ pound bulk Italian sausage for ½ pound of the veal.

Dehydrating, or removing the moisture from foods, intensifies their natural sweetness, especially tomatoes. That sweetness contrasts with the salty olives also added to the veal mix. While these need no sauce to add flavor, I reinforce the tomato flavor by using a sauce with similar ingredients for dipping. Save the oil that's drained off the sun-dried tomatoes and use it in salad dressings or for making homemade mayonnaise or aïoli.

½ cup sun-dried tomatoes packed in olive oil, drained with oil reserved, and chopped
2 shallots, chopped
3 garlic cloves, minced
1 large egg
2 tablespoons whole milk
½ cup seasoned Italian breadcrumbs
¼ cup chopped oil-cured black olives
¼ cup freshly grated Parmesan
2 tablespoons chopped fresh parsley
1 tablespoon chopped fresh oregano or 1 teaspoon dried
1¼ pounds ground veal
Salt and freshly ground black pepper to taste
Vegetable oil spray

For dipping:
1 cup Sun-Dried Tomato Sauce (page 43)

1. Preheat the oven to 450°F. Line a rimmed baking sheet with heavy-duty aluminum foil, and spray the foil with vegetable oil spray.

2. Heat reserved oil in a small skillet over medium-high heat. Add shallots and garlic, and cook, stirring frequently, for 3 minutes, or until shallots are translucent. While vegetables cook, whisk egg and milk in a mixing bowl, and add breadcrumbs, olives, cheese, parsley, and oregano and mix well.

3. Add vegetable mixture and veal to the mixing bowl, season to taste with salt and pepper, and mix well again. Make mixture into 1½-inch meatballs, and arrange meatballs on the prepared pan. Spray tops of meatballs with vegetable oil spray.

4. Bake meatballs for 12 to 15 minutes, or until cooked through. Remove the pan from the oven, and serve immediately, accompanied by a bowl of Sun-dried Tomato Sauce for dipping.

Note: The veal mixture can be prepared up to 1 day in advance and refrigerated, tightly covered. Also, the meatballs can be baked up to 2 days in advance and refrigerated, tightly covered. Reheat them in a 350°F oven, covered, for 10 to 12 minutes, or until hot.

Dilled Scandinavian Veal Meatballs

Makes 4 to 6 servings

Active time:
25 minutes

Start to finish:
50 minutes

VARIATION

Substitute ground pork, chicken, or turkey for the veal.

Veal is used on rare occasions in Scandinavian cooking, with these lightly seasoned meatballs being an exception. The light dill cream sauce is luscious. Serve this with buttered egg noodles.

4 tablespoons (½ stick) unsalted butter, divided
1 small onion, chopped
1 large egg
2 tablespoons whole milk
3 slices white sandwich bread
Pinch ground nutmeg
Pinch ground allspice
Pinch ground ginger
1¼ pounds ground veal
Salt and freshly ground black pepper to taste
3 tablespoons all-purpose flour
1 cup chicken stock
⅔ cup light cream
¼ cup chopped fresh dill
Vegetable oil spray

1. Preheat the oven broiler. Line a rimmed baking sheet with heavy-duty aluminum foil, and spray the foil with vegetable oil spray.

2. Heat 2 tablespoons butter in a large skillet over medium-high heat. Add onion, and cook, stirring

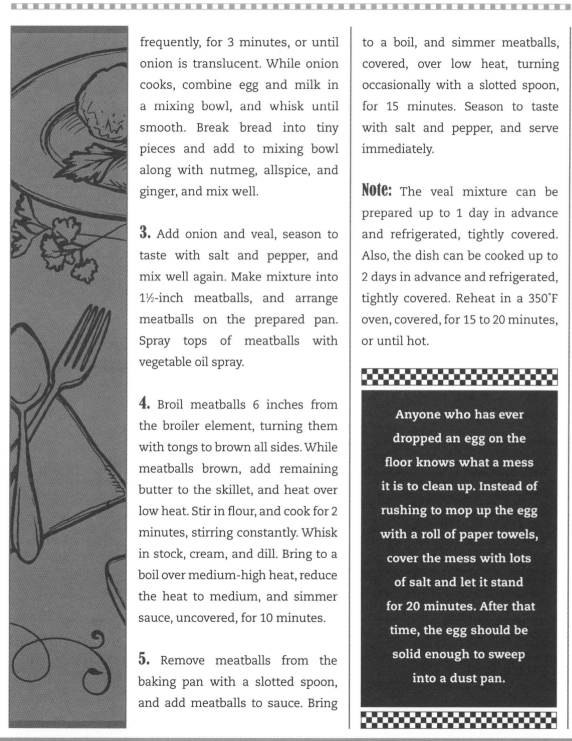

frequently, for 3 minutes, or until onion is translucent. While onion cooks, combine egg and milk in a mixing bowl, and whisk until smooth. Break bread into tiny pieces and add to mixing bowl along with nutmeg, allspice, and ginger, and mix well.

3. Add onion and veal, season to taste with salt and pepper, and mix well again. Make mixture into 1½-inch meatballs, and arrange meatballs on the prepared pan. Spray tops of meatballs with vegetable oil spray.

4. Broil meatballs 6 inches from the broiler element, turning them with tongs to brown all sides. While meatballs brown, add remaining butter to the skillet, and heat over low heat. Stir in flour, and cook for 2 minutes, stirring constantly. Whisk in stock, cream, and dill. Bring to a boil over medium-high heat, reduce the heat to medium, and simmer sauce, uncovered, for 10 minutes.

5. Remove meatballs from the baking pan with a slotted spoon, and add meatballs to sauce. Bring to a boil, and simmer meatballs, covered, over low heat, turning occasionally with a slotted spoon, for 15 minutes. Season to taste with salt and pepper, and serve immediately.

Note: The veal mixture can be prepared up to 1 day in advance and refrigerated, tightly covered. Also, the dish can be cooked up to 2 days in advance and refrigerated, tightly covered. Reheat in a 350°F oven, covered, for 15 to 20 minutes, or until hot.

Anyone who has ever dropped an egg on the floor knows what a mess it is to clean up. Instead of rushing to mop up the egg with a roll of paper towels, cover the mess with lots of salt and let it stand for 20 minutes. After that time, the egg should be solid enough to sweep into a dust pan.

Grilled Chinese Veal Meatballs

Makes 4 to 6 servings

Active time:
20 minutes

Start to finish:
35 minutes

VARIATION

Substitute ground pork, chicken, or turkey for the veal.

Veal is not used in Asian cuisines, but it's delicious when grilled, especially when Asian flavors are used. Some stir-fried vegetables and rice can complete your meal.

8 to 12 (8-inch) bamboo skewers
1 large egg
3 tablespoons soy sauce
2 tablespoons dry sherry
½ cup panko breadcrumbs
½ cup finely chopped water
    chestnuts
6 scallions, white parts and
    2 inches of green tops,
    thinly sliced
2 tablespoons grated fresh ginger
¼ cup chopped fresh cilantro
4 garlic cloves, minced
1¼ pounds ground veal
Freshly ground black pepper to taste
Vegetable oil spray

For dipping:
1 cup Asian Dipping Sauce
    (page 54)

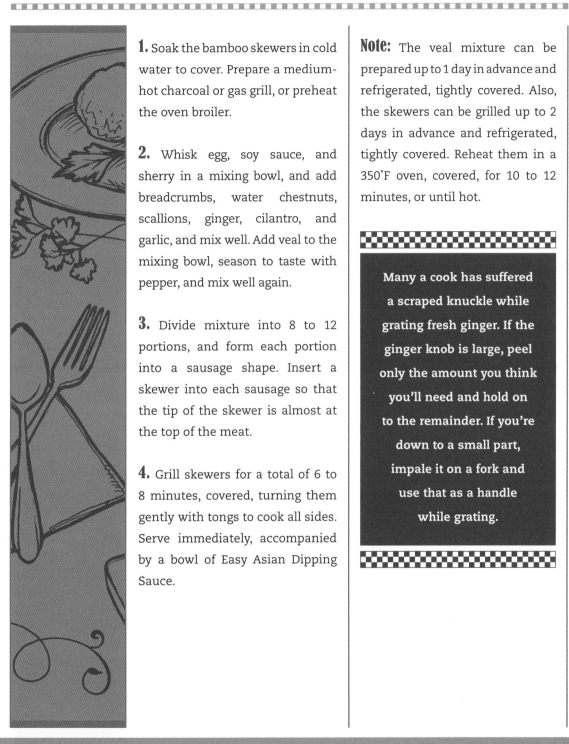

1. Soak the bamboo skewers in cold water to cover. Prepare a medium-hot charcoal or gas grill, or preheat the oven broiler.

2. Whisk egg, soy sauce, and sherry in a mixing bowl, and add breadcrumbs, water chestnuts, scallions, ginger, cilantro, and garlic, and mix well. Add veal to the mixing bowl, season to taste with pepper, and mix well again.

3. Divide mixture into 8 to 12 portions, and form each portion into a sausage shape. Insert a skewer into each sausage so that the tip of the skewer is almost at the top of the meat.

4. Grill skewers for a total of 6 to 8 minutes, covered, turning them gently with tongs to cook all sides. Serve immediately, accompanied by a bowl of Easy Asian Dipping Sauce.

Note: The veal mixture can be prepared up to 1 day in advance and refrigerated, tightly covered. Also, the skewers can be grilled up to 2 days in advance and refrigerated, tightly covered. Reheat them in a 350°F oven, covered, for 10 to 12 minutes, or until hot.

Many a cook has suffered a scraped knuckle while grating fresh ginger. If the ginger knob is large, peel only the amount you think you'll need and hold on to the remainder. If you're down to a small part, impale it on a fork and use that as a handle while grating.

Lamb Meatballs in Curried Coconut Sauce

Makes 4 to 6 servings

Active time: 25 minutes

Start to finish: 55 minutes

VARIATIONS

Substitute ground chuck for the lamb.

Substitute chopped prunes, raisins, or dried cranberries for the dried fruits listed.

Creamy coconut milk, succulent dried fruit, and curry powder create a sauce that transforms these lamb meatballs into an exotic adventure. Serve them over rice pilaf, with a simple vegetable dish such as steamed cauliflower or sautéed green beans.

2 tablespoons Asian sesame oil
8 scallions, white parts and
    2 inches of green tops, chopped
6 garlic cloves, minced
2 tablespoon grated fresh ginger
1 large egg
2 tablespoons soy sauce
½ cup panko breadcrumbs
2 tablespoons chopped fresh cilantro

1¼ pounds ground lamb
Salt and freshly ground black
    pepper to taste
3 tablespoons curry powder
1 (14-ounce) can coconut milk
½ cup chicken stock
½ cup chopped dried apricots
3 tablespoons dried currants
1 tablespoon cornstarch
Vegetable oil spray

1. Preheat the oven broiler. Line a rimmed baking sheet with heavy-duty aluminum foil, and spray the foil with vegetable oil spray.

2. Heat oil in a large skillet over medium-high heat. Add scallions, garlic, and ginger, and cook, stirring frequently, for 3 minutes, or until scallions are translucent. While vegetables cook, combine egg and soy sauce in a mixing bowl, and whisk until smooth. Add breadcrumbs, and cilantro, and mix well.

3. Add ½ of scallion mixture and lamb, season to taste with salt and pepper, and mix well again. Make mixture into 1½-inch meatballs, and arrange meatballs on the prepared pan. Spray tops of meatballs with vegetable oil spray.

4. Broil meatballs 6 inches from the broiler element, turning them with tongs to brown all sides. While meatballs brown, add curry powder to the skillet and cook over low heat, stirring constantly, for 1 minute. Stir in coconut milk, stock, apricots, and currants. Bring to a boil over medium-high heat, reduce the heat to medium, and simmer sauce, uncovered, for 10 minutes.

5. Remove meatballs from the baking pan with a slotted spoon, and add meatballs to sauce. Bring to a boil, and simmer meatballs, covered, over low heat, turning occasionally with a slotted spoon, for 15 minutes. Combine cornstarch and 1 tablespoon cold water in a small bowl, and stir well. Add mixture to sauce, and cook for

an additional 2 minutes, or until lightly thickened. Season to taste with salt and pepper, and serve immediately.

Note: The lamb mixture can be prepared up to 1 day in advance and refrigerated, tightly covered. Also, the dish can be cooked up to 2 days in advance and refrigerated, tightly covered. Reheat in a 350°F oven, covered, for 15 to 20 minutes, or until hot.

While it's a good idea to toss out any dried herb or spice that's been opened for more than six months, abbreviate the life of curry powder to two months. This ground blend, made up of up to 20 herbs and spices, loses its flavor and aroma very quickly.

Grilled Tandoori Lamb Meatballs

Makes 4 to 6 servings

Active time:
15 minutes

Start to finish:
30 minutes

VARIATION

Substitute ground chuck, chicken, or turkey for the lamb.

Indian dishes called *tandoori* mean that they are cooked over high heat in a traditional round tandoor, or oven. Many traditional Indian breads such as naan are also cooked in these ovens. But an outdoor grill does just as good a job, and these are some of the most flavorful morsels you will ever eat.

8 to 12 (8-inch) bamboo skewers
½ cup plain yogurt
1 large egg
3 garlic cloves, minced
3 scallions, chopped
1 tablespoon grated fresh ginger
2 tablespoons paprika
2 teaspoons ground coriander
2 teaspoons ground cumin
1 teaspoon granulated sugar
1 teaspoon ground ginger
⅛ teaspoon ground cinnamon
½ cup plain breadcrumbs
1¼ pounds ground lamb
Salt and cayenne to taste

For dipping:
1 cup Cucumber Raita (page 52)

1. Soak the bamboo skewers in cold water to cover. Prepare a medium-hot charcoal or gas grill, or preheat the oven broiler.

2. Combine yogurt, egg, garlic, scallions, ginger, paprika, coriander, cumin, sugar, ginger, cinnamon, and breadcrumbs, and mix well. Add lamb to the mixing bowl, season to taste with salt and cayenne, and mix well again.

3. Divide mixture into 8 to 12 portions, and form each portion into a sausage shape. Insert a skewer into each sausage so that the tip of the skewer is almost at the top of the meat.

4. Grill skewers for a total of 6 to 8 minutes, uncovered if using a charcoal grill, turning them gently with tongs to cook all sides. Serve immediately, accompanied by a bowl of Cucumber Raita for dipping.

Note: The lamb mixture can be prepared up to 1 day in advance and refrigerated, tightly covered. Also, the skewers can be grilled up to 2 days in advance and refrigerated, tightly covered. Reheat them in a 350°F oven, covered, for 10 to 12 minutes, or until hot.

Ground coriander is the seed of the same plant that produces cilantro as fresh leaves, although each flavor is entirely different. Coriander is one of the world's earliest recorded ingredients. Seeds were discovered in an Egyptian tomb that dates from 960 BCE.

Greek Lamb Meatballs

Makes 4 to 6 servings

Active time:
20 minutes

Start to finish:
45 minutes

VARIATION

Substitute ground chuck for the lamb.

In Greek and Middle Eastern food, mint is used in savory dishes rather than in desserts. When used in moderation, as in this recipe, the flavor enlivens the other herbs but doesn't dominate them. Serve the meatballs accompanied by tabbouleh or a pasta salad.

3 tablespoons olive oil
1 small onion, chopped
3 garlic cloves, minced
1 large egg
2 tablespoons whole milk
1 tablespoon freshly squeezed
    lemon juice
½ cup seasoned Italian breadcrumbs
3 tablespoons chopped fresh
    oregano or 2 teaspoons dried
2 tablespoons chopped fresh parsley
1 tablespoon chopped fresh mint
1¼ pounds ground lamb
Salt and freshly ground black
    pepper to taste
Vegetable oil spray

For dipping:
1 cup Middle Eastern Yogurt Sauce
    (page 51) or purchased hummus

1. Preheat the oven to 450°F. Line a rimmed baking sheet with heavy-duty aluminum foil, and spray the foil with vegetable oil spray.

2. Heat oil in a small skillet over medium-high heat. Add onion and garlic, and cook, stirring frequently, for 3 minutes, or until onion is translucent. While vegetables cook, whisk egg, milk, and lemon juice in a mixing bowl, and add breadcrumbs, oregano, parsley, and mint, and mix well.

3. Add vegetable mixture and lamb to the mixing bowl, season to taste with salt and pepper, and mix well again. Make mixture into 1½-inch meatballs, and arrange meatballs on the prepared pan. Spray tops of meatballs with vegetable oil spray.

4. Bake meatballs for 12 to 15 minutes, or until cooked through. Remove the pan from the oven, and serve immediately, accompanied by a bowl of Middle Eastern Yogurt Sauce for dipping.

Note: The lamb mixture can be prepared up to 1 day in advance and refrigerated, tightly covered. Also, the meatballs can be baked up to 2 days in advance and refrigerated, tightly covered. Reheat them in a 350°F oven, covered, for 10 to 12 minutes, or until hot.

In Greek mythology mint was once a nymph named Mentha. Because she angered Persephone, Pluto's wife, she turned her into this aromatic herb as permanent revenge.

Garlic-Rosemary Lamb Meatballs in Tomato Sauce

Makes 4 to 6 servings

Active time:
20 minutes

Start to finish:
45 minutes

Substitute ground chuck for the lamb.

Rosemary and garlic are my favorite seasonings for lamb, and here they are combined to flavor both the meatballs and the heady red wine sauce in which they're cooked. Serve these with some crusty bread.

¼ cup olive oil

2 large onions, chopped

5 garlic cloves, minced

1 large egg

2 tablespoons whole milk

1 tablespoon freshly squeezed
    lemon juice

½ cup plain breadcrumbs

¼ cup chopped fresh rosemary,
    divided

2 tablespoons chopped fresh parsley

1 tablespoon grated lemon zest

1¼ pounds ground lamb

Salt and freshly ground black
    pepper to taste

1 (15-ounce) can tomato sauce

¾ cup dry red wine

Vegetable oil spray

1. Preheat the oven broiler. Line a rimmed baking sheet with heavy-duty aluminum foil, and spray the foil with vegetable oil spray.

2. Heat oil in a large skillet over medium-high heat. Add onions and garlic and cook, stirring frequently, for 3 minutes, or until onions are translucent. While vegetables cook, combine egg, milk, and lemon juice in a mixing bowl, and whisk until smooth. Add breadcrumbs, 2 tablespoons rosemary, parsley, and lemon zest, and mix well.

3. Add ½ of onion mixture and lamb, season to taste with salt and pepper, and mix well again. Make mixture into 1½-inch meatballs, and arrange meatballs on the prepared pan. Spray tops of meatballs with vegetable oil spray.

4. Broil meatballs 6 inches from the broiler element, turning them with tongs to brown all sides. While meatballs brown, add remaining rosemary, tomato sauce, and wine to the skillet containing remaining onions and garlic. Bring to a boil over medium-high heat, stirring occasionally.

5. Remove meatballs from the baking pan with a slotted spoon, and add meatballs to sauce. Bring to a boil, and simmer the meatballs, covered, over low heat, turning occasionally with a slotted spoon, for 15 minutes. Serve immediately.

Note: The lamb mixture can be prepared up to 1 day in advance and refrigerated, tightly covered. Also, the dish can be made up to 2 days in advance and refrigerated, tightly covered. Reheat it in a 350˚F oven, covered, for 15 to 20 minutes, or until hot.

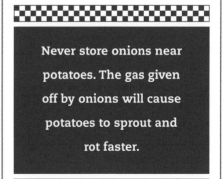

Never store onions near potatoes. The gas given off by onions will cause potatoes to sprout and rot faster.

Spanish Lamb Meatballs in Almond Sauce

Makes 4 to 6 servings

Active time:

20 minutes

Start to finish:

45 minutes

Spanish and Middle Eastern cooking feature many of the same ingredients, stemming from the period of Moorish rule over Spain. One of those ingredients is almonds. Here they add some crunchiness to the sauce.

¼ cup olive oil

1 large onion, chopped

3 garlic cloves, minced

1 large egg

⅔ cup dry red wine, divided

½ cup seasoned Italian breadcrumbs

2 tablespoons chopped fresh parsley

2 tablespoons smoked Spanish paprika

1¼ pounds ground lamb

Salt and freshly ground black pepper to taste

½ cup blanched slivered almonds

1 cup beef stock

Vegetable oil spray

1. Preheat the oven broiler. Line a rimmed baking sheet with heavy-duty aluminum foil, and spray the foil with vegetable oil spray.

2. Heat oil in a large skillet over medium-high heat. Add onion and garlic and cook, stirring frequently, for 3 minutes, or until onion is translucent. While vegetables cook,

combine egg and 2 tablespoons wine, and whisk until smooth. Add breadcrumbs, parsley, and paprika, and mix well.

3. Add ½ of onion mixture and lamb, season to taste with salt and pepper, and mix well again. Make mixture into 1½-inch meatballs, and arrange meatballs on the prepared pan. Spray tops of meatballs with vegetable oil spray.

4. Broil meatballs 6 inches from the broiler element, turning them with tongs to brown all sides. While meatballs brown, combine remaining onions and garlic, almonds, remaining wine, and stock in a blender or food processor, and puree until smooth. Return mixture to the skillet, and bring to a boil over medium-high heat, stirring occasionally. Reduce the heat to low, and simmer sauce for 10 minutes.

5. Remove meatballs from the baking pan with a slotted spoon, and add meatballs to sauce. Bring to a boil, and simmer the meatballs, covered, over low heat, turning occasionally with a slotted spoon, for 15 minutes. Serve immediately.

Note: The lamb mixture can be prepared up to 1 day in advance and refrigerated, tightly covered. Also, the dish can be prepared up to 2 days in advance and refrigerated, tightly covered. Reheat it in a 350°F oven, covered, for 15 to 20 minutes, or until hot.

Botanically speaking, almonds are not a nut, although we certainly treat them as such. They are really a fruit, related to the peach. The fruit is called a *drupe,* and there's a hard woody shell surrounding the seed, which is the almond.

South African Curried Lamb Meatballs

Makes 4 to 6 servings

Active time:
20 minutes

Start to finish:
35 minutes

VARIATION

Substitute ground chuck for the lamb.

These meatballs are based on a meatloaf native to South Africa called *bobotie*. A combination of apple, curry, and almonds lends flavor to the dish. Serve them with braised red cabbage and mashed potatoes.

3 tablespoons unsalted butter

1 medium onion, chopped

1 Granny Smith apple, peeled, cored, and chopped

¼ cup blanched almonds, finely chopped

1 large egg

2 tablespoons whole milk

½ cup plain breadcrumbs

½ cup chopped raisins

2 tablespoons chopped fresh parsley

1 tablespoon curry powder

1 teaspoon granulated sugar

1¼ pounds ground lamb

Salt and freshly ground black pepper to taste

Vegetable oil spray

For dipping:

1 cup Herbed Tomato Sauce (page 38) or purchased marinara sauce, heated

1. Preheat the oven to 450°F. Line a rimmed baking sheet with heavy-duty aluminum foil, and spray the foil with vegetable oil spray.

2. Heat butter in a small skillet over medium-high heat. Add onion, apple, and almonds, and cook, stirring frequently, for 3 minutes, or until onion is translucent. While vegetables cook, whisk egg and milk in a mixing bowl, and add breadcrumbs, raisins, parsley, curry powder, and sugar, and mix well.

3. Add vegetable mixture and lamb to the mixing bowl, season to taste with salt and pepper, and mix well again. Make mixture into 1½-inch meatballs, and arrange meatballs on the prepared pan. Spray tops of meatballs with vegetable oil spray.

4. Bake meatballs for 12 to 15 minutes, or until cooked through. Remove the pan from the oven, and serve immediately, accompanied by a bowl of Herbed Tomato Sauce for dipping.

Note: The lamb mixture can be prepared up to 1 day in advance and refrigerated, tightly covered. Also, the meatballs can be baked up to 2 days in advance and refrigerated, tightly covered. Reheat them in a 350°F oven, covered, for 10 to 12 minutes, or until hot.

While I'm all in favor of advance preparation when cooking, one task you can't do in advance is to grate or chop apples and let them stand, or they will discolor quickly. Prepare apples right before they are to be joined with other ingredients.

Lamb and Goat Cheese Meatballs

Makes 4 to 6 servings

Active time:
20 minutes

Start to finish:
35 minutes

VARIATION

Substitute ground chuck for the lamb.

The sharpness of the goat cheese enlivens the flavor of the herbed lamb encasing it in this adaptation of a Provençal dish. The garlicky mayonnaise sauce in which the meatballs are dipped adds luster to the meal.

2 tablespoons olive oil

2 shallots, chopped

3 garlic cloves, minced

1 large egg

2 tablespoons whole milk

½ cup seasoned Italian breadcrumbs

¼ cup chopped fresh parsley

2 tablespoons chopped fresh basil

1 tablespoon fresh thyme or
    1 teaspoon dried

2 teaspoons ground cumin

1¼ pounds ground lamb

Salt and freshly ground black
    pepper to taste

1 (3.5-ounce) log plain fresh
    goat cheese

Vegetable oil spray

For dipping:
1 cup Easy Aïoli (page 46)

1. Preheat the oven to 450°F. Line a rimmed baking sheet with heavy-duty aluminum foil, and spray the foil with vegetable oil spray.

2. Heat oil in a small skillet over medium-high heat. Add shallots and garlic, and cook, stirring frequently, for 3 minutes, or until shallots are translucent. While vegetables cook, whisk egg and milk in a mixing bowl, and add breadcrumbs, parsley, basil, thyme, and cumin, and mix well.

3. Add vegetable mixture and lamb to the mixing bowl, season to taste with salt and pepper, and mix well again. Measure mixture into heaping 1-tablespoon portions and stick 1 teaspoon goat cheese in the center of each portion. Form portions into 1½-inch meatballs, enclosing the cheese in the center, and arrange meatballs on the prepared pan. Spray tops of meatballs with vegetable oil spray.

4. Bake meatballs for 12 to 15 minutes, or until cooked through. Remove the pan from the oven, and serve immediately, accompanied by a bowl of Easy Aïoli for dipping.

Note: The lamb mixture can be prepared up to 1 day in advance and refrigerated, tightly covered. Also, the meatballs can be baked up to 2 days in advance and refrigerated, tightly covered. Reheat them in a 350°F oven, covered, for 10 to 12 minutes, or until hot.

For this recipe, a less expensive goat cheese is fine. As a general rule, save expensive cheeses for nibbling and use less expensive ones as ingredients. Pregrated cheeses are a real convenience, but the price per pound is far higher than purchasing a block of the same cheese and grating it yourself.

Grilled Lamb and Pistachio Meatballs

Makes 4 to 6 servings

Active time:
20 minutes

Start to finish:
35 minutes

VARIATION

Substitute ground chuck for the lamb.

Cooking with nuts, including bright green pistachio nuts, is an integral part of Middle Eastern cooking. These tasty treats are then grilled for even more flavor.

8 to 12 (8-inch) bamboo skewers
3 tablespoons olive oil
½ cup coarsely chopped pistachio nuts
2 shallots, chopped
3 garlic cloves, chopped
1 large egg
2 tablespoons dry red wine
½ cup seasoned Italian breadcrumbs
2 tablespoons chopped fresh parsley
1 tablespoon fresh thyme or
     1 teaspoon dried
1 tablespoon ground cumin
1 tablespoon ground coriander
2 teaspoons grated lemon zest
1¼ pounds ground lamb
Salt and freshly ground black
     pepper to taste
Vegetable oil spray

For dipping:
1 cup Tahini (page 50) or
     purchased hummus

1. Soak the bamboo skewers in cold water to cover. Prepare a medium-hot charcoal or gas grill, or preheat the oven broiler.

2. Heat oil in a small skillet over medium-high heat. Add pistachio nuts, shallots, and garlic, and cook, stirring frequently, for 3 minutes, or until shallots are translucent. While mixture cooks, whisk egg and wine in a mixing bowl, and add breadcrumbs, parsley, thyme, cumin, coriander, and lemon zest, and mix well.

3. Add nut mixture and lamb to the mixing bowl, season to taste with salt and pepper, and mix well again.

4. Divide mixture into 8 to 12 portions, and form each portion into a sausage shape. Insert a skewer into each sausage so that the tip of the skewer is almost at the top of the meat.

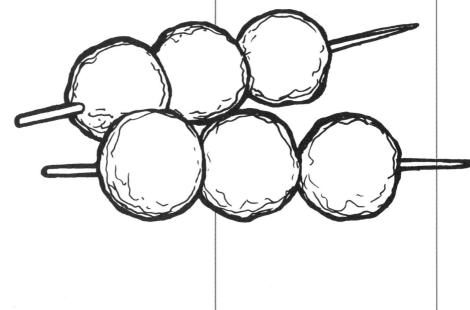

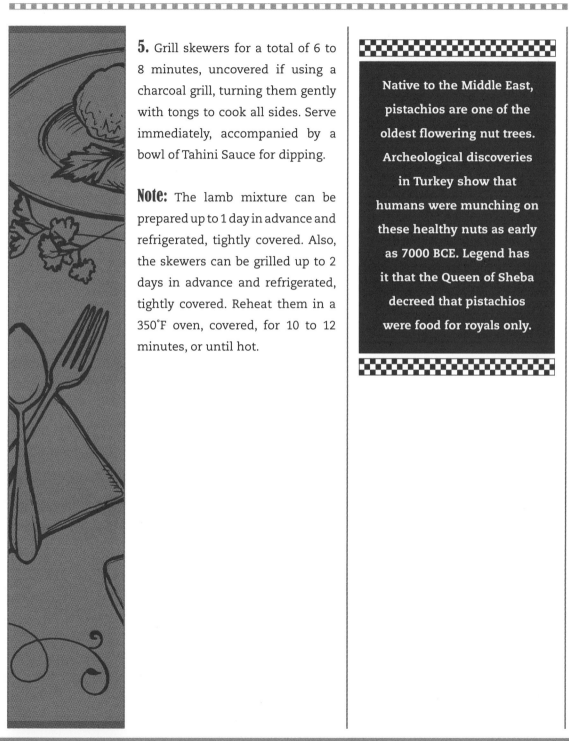

5. Grill skewers for a total of 6 to 8 minutes, uncovered if using a charcoal grill, turning them gently with tongs to cook all sides. Serve immediately, accompanied by a bowl of Tahini Sauce for dipping.

Note: The lamb mixture can be prepared up to 1 day in advance and refrigerated, tightly covered. Also, the skewers can be grilled up to 2 days in advance and refrigerated, tightly covered. Reheat them in a 350°F oven, covered, for 10 to 12 minutes, or until hot.

Native to the Middle East, pistachios are one of the oldest flowering nut trees. Archeological discoveries in Turkey show that humans were munching on these healthy nuts as early as 7000 BCE. Legend has it that the Queen of Sheba decreed that pistachios were food for royals only.

Persian Lamb Meatballs

Makes 4 to 6 servings

Active time:
20 minutes

Start to finish:
50 minutes

VARIATION

Substitute ground chuck for the lamb.

Persian cooking includes the use of dried fruits in savory dishes. The sweet and succulent flavor of the fruit balances the spices also flavoring rich lamb. These meatballs are then simmered in a subtle tomato sauce. Serve them over rice pilaf.

¼ cup olive oil

2 large onions, chopped

3 garlic cloves, minced

2 tablespoons grated fresh ginger

1 large egg

1 (15-ounce) can tomato sauce, divided

½ cup plain breadcrumbs

½ cup finely chopped pitted prunes

2 tablespoons chopped fresh cilantro

2 teaspoons curry powder

1¼ pounds ground lamb

Salt and cayenne to taste

½ cup dry sherry

2 tablespoons ground coriander

1 bay leaf

Vegetable oil spray

1. Preheat the oven broiler. Line a rimmed baking sheet with heavy-duty aluminum foil, and spray the foil with vegetable oil spray.

2. Heat oil in a large skillet over medium-high heat. Add onions, garlic, and ginger, and cook, stirring frequently, for 3 minutes, or until onions are translucent. While vegetables cook, combine egg and 2 tablespoons tomato sauce in a mixing bowl, and whisk until smooth. Add breadcrumbs, prunes, cilantro, and curry powder, and mix well.

3. Add ½ of onion mixture and lamb, season to taste with salt and cayenne, and mix well again. Make mixture into 1½-inch meatballs, and arrange meatballs on the prepared pan. Spray tops of meatballs with vegetable oil spray.

4. Broil meatballs 6 inches from the broiler element, turning them with tongs to brown all sides. While meatballs brown, add remaining tomato sauce, sherry, coriander, and bay leaf to the skillet containing remaining onions and garlic. Bring to a boil over medium-high heat, stirring occasionally. Simmer sauce, uncovered, for 10 minutes.

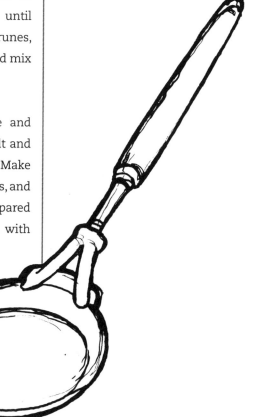

5. Remove meatballs from the baking pan with a slotted spoon, and add meatballs to sauce. Bring to a boil, and simmer the meatballs, covered, over low heat, turning occasionally with a slotted spoon, for 15 minutes. Serve immediately.

Note: The lamb mixture can be prepared up to 1 day in advance and refrigerated, tightly covered. Also, the dish can be prepared up to 2 days in advance and refrigerated, tightly covered. Reheat it in a 350°F oven, covered, for 12 to 18 minutes or until hot.

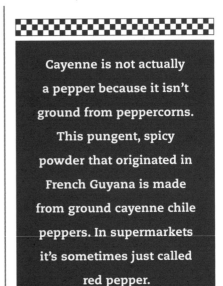

Cayenne is not actually a pepper because it isn't ground from peppercorns. This pungent, spicy powder that originated in French Guyana is made from ground cayenne chile peppers. In supermarkets it's sometimes just called red pepper.

Lamb Meatballs in Herbed Red Wine Sauce

Makes 4 to 6 servings

Active time:
25 minutes

Start to finish:
55 minutes

VARIATION

Substitute ground chuck for the lamb.

Tender morsels of lamb braised in a red wine sauce is one of my favorite winter stews, so I decided to create a comforting dish made with meatballs. Serve these over some couscous or buttered egg noodles.

3 tablespoons unsalted butter

1 medium onion, chopped

1 small carrot, chopped

2 garlic cloves, minced

1 large egg

2 tablespoons whole milk

½ cup seasoned Italian breadcrumbs

3 tablespoons chopped fresh
    rosemary or 1 tablespoon dried

2 tablespoons chopped fresh parsley

1¼ pounds ground lamb

Salt and freshly ground black
    pepper to taste

3 tablespoons all-purpose flour

1¼ cups dry red wine

1 cup beef stock

2 tablespoons tomato paste

1 tablespoon herbes de Provence

Vegetable oil spray

1. Preheat the oven broiler. Line a rimmed baking sheet with heavy-duty aluminum foil, and spray the foil with vegetable oil spray.

2. Heat butter in a large skillet over medium-high heat. Add onion, carrot, and garlic and cook, stirring frequently, for 3 minutes, or until onion is translucent. While vegetables cook, combine egg and milk in a mixing bowl, and whisk until smooth. Add breadcrumbs, rosemary, and parsley, and mix well.

3. Add ½ onion mixture and lamb, season to taste with salt and pepper, and mix well again. Make mixture into 1½-inch meatballs, and arrange meatballs on the prepared pan. Spray tops of meatballs with vegetable oil spray.

4. Broil meatballs 6 inches from the broiler element, turning them with tongs to brown all sides. While meatballs brown, stir flour into the skillet, and cook over low heat for 2 minutes, stirring constantly. Whisk

in wine, stock, tomato paste, and herbes de Provence. Bring to a boil over medium-high heat, reduce the heat to medium, and simmer sauce, uncovered, for 10 minutes.

5. Remove meatballs from the baking pan with a slotted spoon, and add meatballs to sauce. Bring to a boil, and simmer meatballs, covered, over low heat, turning occasionally with a slotted spoon, for 15 minutes. Season to taste with salt and pepper, and serve immediately.

Note: The lamb mixture can be prepared up to 1 day in advance and refrigerated, tightly covered. Also, the dish can be cooked up to 2 days in advance and refrigerated, tightly covered. Reheat in a 350°F oven, covered, for 15 to 20 minutes, or until hot.

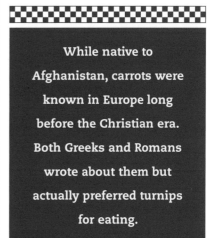

While native to Afghanistan, carrots were known in Europe long before the Christian era. Both Greeks and Romans wrote about them but actually preferred turnips for eating.

Minted Lamb and Feta Meatballs

Makes 4 to 6 servings

Active time:
20 minutes

Start to finish:
35 minutes

VARIATION

Substitute ground chuck for the lamb.

Crumbly, sharp-flavored feta cheese is used in much of Greek cooking and other Mediterranean cuisines. The addition of fresh mint balances the aromatic flavors of spices such as cinnamon and allspice.

2 tablespoons olive oil

2 shallots, chopped

3 garlic cloves, minced

1 large egg

2 tablespoons whole milk

½ cup seasoned Italian breadcrumbs

½ cup crumbled feta cheese

3 tablespoons finely chopped
    fresh mint

1 tablespoon ground cumin

1 teaspoon grated lemon zest

Pinch ground cinnamon

Pinch ground allspice

1¼ pounds ground lamb

Salt and freshly ground black
    pepper to taste

Vegetable oil spray

For dipping:
1 cup Middle Eastern Yogurt Sauce
    (page 51) or purchased hummus

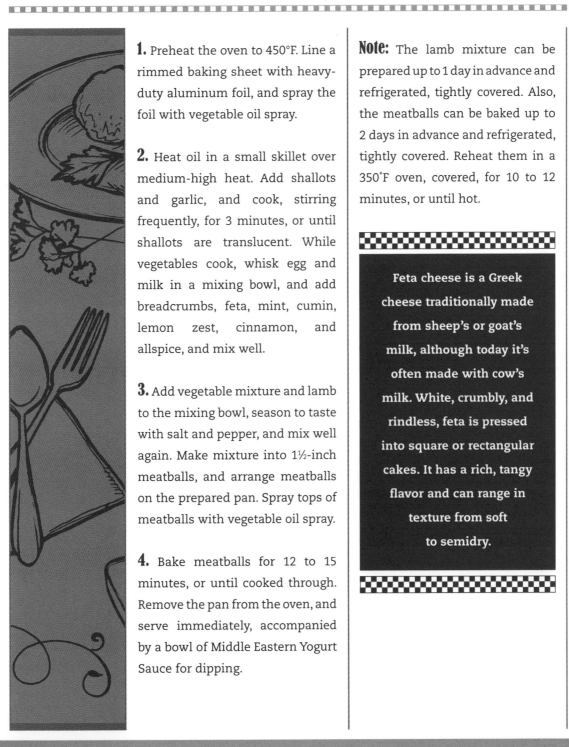

1. Preheat the oven to 450°F. Line a rimmed baking sheet with heavy-duty aluminum foil, and spray the foil with vegetable oil spray.

2. Heat oil in a small skillet over medium-high heat. Add shallots and garlic, and cook, stirring frequently, for 3 minutes, or until shallots are translucent. While vegetables cook, whisk egg and milk in a mixing bowl, and add breadcrumbs, feta, mint, cumin, lemon zest, cinnamon, and allspice, and mix well.

3. Add vegetable mixture and lamb to the mixing bowl, season to taste with salt and pepper, and mix well again. Make mixture into 1½-inch meatballs, and arrange meatballs on the prepared pan. Spray tops of meatballs with vegetable oil spray.

4. Bake meatballs for 12 to 15 minutes, or until cooked through. Remove the pan from the oven, and serve immediately, accompanied by a bowl of Middle Eastern Yogurt Sauce for dipping.

Note: The lamb mixture can be prepared up to 1 day in advance and refrigerated, tightly covered. Also, the meatballs can be baked up to 2 days in advance and refrigerated, tightly covered. Reheat them in a 350°F oven, covered, for 10 to 12 minutes, or until hot.

Feta cheese is a Greek cheese traditionally made from sheep's or goat's milk, although today it's often made with cow's milk. White, crumbly, and rindless, feta is pressed into square or rectangular cakes. It has a rich, tangy flavor and can range in texture from soft to semidry.

Double Your Pleasure:

Meatballs with More than One Meat

In most chapters in this book, the centerpiece of the meatballs recipe is a single meat. It can be a red meat, a white meat, poultry, or even fish, but it's a singular flavor. But that's not the case with the following recipes. Here they are all made from a combination of meats, which adds a degree of complexity to the recipes and a depth of flavor to the resulting dishes.

Making meatballs from a combination of meats is nothing new; that's why as I've mentioned, in many supermarkets you'll find a pre-ground mixture of pork, beef, and veal called "meatloaf mix." In the case of these recipes, however, it should be called "meatball mix." Some of the great meatball recipes, like the Italian-American meatball and the traditional Swedish meatball, are made with a mix of meats.

Mixing beef and pork is a common combination; the beef adds richness while the pork is more subtle and lends its delicacy to the mixture. Most of these recipes are drawn from European cuisines, but you'll find some Latin American and American ones as well.

Basic Italian-American Meatballs

Makes 4 to 6 servings

Active time:
20 minutes

Start to finish:
50 minutes

After years of experimentation these are my favorite meatballs. The mixture of herbs and spices give them a complex flavor, and the cheeses add moisture.

2 tablespoons olive oil

1 small onion, finely chopped

3 garlic cloves, minced

¼ teaspoon crushed red pepper flakes

1 large egg

2 tablespoons whole milk

½ cup seasoned Italian breadcrumbs

¼ cup freshly grated Parmesan

¼ cup grated whole-milk mozzarella

2 tablespoons chopped fresh parsley

1 teaspoon Italian seasoning

½ pound ground pork

½ pound ground chuck

¼ pound ground veal

Salt and freshly ground black pepper to taste

2 cups Herbed Tomato Sauce (page 38) or purchased marinara sauce

Vegetable oil spray

VARIATIONS

For traditional spaghetti and meatballs, cook ½ to 1 pound pasta, and pass some freshly grated Parmesan on the side.

Cut the cooked meatballs into small pieces and use as a pizza topping.

For a meatball sandwich, make an indentation in the center of a roll or section of bread to accommodate the size of the meatballs. Then top the meatballs with grated or sliced mozzarella and bake the sandwich in a 375°F oven for 10 to 12 minutes, or until meatballs are hot and cheese melts.

1. Preheat the oven broiler. Line a rimmed baking sheet with heavy-duty aluminum foil, and spray the foil with vegetable oil spray.

2. Heat oil in a large skillet over medium-high heat. Add onion, garlic, and red pepper flakes, and cook, stirring frequently, for 3 minutes, or until onion is translucent. Combine egg and milk in a mixing bowl, and whisk until smooth. Add breadcrumbs, Parmesan, mozzarella cheese, parsley, and Italian seasoning, and mix well.

3. Add onion mixture, pork, beef, and veal, season to taste with salt and pepper, and mix well again. Make mixture into 1½-inch meatballs, and arrange meatballs on the prepared pan. Spray tops of meatballs with vegetable oil spray.

4. Broil meatballs 6 inches from the broiler element, turning them with tongs to brown all sides. While meatballs brown, heat Herbed Tomato Sauce in the skillet in which the vegetables cooked.

5. Remove meatballs from the baking pan with a slotted spoon, and add meatballs to sauce. Bring to a boil, and simmer meatballs, covered, over low heat, turning occasionally with a slotted spoon, for 15 minutes. Season to taste with salt and pepper, and serve immediately.

Note: The meatball mixture can be prepared up to 1 day in advance and refrigerated, tightly covered. Also, the dish can be cooked up to 2 days in advance and refrigerated, tightly covered. Reheat in a 350°F oven, covered, for 15 to 20 minutes, or until hot.

Seasoned Italian breadcrumbs are first toasted then seasoned with parsley, other herbs, garlic, and Parmesan. If you only have plain breadcrumbs, created seasoned ones by adding 1 teaspoon Italian seasoning, ½ teaspoon garlic powder, and 3 tablespoons Parmesan to each 1 cup plain breadcrumbs.

One-Step Meatball Lasagna

Makes 6 to 8 servings

**Active time:
15 minutes**

**Start to finish:
1¼ hours**

VARIATION

Use any other meatball recipe in this book that is finished or dipped into a tomato sauce.

Once you have a cache of meatballs in the freezer, there's no end to how you can use them. This easy lasagna is one option, and it's made with par-boiled lasagna noodles so it's not necessary to cook the pasta first.

1 recipe Basic Italian-American Meatballs (page 254)
1½ cups water
1 (1-pound) box precooked lasagna noodles
1 (15-ounce) container part-skim ricotta
½ pound grated mozzarella
1 cup freshly grated Parmesan

1. Preheat the oven to 350°F. Grease a 9 x 13-inch baking pan.

2. Remove meatballs from sauce, cut in half, and set aside. Add water to sauce, and stir well. Spread 1 cup sauce in bottom of prepared pan. Arrange ⅓ noodles, slightly overlapping if necessary, atop sauce. Spread ½ of ricotta over noodles. Sprinkle with ½ of mozzarella cheese, ½ of meatballs, and ¼ cup Parmesan. Top with 1 cup sauce. Repeat layering with noodles, ricotta, mozzarella, meatballs, and ¼ cup Parmesan. Arrange remaining noodles over. Spoon remaining sauce over, covering completely. Sprinkle with remaining ½ cup Parmesan. Cover pan tightly with aluminum foil, and place the pan on a baking sheet.

3. Bake for 1 hour, or until noodles are tender and dish is bubbly. Increase the oven temperature to 400°F, remove and discard the foil, and bake for an additional 10 to 12 minutes, or until top is browned. Allow lasagna to rest for 5 minutes, then serve immediately.

Note: The dish can be cooked up to 2 days in advance and refrigerated, tightly covered. Reheat in 350° F oven, covered, for 30 to 40 minutes.

Be sure to buy the right lasagna noodles for this dish. The pre-cooked noodles are fairly new to the market, and they are what they say: noodles that are partially cooked to rid them of some of the starch, and then dehydrated. Regular lasagna noodles will not cook as well.

Spinach-Parmesan Meatballs

Makes 4 to 6 servings

Active time:
20 minutes

Start to finish:
35 minutes

VARIATION

Substitute ground chicken or turkey for all or any of the meats above.

While you can serve these on top of spaghetti with more sauce, I make them cocktail size for hors d'oeuvre and use the sauce for dipping.

2 tablespoons olive oil

2 shallots, chopped

2 garlic cloves, minced

1 celery rib, finely chopped

½ (10-ounce) package frozen chopped spinach, thawed and squeezed dry

1 large egg

2 tablespoons whole milk

½ cup seasoned Italian breadcrumbs

⅓ cup freshly grated Parmesan

2 tablespoons chopped fresh parsley

2 tablespoons chopped fresh oregano or 2 teaspoons dried

1¼ pounds meatloaf mix (or some proportion of ground pork, veal, and beef)

Salt and crushed red pepper flakes to taste

Vegetable oil spray

For dipping:

1 cup Herbed Tomato Sauce (page 38) or purchased marinara sauce, heated

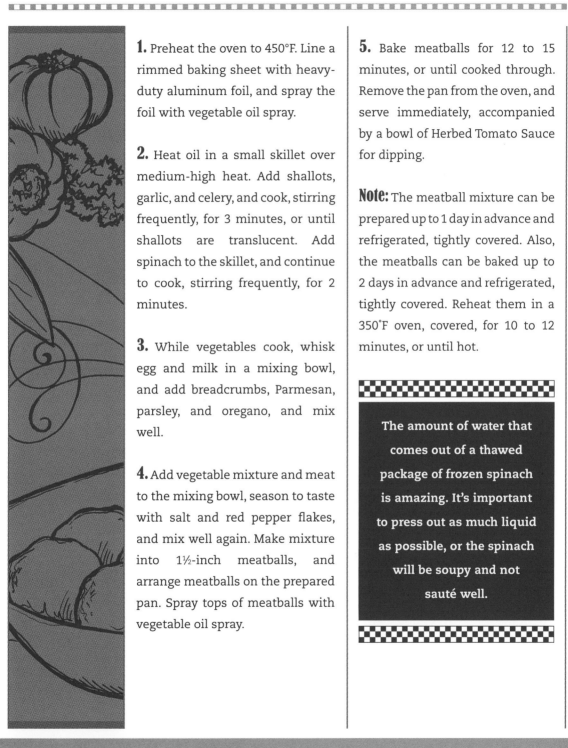

1. Preheat the oven to 450°F. Line a rimmed baking sheet with heavy-duty aluminum foil, and spray the foil with vegetable oil spray.

2. Heat oil in a small skillet over medium-high heat. Add shallots, garlic, and celery, and cook, stirring frequently, for 3 minutes, or until shallots are translucent. Add spinach to the skillet, and continue to cook, stirring frequently, for 2 minutes.

3. While vegetables cook, whisk egg and milk in a mixing bowl, and add breadcrumbs, Parmesan, parsley, and oregano, and mix well.

4. Add vegetable mixture and meat to the mixing bowl, season to taste with salt and red pepper flakes, and mix well again. Make mixture into 1½-inch meatballs, and arrange meatballs on the prepared pan. Spray tops of meatballs with vegetable oil spray.

5. Bake meatballs for 12 to 15 minutes, or until cooked through. Remove the pan from the oven, and serve immediately, accompanied by a bowl of Herbed Tomato Sauce for dipping.

Note: The meatball mixture can be prepared up to 1 day in advance and refrigerated, tightly covered. Also, the meatballs can be baked up to 2 days in advance and refrigerated, tightly covered. Reheat them in a 350°F oven, covered, for 10 to 12 minutes, or until hot.

The amount of water that comes out of a thawed package of frozen spinach is amazing. It's important to press out as much liquid as possible, or the spinach will be soupy and not sauté well.

Italian Beef and Sausage Meatballs

Makes 4 to 6 servings

Active time: 20 minutes

Start to finish: 35 minutes

VARIATION

Substitute ground chicken or turkey for all or any of the meats above.

The inclusion of sun-dried tomatoes and wine, herbs, and cheese gives the meatballs a hearty flavor. By using sausage in the meat mixture the complexity of the flavor is further increased. Serve them over pasta or by themselves with a tossed salad.

½ cup sun-dried tomatoes, packed in olive oil

2 shallots, chopped

3 garlic cloves, minced

1 large egg

3 tablespoons dry red wine

½ cup seasoned Italian breadcrumbs

⅓ cup grated whole milk mozzarella

2 tablespoons chopped fresh parsley

1 tablespoon chopped fresh oregano or 1 teaspoon dried

¾ pound ground chuck

½ pound sweet or spicy bulk Italian pork sausage

Salt and freshly ground black pepper to taste

Vegetable oil spray

For dipping:

1 cup Herbed Tomato Sauce (page 38) or purchased marinara sauce, heated

1. Preheat the oven to 450°F. Line a rimmed baking sheet with heavy-duty aluminum foil, and spray the foil with vegetable oil spray. Drain sun-dried tomatoes, pressing with the back of a spoon to extract as much liquid as possible. Reserve oil, chop tomatoes finely, and set aside.

2. Heat reserved oil in a small skillet over medium-high heat. Add shallots and garlic, and cook, stirring frequently, for 3 minutes, or until shallots are translucent. While vegetables cook, whisk egg and wine in a mixing bowl, and add breadcrumbs, cheese, parsley, and oregano, and mix well.

3. Add vegetable mixture, beef, and sausage to the mixing bowl, season to taste with salt and pepper, and mix well again. Make mixture into 1½-inch meatballs, and arrange meatballs on the prepared pan. Spray tops of meatballs with vegetable oil spray.

4. Bake meatballs for 12 to 15 minutes, or until cooked through. Remove the pan from the oven, and serve immediately, accompanied by a bowl of Herbed Tomato Sauce for dipping.

Note: The meatball mixture can be prepared up to 1 day in advance and refrigerated, tightly covered. Also, the meatballs can be baked up to 2 days in advance and refrigerated, tightly covered. Reheat them in a 350°F oven, covered, for 10 to 12 minutes, or until hot.

Of all the convenience products on the market, perhaps one of the worst is minced garlic. It comes packed in both oil and water, and you should always avoid using it because the flavor isn't good. On the other hand, some supermarkets carry small packages of whole garlic cloves that are peeled. These are great, and you can use them in any recipe.

Sicilian Meatballs

Makes 4 to 6 servings

Active time:
20 minutes

Start to finish:
45 minutes

The use of pine nuts and dried currants is characteristic of Sicilian cuisine; it comes from the Arabic influence from North Africa sustained in the region. The combination of Italian sausage and ground pork, with vegetables and herbs, is joined by these two special ingredients in these meatballs.

2 tablespoons olive oil
½ small red onion, chopped
2 garlic cloves, minced
1 large egg
2 tablespoons whole milk
½ cup seasoned Italian breadcrumbs
¼ cup freshly grated Parmesan
¼ cup pine nuts, toasted
3 tablespoons dried currants
2 tablespoons chopped fresh oregano or 2 teaspoons dried
2 tablespoons chopped fresh parsley
¾ pound ground pork
½ pound sweet or spicy bulk Italian sausage
Salt and freshly ground black pepper to taste
2 cups Herbed Tomato Sauce (page 38) or purchased marinara sauce
Vegetable oil spray

1. Preheat the oven broiler. Line a rimmed baking sheet with heavy-duty aluminum foil, and spray the foil with vegetable oil spray.

2. Heat oil in a large skillet over medium-high heat. Add onion and garlic, and cook, stirring frequently, for 3 minutes, or until onion is translucent. Combine egg and milk in a mixing bowl, and whisk until smooth. Add breadcrumbs, Parmesan, pine nuts, currants, oregano, and parsley, and mix well.

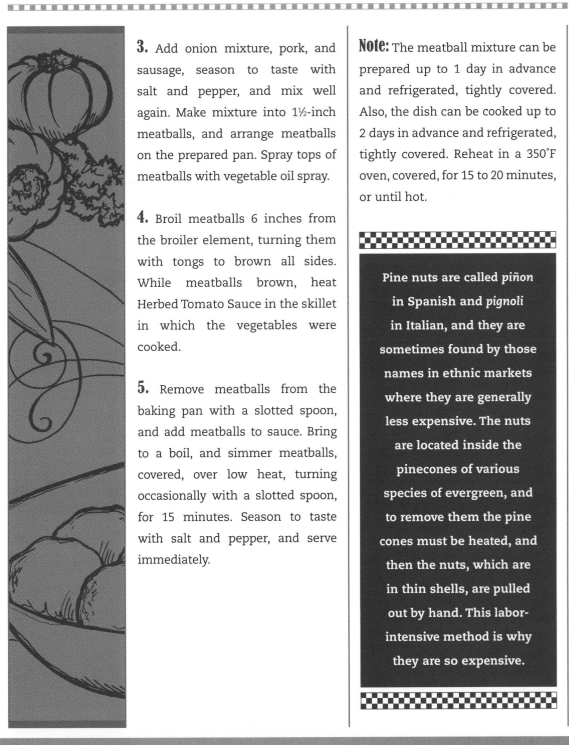

3. Add onion mixture, pork, and sausage, season to taste with salt and pepper, and mix well again. Make mixture into 1½-inch meatballs, and arrange meatballs on the prepared pan. Spray tops of meatballs with vegetable oil spray.

4. Broil meatballs 6 inches from the broiler element, turning them with tongs to brown all sides. While meatballs brown, heat Herbed Tomato Sauce in the skillet in which the vegetables were cooked.

5. Remove meatballs from the baking pan with a slotted spoon, and add meatballs to sauce. Bring to a boil, and simmer meatballs, covered, over low heat, turning occasionally with a slotted spoon, for 15 minutes. Season to taste with salt and pepper, and serve immediately.

Note: The meatball mixture can be prepared up to 1 day in advance and refrigerated, tightly covered. Also, the dish can be cooked up to 2 days in advance and refrigerated, tightly covered. Reheat in a 350°F oven, covered, for 15 to 20 minutes, or until hot.

Pine nuts are called *piñon* in Spanish and *pignoli* in Italian, and they are sometimes found by those names in ethnic markets where they are generally less expensive. The nuts are located inside the pinecones of various species of evergreen, and to remove them the pine cones must be heated, and then the nuts, which are in thin shells, are pulled out by hand. This labor-intensive method is why they are so expensive.

Mediterranean Meatballs

Makes 4 to 6 servings

Active time: 25 minutes

Start to finish: 1¾ hours, including 1 hour to chill mixture

VARIATION

Make the meatballs with buckwheat groats or couscous.

These meatballs, made with cracked-wheat bulgur, which adds texture as well as the healthful goodness of grains, comes from the Greek islands. They are made with a combination of lamb and beef, and then poached in a spiced tomato sauce.

1 large egg
⅔ cup dry red wine, divided
½ cup cracked-wheat bulgur
⅔ cup chopped fresh parsley, divided
3 scallions, white parts and
    2 inches of green tops, chopped
4 garlic cloves, minced, divided
2 teaspoons ground cumin
2 teaspoons ground coriander
¾ pound ground lamb
½ pound ground beef
Salt and freshly ground black
    pepper to taste
¼ cup olive oil
1 medium onion, diced
1 (28-ounce) can crushed tomatoes
    in tomato puree
1 (3-inch) cinnamon stick
1 bay leaf
Vegetable oil spray

1. Preheat the oven broiler. Line a rimmed baking sheet with heavy-duty aluminum foil, and spray the foil with vegetable oil spray.

2. Combine egg and 2 tablespoons wine in a mixing bowl, and whisk until smooth. Add bulgur, ½ cup parsley, scallions, 2 garlic cloves, cumin, and coriander, and mix well.

3. Add lamb and beef, season to taste with salt and pepper, and knead mixture for 2 minutes. Refrigerate mixture for 1 hour.

4. While mixture chills, heat olive oil in a large skillet over medium-high heat. Add onion and remaining 2 garlic cloves, and cook, stirring frequently, for 3 minutes, or until onion is translucent. Add remaining wine, tomatoes, cinnamon stick, and bay leaf, and bring to a boil over medium-high heat, stirring occasionally. Reduce the heat to low and simmer sauce, uncovered, for 10 minutes.

5. Make mixture into 1½-inch meatballs, and arrange meatballs on the prepared pan. Spray tops of meatballs with vegetable oil spray. Broil meatballs 6 inches from the broiler element, turning them with tongs to brown all sides. Remove meatballs from the baking pan with a slotted spoon, and add meatballs to sauce. Bring to a boil, and simmer meatballs, covered, over low heat, turning occasionally with a slotted spoon, for 15 minutes. Remove and discard cinnamon stick and bay leaf, season to taste with salt and pepper, and serve immediately.

Note: The meatball mixture can be prepared up to 1 day in advance and refrigerated, tightly covered. Also, the dish can be cooked up to 2 days in advance and refrigerated, tightly covered. Reheat in a 350°F oven, covered, for 15 to 20 minutes, or until hot.

Bay leaves should always be discarded from a dish before serving. Although they add a pungent and woodsy flavor and aroma to dishes, they can be quite a bitter mouthful if you accidentally eat one. That's also why bay leaves are always added whole. If they were broken into pieces, it would be a real scavenger hunt to retrieve them.

Lemony Greek Meatballs

Makes 4 to 6 servings

Active time:
20 minutes

Start to finish:
35 minutes

VARIATION

Substitute ground chicken or turkey for any or all of the meats used above. If using poultry, cook with white wine rather than red.

Garlic, oregano, and lemon form almost a holy trinity in Greek cuisine, and in this case they are joined by red wine to become a simple sauce. The meat component of these meatballs is a combination of beef and lamb.

2 tablespoons olive oil

½ small red onion, finely chopped

3 garlic cloves, minced

1 large egg

2 tablespoons whole milk

½ cup seasoned Italian breadcrumbs

¼ cup chopped fresh parsley, divided

2 tablespoons chopped fresh
    oregano or 2 teaspoons dried

¾ pound ground lamb

½ pound ground chuck

Salt and freshly ground black
    pepper to taste

1 cup dry red wine

2 tablespoons freshly squeezed
    lemon juice

Vegetable oil spray

1. Preheat the oven to 450°F. Line a rimmed baking sheet with heavy-duty aluminum foil, and spray the foil with vegetable oil spray.

2. Heat oil in a small skillet over medium-high heat. Add onion and garlic, and cook, stirring frequently, for 3 minutes, or until onion is translucent. While vegetables cook, whisk egg and milk in a mixing bowl, and add breadcrumbs, ½ of parsley, and oregano, and mix well.

3. Add ½ of vegetable mixture, lamb, and beef to the mixing bowl, season to taste with salt and pepper, and mix well again. Make mixture into 1½-inch meatballs, and arrange meatballs on the prepared pan. Spray tops of meatballs with vegetable oil spray.

4. Bake meatballs for 12 to 15 minutes, or until cooked through. While meatballs bake, add wine to the skillet with remaining onion mixture, and bring to a boil over high heat, stirring occasionally. Cook until liquid is reduced by ½, then add remaining 2 tablespoons parsley and lemon juice, and cook for an additional 2 minutes, stirring occasionally. Season to taste with salt and pepper.

5. Remove the pan from the oven, and place meatballs in a shallow bowl. Pour wine mixture over meatballs, stirring to coat them well, and serve immediately.

Note: The meatball mixture can be prepared up to 1 day in advance and refrigerated, tightly covered. Also, the meatballs can be baked up to 2 days in advance and refrigerated, tightly covered. Reheat them in a 350°F oven, covered, for 10 to 12 minutes, or until hot.

To reduce a sauce is like to reduce your body; it's losing weight. In this case, it's liquid that's boiled down so it loses some of its water through evaporation. This reduction, as the process is known, intensifies the flavor of the resulting liquid while shrinking its volume.

Grilled Greek Meatballs

Makes 4 to 6 servings

Active time:
20 minutes

Start to finish:
35 minutes

In Greek, meatballs have a different name depending on how they're cooked. While *keftedes* are fried or grilled meatballs such as these, meatballs in a sauce are called *yuvarlakia*.

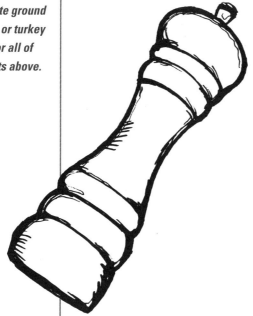

8 to 12 (8-inch) bamboo skewers

3 tablespoons olive oil

2 shallots, chopped

3 garlic cloves, chopped

1 large egg

2 tablespoons freshly squeezed lemon juice

1 tablespoon tomato paste

½ cup seasoned Italian breadcrumbs

2 tablespoons chopped fresh parsley

2 tablespoons chopped fresh mint

1 tablespoon fresh thyme or 1 teaspoon dried

1 tablespoon chopped fresh oregano or 1 teaspoon dried

1 teaspoon grated lemon zest

¾ pound ground chuck

¾ pound ground lamb

Salt and freshly ground black pepper to taste

Vegetable oil spray

For dipping:

1 cup Greek Feta Sauce (page 49) or purchased hummus

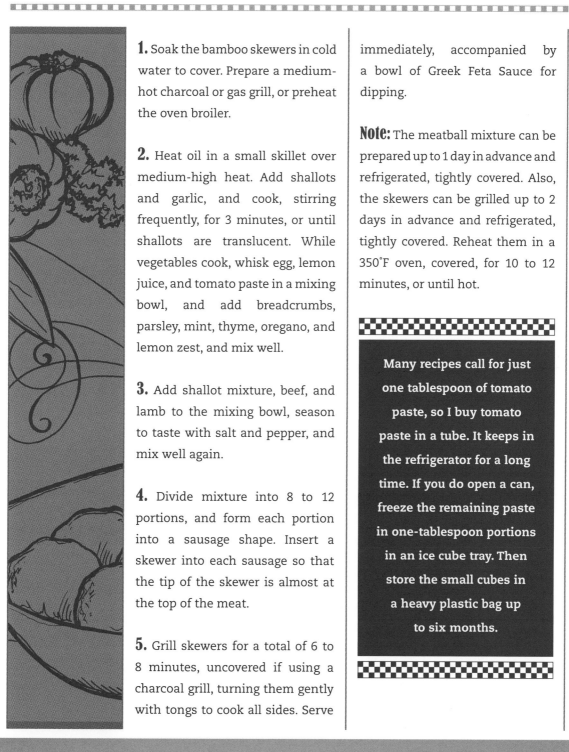

1. Soak the bamboo skewers in cold water to cover. Prepare a medium-hot charcoal or gas grill, or preheat the oven broiler.

2. Heat oil in a small skillet over medium-high heat. Add shallots and garlic, and cook, stirring frequently, for 3 minutes, or until shallots are translucent. While vegetables cook, whisk egg, lemon juice, and tomato paste in a mixing bowl, and add breadcrumbs, parsley, mint, thyme, oregano, and lemon zest, and mix well.

3. Add shallot mixture, beef, and lamb to the mixing bowl, season to taste with salt and pepper, and mix well again.

4. Divide mixture into 8 to 12 portions, and form each portion into a sausage shape. Insert a skewer into each sausage so that the tip of the skewer is almost at the top of the meat.

5. Grill skewers for a total of 6 to 8 minutes, uncovered if using a charcoal grill, turning them gently with tongs to cook all sides. Serve immediately, accompanied by a bowl of Greek Feta Sauce for dipping.

Note: The meatball mixture can be prepared up to 1 day in advance and refrigerated, tightly covered. Also, the skewers can be grilled up to 2 days in advance and refrigerated, tightly covered. Reheat them in a 350°F oven, covered, for 10 to 12 minutes, or until hot.

Many recipes call for just one tablespoon of tomato paste, so I buy tomato paste in a tube. It keeps in the refrigerator for a long time. If you do open a can, freeze the remaining paste in one-tablespoon portions in an ice cube tray. Then store the small cubes in a heavy plastic bag up to six months.

Swedish Meatballs

Makes 4 to 6 servings

Active time: 20 minutes

Start to finish: 45 minutes

VARIATIONS

Substitute ground chicken or turkey for any or all of the meats used above.

Add ¼ cup chopped fresh dill to the sauce.

Allspice and nutmeg, in addition to a combination of meats and a creamed sauce, are what defines the quintessential Swedish meatball, called *köttbullar* in Sweden. Variations on this recipe have been served at American cocktail parties for generations.

4 tablespoons (½ stick) unsalted butter, divided
1 small onion, chopped
¼ cup milk
1 large egg
1 large egg yolk
3 slices fresh white bread
¼ teaspoon ground allspice
¼ teaspoon freshly grated nutmeg
Pinch ground ginger

¾ pound ground pork
½ pound ground chuck
Salt and freshly ground black pepper to taste
¼ cup all-purpose flour
2½ cups beef stock
½ cup heavy cream
Vegetable oil spray

1. Preheat the oven broiler. Line a rimmed baking sheet with heavy-duty aluminum foil, and spray the foil with vegetable oil spray.

2. Heat 2 tablespoons butter in a large skillet over medium-high heat. Add onion, and cook, stirring frequently, for 3 minutes, or until onion is translucent. Combine milk, egg, and egg yolk in a mixing bowl, and whisk until smooth. Break bread into tiny pieces and add to mixing bowl along with allspice, nutmeg, and ginger, and mix well.

3. Add onion, pork, and beef, season to taste with salt and pepper, and mix well again. Make mixture into 1½-inch meatballs, and arrange meatballs on the prepared pan. Spray tops of meatballs with vegetable oil spray.

4. Broil meatballs 6 inches from the broiler element, turning them with tongs to brown all sides. While meatballs brown, add remaining butter to the skillet and heat over low heat. Stir flour into the skillet, and cook over low heat for 2 minutes, stirring constantly. Raise the heat to medium-high, whisk in stock and cream, and bring to a boil over medium-high heat, whisking constantly.

5. Remove meatballs from the baking pan with a slotted spoon, and add meatballs to sauce. Bring to a boil, and simmer meatballs, covered, over low heat, turning occasionally with a slotted spoon, for 15 minutes. Season to taste with salt and pepper, and serve immediately.

Note: The meatball mixture can be prepared up to 1 day in advance and refrigerated, tightly covered. Also, the dish can be cooked up to 2 days in advance and refrigerated, tightly covered. Reheat in a 350°F oven, covered, for 15 to 20 minutes, or until hot.

Nutmeg is the seed of a tropical evergreen native to the Spice Islands that was most popular with European aristocracy beginning in the fifteenth century. When the fruit of the tree is split, it reveals the inch-long nutmeg seed surrounded by a lacy membrane that is ground into mace, a spice similar in flavor.

Mustard Dill Meatballs

Makes 4 to 6 servings

Active time:
15 minutes

Start to finish:
30 minutes

VARIATION

Substitute ground chicken or turkey for any or all of the meats used above.

Here's another Scandinavian meatball preparation with fresh dill as well as sharp mustard and spices. Serve them with a dipping sauce containing sour cream and the same flavors.

1 large egg
¾ cup sour cream, divided
1 tablespoon mayonnaise
3 slices seeded rye bread, broken
    in small pieces
⅓ cup chopped dill, divided
3 tablespoons Dijon mustard,
    divided
2 scallions, white parts and
    2 inches of green tops, chopped
Pinch ground allspice
Pinch ground nutmeg
¾ pound ground pork
½ pound ground veal
Salt and freshly ground black
    pepper to taste
Vegetable oil spray

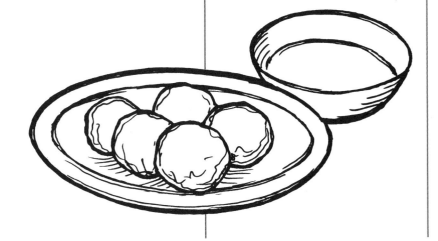

1. Preheat the oven to 450°F. Line a rimmed baking sheet with heavy-duty aluminum foil, and spray the foil with vegetable oil spray.

2. Whisk egg, ¼ cup sour cream, and mayonnaise in a mixing bowl. Add bread, 2 tablespoons dill, 1 tablespoon mustard, scallions, allspice, and nutmeg, and mix well.

3. Add pork and veal to the mixing bowl, season to taste with salt and pepper, and mix well again. Make mixture into 1½-inch meatballs, and arrange meatballs on the prepared pan. Spray tops of meatballs with vegetable oil spray.

4. Bake meatballs for 12 to 15 minutes, or until cooked through. While meatballs bake, combine remaining sour cream, remaining dill, and remaining mustard in a small bowl, and whisk well.

5. Remove the pan from the oven, and serve immediately, accompanied by the bowl of sauce for dipping.

Note: The meatball mixture can be prepared up to 1 day in advance and refrigerated, tightly covered. Also, the meatballs can be baked up to 2 days in advance and refrigerated, tightly covered. Reheat them in a 350°F oven, covered, for 10 to 12 minutes, or until hot.

If using white bread or bread crumbs instead of rye bread, add a teaspoon or two of caraway seeds to the meat mixture. Rye bread adds caraway flavor as well as texture.

Bacon-Studded Meatballs in Wine Sauce

Makes 4 to 6 servings

Active time:
20 minutes

Start to finish:
45 minutes

VARIATION

Substitute ground chicken or turkey for any or all of the meats used above. If using poultry, substitute chicken stock and white wine for the beef stock and red wine.

These meatballs make a hearty entree for a cold fall evening, especially if they are served over buttered egg noodles so none of the sauce is left behind. The flavor of hearty bacon, herbs, and heady cheeses enlivens the meat mix.

¼ *pound bacon, cut into ⅛-inch slices*
1 *medium onion, chopped*
2 *garlic cloves, minced*
1 *large egg*
2 *tablespoons whole milk*
½ *cup plain breadcrumbs*
½ *cup grated Swiss cheese*
¼ *cup freshly grated Parmesan*
2 *tablespoons chopped fresh parsley*
1 *tablespoon fresh thyme or*
     1 *teaspoon dried*
¾ *pound ground beef*
½ *pound ground pork*
Salt and freshly ground black pepper to taste
1 *cup beef stock*
1 *cup dry red wine*
2 *teaspoons cornstarch*
Vegetable oil spray

1. Preheat the oven broiler. Line a rimmed baking sheet with heavy-duty aluminum foil, and spray the foil with vegetable oil spray.

2. Cook bacon in a large skillet over medium-high heat until crisp. Remove bacon from the skillet with a slotted spoon, and drain on paper towels. Discard all but 2 tablespoons bacon grease from the skillet, and add onion and garlic. Cook, stirring frequently, for 3 minutes, or until onion is translucent. Set aside.

3. Combine egg and milk in a mixing bowl, and whisk well. Add breadcrumbs, Swiss cheese, ¼ cup Parmesan, parsley, and thyme, and mix well.

4. Add onion mixture, bacon, beef, and pork, season to taste with salt and pepper, and mix well again. Make mixture into 1½-inch meatballs, and arrange meatballs on the prepared pan. Spray tops of meatballs with vegetable oil spray.

5. Broil meatballs 6 inches from the broiler element, turning them with tongs to brown all sides. While meatballs brown, add beef stock and wine to the skillet, and bring to a boil over high heat. Reduce the heat to medium-high, and cook until reduced by ⅓.

6. Remove meatballs from the baking pan with a slotted spoon, and add meatballs to sauce. Bring to a boil, and simmer meatballs, covered, over low heat, turning occasionally with a slotted spoon, for 15 minutes. Combine cornstarch with 1 tablespoon cold water in a small cup. Add mixture to sauce, and simmer for 2 minutes, or until slightly thickened. Season to taste with salt and pepper, and serve immediately.

Note: The meatball mixture can be prepared up to 1 day in advance and refrigerated, tightly covered. Also, the dish can be cooked up to 2 days in advance and refrigerated, tightly covered. Reheat in a 350°F oven, covered, for 15 to 20 minutes, or until hot.

To store bacon so a few slices can be used at a time, roll up the bacon in tight cylinders of 2 to 4 strips, and freeze them in a heavy resealable plastic bag. You can then defrost them in the microwave in a matter of a few seconds.

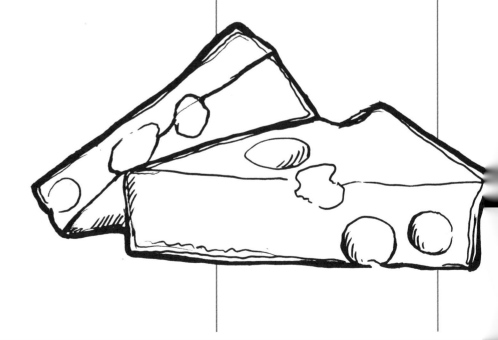

Spanish Meatballs in Tomato-Garlic Sauce

Makes 4 to 6 servings

Active time:
20 minutes

Start to finish:
50 minutes

VARIATION

Substitute ground chicken or turkey for any or all of the meats. If using poultry, substitute white wine for the red wine.

Small meatballs in tomato sauce are one of the traditional small bites served in Spanish tapas bars. I like them accompanied by dry sherry as they do in Spain. You can serve these as an hors d'oeuvre or over some pasta for dinner with a tossed salad.

¼ cup olive oil

1 large onion, finely chopped

1 large red bell pepper, seeds and
    ribs removed, and finely chopped

6 garlic cloves, minced

1 large egg

½ cup dry red wine, divided

½ cup plain breadcrumbs

⅓ cup chopped fresh parsley, divided

2 tablespoons smoked Spanish
    paprika

¾ pound ground chuck

¾ pound ground pork

Salt and freshly ground black
    pepper to taste

1 (28-ounce) can crushed tomatoes
    in tomato puree

1 tablespoon dried oregano

Vegetable oil spray

1. Preheat the oven broiler. Line a rimmed baking sheet with heavy-duty aluminum foil, and spray the foil with vegetable oil spray.

2. Heat oil in a large skillet over medium-high heat. Add onion, bell pepper, and garlic, and cook, stirring frequently, for 3 minutes, or until onion is translucent. Combine egg and 3 tablespoons wine in a mixing bowl, and whisk until smooth. Add breadcrumbs, ¼ cup parsley, and paprika, and mix well.

3. Add ½ of onion mixture, beef, and pork, season to taste with salt and pepper, and mix well again. Make mixture into 1½-inch meatballs, and arrange meatballs on the prepared pan. Spray tops of meatballs with vegetable oil spray.

4. Broil meatballs 6 inches from the broiler element, turning them with tongs to brown all sides. While meatballs brown, add remaining wine, tomatoes, and oregano to the skillet with remaining onion mixture. Bring to a boil over medium-high heat, stirring occasionally, then reduce the heat to medium, and simmer sauce, uncovered, for 10 minutes.

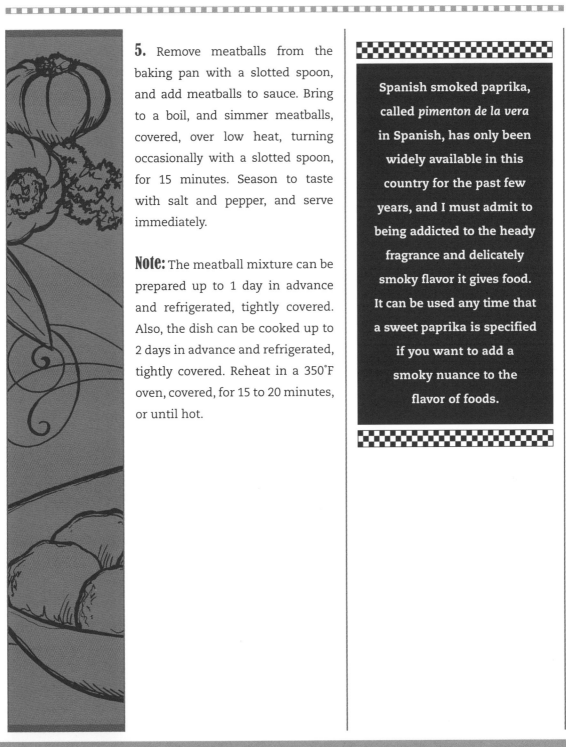

5. Remove meatballs from the baking pan with a slotted spoon, and add meatballs to sauce. Bring to a boil, and simmer meatballs, covered, over low heat, turning occasionally with a slotted spoon, for 15 minutes. Season to taste with salt and pepper, and serve immediately.

Note: The meatball mixture can be prepared up to 1 day in advance and refrigerated, tightly covered. Also, the dish can be cooked up to 2 days in advance and refrigerated, tightly covered. Reheat in a 350°F oven, covered, for 15 to 20 minutes, or until hot.

Spanish smoked paprika, called *pimenton de la vera* in Spanish, has only been widely available in this country for the past few years, and I must admit to being addicted to the heady fragrance and delicately smoky flavor it gives food. It can be used any time that a sweet paprika is specified if you want to add a smoky nuance to the flavor of foods.

Grilled Barbecued Mustard Meatballs

Makes 4 to 6 servings

Active time:
15 minutes

Start to finish:
30 minutes

VARIATION

Substitute ground chicken or turkey for any or all of the meats.

This is an all-American meatball flavored with a number of herbs and spices and grilled as skewers of meat. The extra mustard added to the barbecue sauce gives them a sharp bite.

8 to 12 (8-inch) bamboo skewers
1 large egg
2 tablespoons whole milk
3 slices seeded rye bread, broken
   into small pieces
3 scallions, white parts and
   2 inches of green tops, chopped
2 tablespoons chopped fresh parsley
2 teaspoons fresh thyme or
   ½ teaspoon dried
¼ teaspoon ground allspice
Pinch of ground nutmeg
¾ pound ground chuck
½ pound ground pork
Salt and freshly ground black
   pepper to taste
1 cup Southern Barbecue Sauce
   (page 39) or purchased barbecue
   sauce
¼ cup Dijon mustard

1. Soak the bamboo skewers in cold water to cover. Prepare a medium-hot charcoal or gas grill, or preheat the oven broiler.

2. Whisk egg and milk in a mixing bowl, and add bread, scallions, parsley, thyme, allspice, and nutmeg, and mix well. Add beef and pork to the mixing bowl, season to taste with salt and pepper, and mix well again.

3. Divide mixture into 8 to 12 portions, and form each portion into a sausage shape. Insert a skewer into each sausage so that the tip of the skewer is almost at the top of the meat.

4. Combine Southern Barbecue Sauce and mustard in a mixing bowl, and whisk well. Divide mixture into 2 bowls.

5. Grill skewers for a total of 8 to 10 minutes, uncovered if using a charcoal grill, turning them gently with tongs to cook all sides, and basting with barbecue sauce mixture. Serve immediately, discard sauce used for basting, and serve with other bowl of barbecue sauce for dipping.

Note: The meatball mixture can be prepared up to 1 day in advance and refrigerated, tightly covered. Also, the skewers can be grilled up to 2 days in advance and refrigerated, tightly covered. Reheat them in a 350°F oven, covered, for 10 to 12 minutes, or until hot.

> Allspice got its name because its flavor is reminiscent of a combination of cinnamon, nutmeg, and cloves. It comes from small berries of a pimiento tree native to the West Indies, and it was considered a luxury during the centuries of the spice trade.

Grilled Cajun Cheddar Meatballs

Makes 4 to 6 servings

Active time:
20 minutes

Start to finish:
35 minutes

VARIATION

For milder meatballs, omit the andouille and use bulk pork sausage, or omit the sausage entirely and add more pork.

These meatballs combine ground beef with cheese and andouille sausage, a spicy, smoked Louisiana pork sausage used in Cajun cooking. If andouille is unavailable, use another smoked pork sausage such as kielbasa, and add a bit of extra cayenne when seasoning the dish. This is a hearty dish that has been fed to crowds at many of my Super Bowl parties.

8 to 12 (8-inch) bamboo skewers
½ pound smoked andouille sausage, casings removed, if necessary
2 tablespoons olive oil
1 large onion, chopped
2 garlic cloves, minced
1 large egg
2 tablespoons whole milk
1 tablespoon Worcestershire sauce
½ cup plain breadcrumbs
½ cup grated sharp cheddar cheese
¾ pound ground chuck
Salt and freshly ground black pepper to taste
Vegetable oil spray

For dipping:
1 cup Remoulade Sauce (page 45)

1. Soak the bamboo skewers in cold water to cover. Prepare a medium-hot charcoal or gas grill, or preheat the oven broiler.

2. Cut sausage into ¾-inch chunks, and chop finely in a food processor using on-and-off pulsing. Set aside.

3. Heat oil in a small skillet over medium-high heat. Add onion and garlic, and cook, stirring frequently, for 3 minutes, or until onion is translucent. While vegetables cook, whisk egg, milk, and Worcestershire sauce in a mixing bowl, add breadcrumbs and cheese, and mix well.

4. Add onion mixture, beef, and sausage to the mixing bowl, season to taste with salt and pepper, and mix well again.

5. Divide mixture into 8 to 12 portions, and form each portion into a sausage shape. Insert a skewer into each sausage so that the tip of the skewer is almost at the top of the meat.

6. Grill skewers for a total of 6 to 8 minutes, uncovered if using a charcoal grill, turning them gently with tongs to cook all sides. Serve immediately, accompanied by a bowl of Remoulade Sauce for dipping.

Note: The meatball mixture can be prepared up to 1 day in advance and refrigerated, tightly covered. Also, the skewers can be grilled up to 2 days in advance and refrigerated, tightly covered. Reheat them in a 350°F oven, covered, for 10 to 12 minutes, or until hot.

Muffuletta Meatballs

Makes 4 to 6 servings

Active time:
15 minutes

Start to finish:
30 minutes

VARIATION

Substitute ground chicken or turkey for the ground pork, but continue to use the same cold cuts.

The muffuletta sandwich, on which these meatballs are based, is a submarine sandwich with layers of cold cuts topped with cheese and an olive salad. The Central Grocery in New Orleans' French Quarter has been making them since 1906, but they're available throughout the city. These meatballs have so much going on in them that no sauce is necessary. Accompany them with toothpicks.

1 large egg
2 tablespoons whole milk
2 slices white bread, torn into
    small pieces
¼ pound ham, finely chopped
¼ pound Genoa or hard salami,
    finely chopped
½ cup chopped pimiento-stuffed
    green olives
½ cup grated Fontina
2 garlic cloves, minced
2 tablespoons chopped fresh parsley
1 tablespoon white wine vinegar
2 teaspoons chopped fresh oregano
    or ½ teaspoon dried
¾ pound ground pork
Salt and cayenne to taste
Vegetable oil spray

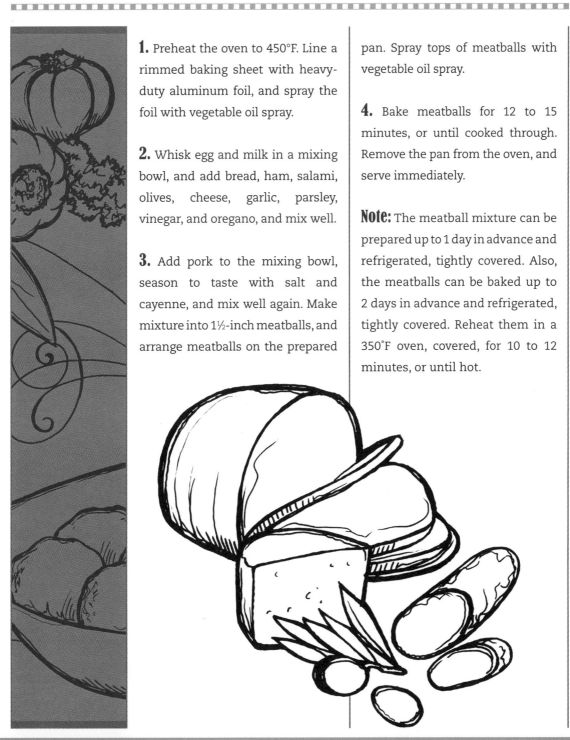

1. Preheat the oven to 450°F. Line a rimmed baking sheet with heavy-duty aluminum foil, and spray the foil with vegetable oil spray.

2. Whisk egg and milk in a mixing bowl, and add bread, ham, salami, olives, cheese, garlic, parsley, vinegar, and oregano, and mix well.

3. Add pork to the mixing bowl, season to taste with salt and cayenne, and mix well again. Make mixture into 1½-inch meatballs, and arrange meatballs on the prepared pan. Spray tops of meatballs with vegetable oil spray.

4. Bake meatballs for 12 to 15 minutes, or until cooked through. Remove the pan from the oven, and serve immediately.

Note: The meatball mixture can be prepared up to 1 day in advance and refrigerated, tightly covered. Also, the meatballs can be baked up to 2 days in advance and refrigerated, tightly covered. Reheat them in a 350°F oven, covered, for 10 to 12 minutes, or until hot.

Barbecued Pumpernickel Meatballs

Makes 4 to 6 servings

Active time:
20 minutes

Start to finish:
45 minutes

VARIATION

Substitute ground chicken or turkey for any or all of the meats.

This recipe is an updated—water chestnuts and lot of herbs are added—version of a classic hors d'oeuvre served at cocktail parties in the mid-1950s.

If you don't have water chestnuts on hand, you can always substitute diced celery in a recipe such as this one. In the short time it takes to cook these meatballs the celery will not be cooked through and will still remain crunchy.

2 tablespoons vegetable oil

½ small red onion, finely chopped

½ green bell pepper, seeds and ribs removed, and finely chopped

2 garlic cloves, minced

1 large egg

2 tablespoons Worcestershire sauce

¼ teaspoon hot red pepper sauce, or to taste

3 slices pumpernickel bread, broken into little pieces

½ cup chopped water chestnuts

2 tablespoons chopped fresh sage or 2 teaspoons dried

1 tablespoon smoked Spanish paprika

¾ pound ground beef

½ pound ground lamb

Salt and freshly ground black pepper to taste

1 cup dry red wine

1 cup Southern Barbecue Sauce (page 39) or purchased barbecue sauce

Vegetable oil spray

1. Preheat the oven broiler. Line a rimmed baking sheet with heavy-duty aluminum foil, and spray the foil with vegetable oil spray.

2. Heat oil in a large skillet over medium-high heat. Add onion, bell pepper, and garlic, and cook, stirring frequently, for 3 minutes, or until onion is translucent. Combine egg, Worcestershire sauce, and hot red pepper sauce in a mixing bowl, and whisk until smooth. Add bread, water chestnuts, sage, and paprika, and mix well.

3. Add onion mixture, beef, and lamb, season to taste with salt and pepper, and mix well again. Make mixture into 1½-inch meatballs, and arrange meatballs on the prepared pan. Spray tops of meatballs with vegetable oil spray.

4. Broil meatballs 6 inches from the broiler element, turning them with tongs to brown all sides. While meatballs brown, pour wine into the skillet, bring to a boil over high heat, and boil until liquid is reduced by ½. Turn off the heat, and stir in barbecue sauce.

5. Remove meatballs from the baking pan with a slotted spoon, and add meatballs to sauce. Bring to a boil, and simmer meatballs, covered, over low heat, turning occasionally with a slotted spoon, for 15 minutes. Season to taste with salt and pepper, and serve immediately.

Note: The meatball mixture can be prepared up to 1 day in advance and refrigerated, tightly covered. Also, the dish can be cooked up to 2 days in advance and refrigerated, tightly covered. Reheat in a 350°F oven, covered, for 15 to 20 minutes, or until hot.

Sweet-and-Sour Tex-Mex Meatballs

Makes 4 to 6 servings

Active time: 20 minutes

Start to finish: 45 minutes

VARIATION

Substitute ground chicken or turkey for any or all of the meats.

These meatballs are cooked in a combination of jalapeño pepper jelly and bottled chili sauce, which have sweet and sour flavors. Crushed tortilla chips add crunchy texture.

2 tablespoons olive oil

1 small onion, finely chopped

½ red bell pepper, seeds and ribs removed, and finely chopped

4 garlic cloves, minced

1 large egg

1 (8-ounce) can tomato sauce, divided

¾ cup crushed tortilla chips

3 tablespoons chopped fresh cilantro

3 tablespoons canned diced mild green chiles, drained

1 tablespoon dried oregano

2 teaspoons ground cumin

¾ pound ground chuck

½ pound ground pork

Salt and freshly ground black pepper to taste

½ cup chili sauce

½ cup jalapeño pepper jelly

Vegetable oil spray

1. Preheat the oven broiler. Line a rimmed baking sheet with heavy-duty aluminum foil, and spray the foil with vegetable oil spray.

2. Heat oil in a large skillet over medium-high heat. Add onion, bell pepper, and garlic, and cook, stirring frequently, for 3 minutes, or until onion is translucent. Combine egg and 2 tablespoons tomato sauce in a mixing bowl, and whisk until smooth. Add crushed tortilla chips, cilantro, chiles, oregano, and cumin, and mix well.

3. Add ½ of onion mixture, beef, and pork, season to taste with salt and pepper, and mix well again. Make mixture into 1½-inch meatballs, and arrange meatballs on the prepared pan. Spray tops of meatballs with vegetable oil spray.

4. Broil meatballs 6 inches from the broiler element, turning them with tongs to brown all sides. While meatballs brown, add remaining tomato sauce, chili sauce, and jelly to the onion mixture remaining in the skillet, and bring to a boil over medium-high heat, stirring occasionally.

5. Remove meatballs from the baking pan with a slotted spoon, and add meatballs to sauce. Bring to a boil, and simmer meatballs, covered, over low heat, turning occasionally with a slotted spoon, for 15 minutes. Season to taste with salt and pepper, and serve immediately.

Note: The meatball mixture can be prepared up to 1 day in advance and refrigerated, tightly covered. Also, the dish can be cooked up to 2 days in advance and refrigerated, tightly covered. Reheat in a 350°F oven, covered, for 15 to 20 minutes, or until hot.

Cumin is sometimes found in markets under its Spanish name, *comino*. The seeds from which it's ground are the dried fruit from a plant in the parsley family, which is very aromatic. It's one of the major ingredients in commercial chili powder, so substitute chili powder if necessary.

Mushroom Meatballs

Makes 4 to 6 servings

Active time:
25 minutes

Start to finish:
40 minutes

VARIATIONS

Substitute ground chicken or turkey for any or all of the meats.

For more flavor, use bottled chili sauce rather than ketchup.

These meatballs are the round and ground version of old-fashioned American meatloaf, down to the ketchup glaze. They're homey, inviting, and a great brunch dish. Serve them with mashed potatoes and creamed spinach.

2 tablespoons unsalted butter
2 tablespoons olive oil
1 small onion, chopped
2 garlic cloves, minced
½ pound mushrooms, wiped with
    a damp paper towel, trimmed,
    and chopped
1 large egg
¾ cup ketchup, divided
2 tablespoons whole milk
½ cup uncooked oatmeal
    (not instant)
2 tablespoons chopped fresh parsley
2 tablespoons Worcestershire sauce
2 teaspoons fresh thyme or
    ½ teaspoon dried
¾ pound ground pork
½ pound ground veal
Salt and freshly ground black
    pepper to taste
Vegetable oil spray

1. Preheat the oven to 450°F. Line a rimmed baking sheet with heavy-duty aluminum foil, and spray the foil with vegetable oil spray.

2. Heat butter and oil in a large skillet over medium-high heat. Add onion and garlic, and cook, stirring frequently, for 2 minutes. Add mushrooms, and cook for 5 to 7 minutes, or until mushrooms are soft. Set aside.

3. While vegetables cook, whisk egg, ¼ cup ketchup, and milk in a mixing bowl. Add oatmeal, parsley, Worcestershire sauce, and thyme, and mix well. Add vegetable mixture, pork, and veal to the mixing bowl, season to taste with salt and pepper, and mix well again. Make mixture into 1½-inch meatballs, and arrange meatballs on the prepared pan. Spray tops of meatballs with vegetable oil spray.

4. Bake meatballs for 12 to 15 minutes, or until cooked through. While meatballs bake, heat remaining ketchup in the skillet over medium heat. Remove the pan from the oven, and add meatballs to the skillet, stirring to glaze them with ketchup. Serve immediately.

Note: The meatball mixture can be prepared up to 1 day in advance and refrigerated, tightly covered. Also, the meatballs can be baked up to 2 days in advance and refrigerated, tightly covered. Reheat them in a 350°F oven, covered, for 10 to 12 minutes, or until hot.

An easy way to slice and dice mushrooms is with an egg slicer. The slices will be even so they will cook at the same rate. If you slice them in one direction and then reverse the slices you can chop them.

Mexican Beef and Chorizo Meatballs

Makes 4 to 6 servings

Active time:
20 minutes

Start to finish:
35 minutes

VARIATION

Substitute Portuguese linguiça for the chorizo, and use ground pork in place of the beef.

Chorizo is a flavorful sausage used in both Mexico and Spain, and when combined with ground beef and spices, it creates a memorable meatball. These meatballs also include a number of aromatic spices and some jalapeño Jack cheese for an added kick.

3 tablespoons olive oil

¼ small red onion, chopped

3 garlic cloves, minced

1 large egg

2 tablespoons whole milk

¼ cup plain breadcrumbs

¾ cup grated jalapeño Jack cheese

3 tablespoons chopped fresh cilantro

1 tablespoon chili powder

2 teaspoon ground cumin

1 teaspoon dried oregano

1 pound ground chuck

½ pound chorizo, casings removed, if necessary

Salt and cayenne to taste

Vegetable oil spray

For dipping:
1 cup Creamy Chipotle Sauce (page 47) or bottled salsa

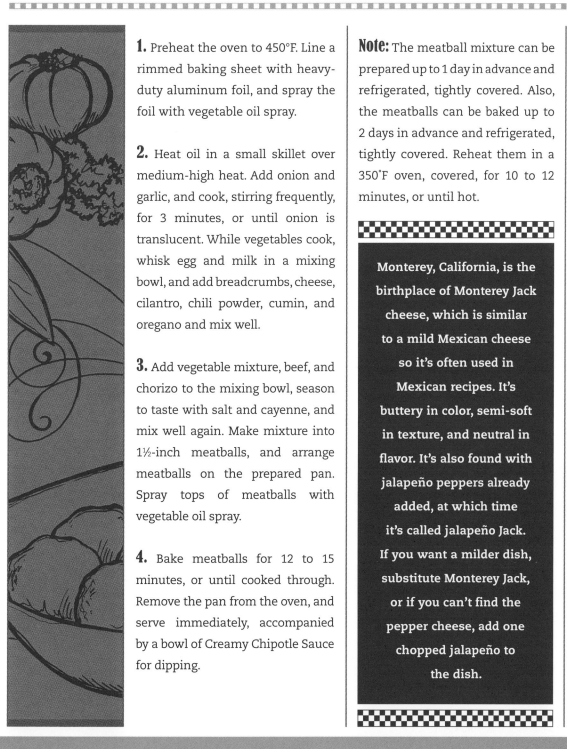

1. Preheat the oven to 450°F. Line a rimmed baking sheet with heavy-duty aluminum foil, and spray the foil with vegetable oil spray.

2. Heat oil in a small skillet over medium-high heat. Add onion and garlic, and cook, stirring frequently, for 3 minutes, or until onion is translucent. While vegetables cook, whisk egg and milk in a mixing bowl, and add breadcrumbs, cheese, cilantro, chili powder, cumin, and oregano and mix well.

3. Add vegetable mixture, beef, and chorizo to the mixing bowl, season to taste with salt and cayenne, and mix well again. Make mixture into 1½-inch meatballs, and arrange meatballs on the prepared pan. Spray tops of meatballs with vegetable oil spray.

4. Bake meatballs for 12 to 15 minutes, or until cooked through. Remove the pan from the oven, and serve immediately, accompanied by a bowl of Creamy Chipotle Sauce for dipping.

Note: The meatball mixture can be prepared up to 1 day in advance and refrigerated, tightly covered. Also, the meatballs can be baked up to 2 days in advance and refrigerated, tightly covered. Reheat them in a 350°F oven, covered, for 10 to 12 minutes, or until hot.

Monterey, California, is the birthplace of Monterey Jack cheese, which is similar to a mild Mexican cheese so it's often used in Mexican recipes. It's buttery in color, semi-soft in texture, and neutral in flavor. It's also found with jalapeño peppers already added, at which time it's called jalapeño Jack. If you want a milder dish, substitute Monterey Jack, or if you can't find the pepper cheese, add one chopped jalapeño to the dish.

CLUCK AND GOBBLE:

MEATBALLS WITH

CHICKEN AND TURKEY

Famed nineteenth-century French gastronome, Jean Anthelme Brillat-Savarin, once wrote that "poultry is for the cook what canvas is for the painter." Its inherently mild flavor takes to many methods of seasoning, and it is relatively quick to cook.

Ground chicken and turkey are relatively new on the market and have become increasingly popular as people cut back on saturated fat in their diets. Ground chicken and turkey are interchangeable in this chapter's recipes. If I suggest one rather than the other, that's based purely on personal preference.

Because these foods are somewhat new, many of the recipes that utilize them—including some in this chapter—are adaptations from other meats, most noticeably pork, which has an equally delicate flavor. So in addition to these recipes, look at those in Chapter 5; any recipe made with ground pork (rather than sausage or ham) can also be made with chicken and turkey.

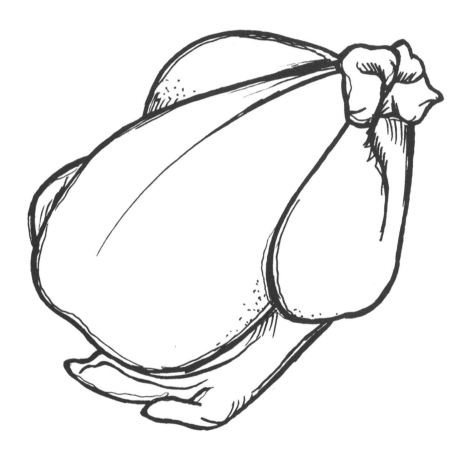

Herbed Turkey Meatballs

Makes 4 to 6 servings

**Active time:
15 minutes**

**Start to finish:
30 minutes**

Make the meatballs with ground pork, ground veal, or some combination of the two.

Fresh apple adds moisture as well as a slightly sweet flavor to these lean meatballs flavored with a variety of herbs and spices. Serve them with potato salad during the summer or some mashed potatoes during colder months.

1 large egg

2 tablespoons whole milk

½ cup plain breadcrumbs

¼ cup grated Monterey Jack cheese

1 Golden Delicious or Granny Smith
   apple, peeled, cored, and grated

3 tablespoons chopped fresh sage
   or 1 tablespoon dried

2 tablespoons chopped fresh parsley

1 tablespoon fresh thyme or
   1 teaspoon dried

Pinch of ground allspice

1¼ pounds ground turkey

Salt and freshly ground black
   pepper to taste

Vegetable oil spray

For dipping:

1 cup Southern Barbecue Sauce
   (page 39) or commercial
   barbecue sauce, heated

1. Preheat the oven to 450°F. Line a rimmed baking sheet with heavy-duty aluminum foil, and spray the foil with vegetable oil spray.

2. Whisk egg and milk in a mixing bowl, and add breadcrumbs, cheese, apple, sage, parsley, thyme, and allspice, and mix well. Add turkey, season to taste with salt and pepper, and mix well again. Make mixture into 1½-inch meatballs, and arrange meatballs on the prepared pan. Spray tops of meatballs with vegetable oil spray.

3. Bake meatballs for 12 to 15 minutes, or until cooked through and no longer pink. Remove the pan from the oven, and serve immediately, accompanied by a bowl of Southern Barbecue Sauce for dipping.

Note: The meatball mixture can be prepared up to 1 day in advance and refrigerated, tightly covered. Also, the meatballs can be baked up to 2 days in advance and refrigerated, tightly covered. Reheat them in a 350°F oven, covered, for 10 to 12 minutes, or until hot.

Chicken Croquettes

Makes 4 to 6 servings

Active time: 20 minutes

Start to finish: 1½ hours, including 1 hour to chill mixture

Croquettes of all types are a way to stretch leftovers. Chopped food is folded into a thick white sauce, formed into balls, and fried. They are very easy to make.

4 tablespoons (½ stick) unsalted butter
2 shallot, finely chopped
1 cup all-purpose flour, divided
⅔ cup milk
⅔ cup chicken stock
3 cups finely chopped cooked chicken
2 tablespoons chopped fresh parsley
1 tablespoon Cajun seasoning
2 large eggs, lightly beaten
1 cup plain breadcrumbs
3 cups vegetable oil for frying

For dipping:
1 cup Herbed Tomato Sauce (page 38), heated, or Creamy Chipotle Sauce (page 47)

1. Heat butter in a saucepan over medium heat. Add shallots and cook, stirring frequently, for 2 minutes. Add ⅓ cup flour, reduce the heat to low, and cook for 2 minutes, stirring constantly. Whisk in milk and stock, and bring to a boil over medium heat, whisking constantly. Reduce the heat to low, and simmer sauce for 2 minutes. Remove the pan from the heat.

2. Stir chicken, parsley, and Cajun seasoning into sauce, and transfer mixture to a 9 x 13-inch baking pan. Spread mixture evenly, and refrigerate loosely covered with plastic wrap for 30 minutes or until cold.

3. Place remaining flour on a sheet of plastic wrap, combine egg and 2 tablespoons water in a shallow bowl, and place breadcrumbs on another sheet of plastic wrap. With wet hands, form mixture into 2-inch balls. Dust balls with flour,

VARIATIONS

Replace the chicken with turkey.

Use chopped ham, omitting the Cajun seasoning and adding 1 tablespoon chopped fresh sage, salt, and pepper.

Use chopped fish or seafood —salmon, cod, halibut, shrimp, and crab all work well—and omit the Cajun seasoning and add 1 tablespoon Old Bay seasoning.

dip into egg mixture, and dip into breadcrumbs, pressing to ensure crumbs adhere. Refrigerate balls for 30 minutes.

4. Heat oil in a saucepan over medium-high heat to 375°F. Add croquettes, being careful not to crowd the pan. Cook croquettes for a total of 3 to 5 minutes, or until browned. Remove croquettes from the pan with a slotted spoon, and drain well on paper towels. Serve immediately, accompanied by a bowl of Herbed Tomato Sauce or Creamy Chipotle Sauce for dipping.

Note: The croquettes can be prepared for frying up to 1 day in advance and refrigerated, tightly covered. They can also be fried in advance; reheat them in a 375°F oven for 10 to 12 minutes or until hot and crusty again.

As a general rule, the thinner the layer of food, the faster it chills. That's why this croquette mixture is transferred to a baking pan rather than being chilled in a saucepan. For large quantities of liquid like soups or stews, portion them into pint and quart containers to speed chilling.

Grilled Spicy Southwestern Turkey Meatballs

Makes 4 to 6 servings

Active time: 15 minutes

Start to finish: 30 minutes

VARIATIONS

Replace the turkey with ground pork or ground veal.

Substitute some uncooked chicken sausage for some of the ground turkey.

Try these spicy morsels with guacamole and stewed beans. The crushed tortilla chips add texture and well as flavor, and chilled beer is your best beverage.

8 to 12 (8-inch) bamboo skewers

1 large egg

1 cup Mexican Tomato Sauce (page 48), divided

½ cup finely crushed tortilla chips

6 scallions, white parts and 3 inches of green tops, chopped

4 garlic cloves, minced

3 tablespoons chopped fresh cilantro

2 teaspoons finely chopped chipotle chiles in adobo sauce

2 teaspoons ground cumin

1 teaspoon dried oregano

1¼ pounds ground turkey

Salt and freshly ground black pepper to taste

1. Soak the bamboo skewers in cold water to cover. Prepare a medium-hot charcoal or gas grill, or preheat the oven broiler.

2. Whisk egg and 2 tablespoons Mexican Tomato Sauce in a mixing bowl, and add crushed tortilla chips, scallions, garlic, cilantro, chipotle chiles, cumin, and oregano, and mix well. Add turkey to the mixing bowl, season to taste with salt and pepper, and mix well again.

3. Divide mixture into 8 to 12 portions, and form each portion into a sausage shape. Insert a skewer into each sausage so that the tip of the skewer is almost at the top of the meat.

4. Grill skewers for a total of 8 to 10 minutes, uncovered if using a charcoal grill, turning them gently with tongs to cook all sides; grill until cooked through and no longer pink. Heat remaining Mexican Tomato Sauce in a small saucepan over medium-high heat, stirring occasionally. Serve immediately, accompanied by the bowl of heated sauce for dipping.

Note: The meatball mixture can be prepared up to 1 day in advance and refrigerated, tightly covered. Also, the skewers can be grilled up to 2 days in advance and refrigerated, tightly covered. Reheat them in a 350°F oven, covered, for 10 to 12 minutes, or until hot.

In Spain and Latin American countries, the word for meatballs is *albóndigas*, which comes from the Arabic *al-bunduq*, which literally means hazelnut, but came to mean any small round object.

Santa Fe Chicken Meatballs

Makes 4 to 6 servings

Active time:
20 minutes

Start to finish:
35 minutes

While not traditionally Mexican, these meatballs contain some characteristically Southwestern flavors, such as cilantro, chili powder, and cumin.

Since bell peppers contain a lot of water, shake them in a colander before adding them to a pan to cook. Then they'll cook evenly with the onions and other ingredients.

2 tablespoons olive oil

1 small onion, chopped

½ red bell pepper, seeds and ribs removed, and chopped

3 garlic cloves, minced

1 large egg

2 tablespoons sour cream

2 tablespoons chili sauce or ketchup

¾ cup finely crushed tortilla chips

¼ cup chopped fresh cilantro

1 tablespoon chili powder

1 tablespoon smoked Spanish paprika

1 teaspoon ground cumin

1¼ pounds ground chicken

Salt and freshly ground black pepper to taste

Vegetable oil spray

For dipping:

1 cup Creamy Chipotle Sauce (page 47)

1. Preheat the oven to 450°F. Line a rimmed baking sheet with heavy-duty aluminum foil, and spray the foil with vegetable oil spray.

2. Heat oil in a small skillet over medium-high heat. Add onion, bell pepper, and garlic, and cook, stirring frequently, for 3 minutes, or until onion is translucent.

3. While vegetables cook, whisk egg, sour cream, and chili sauce in a mixing bowl, add crushed tortilla chips, cilantro, chili powder, paprika, and cumin, and mix well. Add onion mixture and chicken to the mixing bowl, season to taste with salt and pepper, and mix well again. Make mixture into 1½-inch meatballs, and arrange meatballs on the prepared pan. Spray tops of meatballs with vegetable oil spray.

4. Bake meatballs for 12 to 15 minutes, or until cooked through and no longer pink. Remove the pan from the oven, and serve immediately, accompanied by a bowl of Creamy Chipotle Sauce for dipping.

Note: The chicken mixture can be prepared up to 1 day in advance and refrigerated, tightly covered. Also, the meatballs can be baked up to 2 days in advance and refrigerated, tightly covered. Reheat them in a 350°F oven, covered, for 10 to 12 minutes, or until hot.

Grilled Cranberry-Maple Turkey Meatballs

Makes 4 to 6 servings

Active time:
15 minutes

Start to finish:
30 minutes

VARIATIONS

Replace the turkey with ground pork or ground veal.

Substitute chopped dried apricots or dried currants for the cranberries.

Add some hot red pepper sauce to the barbecue sauce for a spicier dish.

Cranberries and maple are treasured New England foods, and they are joined in this recipe. The quickly grilled skewers also include some grated apple for moisture and some crushed cornflakes to add a crunchy texture.

8 to 12 (8-inch) bamboo skewers
1 large egg
2 tablespoons whole milk
½ cup crushed corn flakes
1 Golden Delicious apple, peeled, cored, and grated
¼ cup chopped dried cranberries
2 teaspoons dry mustard, divided
½ teaspoon dried thyme
1¼ pounds ground turkey
Salt and freshly ground black pepper to taste
½ cup barbecue sauce
½ cup pure maple syrup
½ cup cider vinegar
¼ cup finely chopped dried cranberries
1 teaspoon grated lemon zest
½ teaspoon ground cinnamon
½ teaspoon ground ginger

1. Soak the bamboo skewers in cold water to cover. Prepare a medium-hot charcoal or gas grill, or preheat the oven broiler.

2. Whisk egg and milk in a mixing bowl, and add crushed corn flakes, apple, cranberries, 1 teaspoon mustard, and thyme, and mix well. Add turkey to the mixing bowl, season to taste with salt and pepper, and mix well again.

3. Combine barbecue sauce, maple syrup, cider vinegar, lemon zest, cinnamon, ginger, and remaining 1 teaspoon mustard in a small saucepan. Bring to a boil over medium-high heat, stirring occasionally. Reduce the heat to low, and simmer sauce for 3 minutes, stirring occasionally. Divide sauce into 2 small bowls.

4. Divide turkey mixture into 8 to 12 portions, and form each portion into a sausage shape. Insert a skewer into each sausage so that the tip of the skewer is almost at the top of the meat.

5. Grill skewers for a total of 8 to 10 minutes, uncovered if using a charcoal grill, turning them gently with tongs to cook all sides, basting with barbecue sauce every 2 minutes. Grill until cooked through and no longer pink. Discard sauce used for basting, and serve immediately, accompanied by the second bowl of sauce for dipping.

Note: The meatball mixture can be prepared up to 1 day in advance and refrigerated, tightly covered. Also, the skewers can be grilled up to 2 days in advance and refrigerated, tightly covered. Reheat them in a 350°F oven, covered, for 10 to 12 minutes, or until hot.

Cranberries are native to the Cape Cod area, and it's possible the Pilgrims ate them in some form at the first Thanksgiving dinner in 1621. But our word cranberry is not English; it's a corruption from the Dutch *kranbeere*, or craneberry, because the stamen resembled a beak.

Curried Turkey Meatballs with Dried Currants and Toasted Almonds

Makes 4 to 6 servings

Active time:
20 minutes

Start to finish:
50 minutes

VARIATIONS

Replace the turkey with ground pork or ground veal.

Substitute some uncooked chicken sausage for some of the ground turkey.

This is a meatball version of Country Captain, a chicken dish that dates back to Colonial times. Some food historians say it originated in Savannah, Georgia, a major port for the spice trade. Serve it over rice to enjoy the gravy.

1 large egg

2 tablespoons whole milk

½ cup plain breadcrumbs

½ cup chopped almonds, toasted in a 350°F oven for 5 minutes

2 tablespoons chopped fresh parsley

1¼ pounds ground turkey

Salt and freshly ground black pepper to taste

3 tablespoons vegetable oil

1 large onion, diced

1 red bell pepper, seeds and ribs removed, and diced

2 garlic cloves, minced

2 tablespoons curry powder

½ teaspoon ground ginger

½ teaspoon dried thyme

1 (14.5-ounce) can diced tomatoes, drained

¼ cup dry sherry

1½ cups chicken stock

⅔ cup dried currants

2 teaspoons cornstarch

Vegetable oil spray

1. Preheat the oven broiler. Line a rimmed baking sheet with heavy-duty aluminum foil, and spray the foil with vegetable oil spray.

2. Combine egg and milk in a mixing bowl, and whisk until smooth. Add breadcrumbs, almonds, and parsley, and mix well. Add turkey, and season to taste with salt and pepper. Make mixture into 1½-inch meatballs, and arrange meatballs on the prepared pan. Spray tops of meatballs with vegetable oil spray.

3. Heat oil in a large skillet over medium-high heat. Add onion, bell pepper, and garlic, and cook, stirring frequently, for 3 minutes, or until onion is translucent. Add curry powder, ginger, and thyme to the skillet and cook, stirring constantly, for 1 minute. Add tomatoes, sherry, chicken stock, and currants and bring to a boil, stirring occasionally. Reduce the heat to low and simmer sauce, uncovered, for 10 minutes, stirring occasionally.

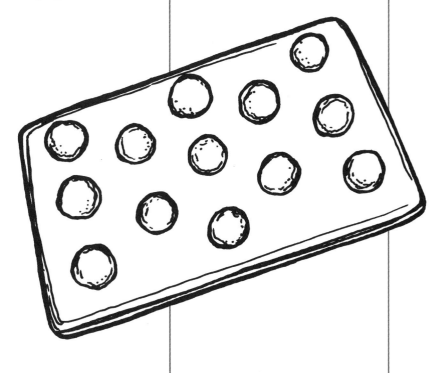

4. Broil meatballs 6 inches from the broiler element, turning them with tongs to brown all sides. Remove meatballs from the baking pan with a slotted spoon, and add meatballs to sauce. Bring to a boil, and simmer meatballs, covered, over low heat, turning occasionally with a slotted spoon, for 15 minutes or until meatballs are cooked through and no longer pink. Combine cornstarch and 1 tablespoon cold water in a small cup, and stir well. Add mixture to the skillet, and simmer for 2 minutes, or until slightly thickened. Season to taste with salt and pepper, and serve immediately.

Note: The turkey mixture can be prepared up to 1 day in advance and refrigerated, tightly covered. Also, the dish can be cooked up to 2 days in advance and refrigerated, tightly covered. Reheat it in a 350°F oven, covered, for 15 to 20 minutes, or until hot.

Heat releases the flavors and aromas of dried herbs and spices. For blends such as curry powder or chili powder, it also removes any "raw" taste. Add these dried ingredients to the skillet at the beginning of the cooking process. Add fresh herbs toward the end.

Chicken Meatballs Piccata

Makes 4 to 6 servings

Active time:
20 minutes

Start to finish:
50 minutes

VARIATIONS

Replace the chicken with ground pork or ground veal.

Substitute freshly squeezed lime juice for the lemon juice.

Boil some pasta, because you're going to want to savor every drop of this luscious lemony sauce dotted with tangy capers. Serve with a light, dry white wine and a tossed salad.

2 tablespoons olive oil

1 small onion, chopped

3 garlic cloves, minced

1 large egg

2 tablespoons whole milk

½ cup seasoned Italian breadcrumbs

½ cup chopped fresh parsley, divided

1 teaspoon Italian seasoning

1¼ pounds ground chicken

Salt and freshly ground black
    pepper to taste

2 tablespoons unsalted butter

3 tablespoons all-purpose flour

1½ cups chicken stock

⅓ cup freshly squeezed lemon juice

¼ cup small capers, drained and
    rinsed

Vegetable oil spray

1. Preheat the oven broiler. Line a rimmed baking sheet with heavy-duty aluminum foil, and spray the foil with vegetable oil spray.

2. Heat oil in a large skillet over medium-high heat. Add onion and garlic, and cook, stirring frequently, for 3 minutes, or until onion is translucent. While vegetables cook, whisk egg and milk in a mixing bowl, add breadcrumbs, 2 tablespoons parsley, and Italian seasoning, and mix well.

3. Add ½ of vegetable mixture and chicken to the mixing bowl, season to taste with salt and pepper, and mix well again. Make mixture into 1½-inch meatballs, and arrange meatballs on the prepared pan. Spray tops of meatballs with vegetable oil spray.

4. Broil meatballs 6 inches from the broiler element, turning them with tongs to brown all sides.

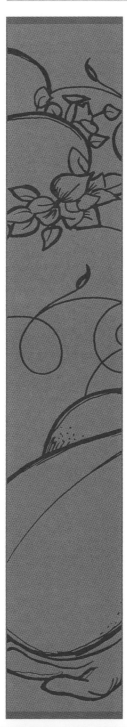

5. While meatballs brown, add butter to the vegetables remaining in the skillet over medium-high heat. Reduce the heat to low, stir in flour and cook, stirring constantly, for 2 minutes. Whisk in stock and lemon juice, and bring to a boil over medium-high heat, whisking constantly. Stir in remaining parsley and capers, and simmer 3 minutes, uncovered.

6. Remove meatballs from the baking pan with a slotted spoon, and add meatballs to sauce. Bring to a boil, and simmer meatballs, covered, over low heat, turning occasionally with a slotted spoon, for 15 minutes or until meatballs are cooked through and no longer pink. Serve immediately.

Note: The chicken mixture can be prepared up to 1 day in advance and refrigerated, tightly covered. Also, the dish can be cooked up to 2 days in advance and refrigerated, tightly covered. Reheat it in a 350°F oven, covered, for 15 to 20 minutes, or until hot.

To get the maximum amount of juice from citrus fruits, roll them back and forth on a counter or prick the skin and microwave them on high power for 30 seconds.

Chicken Meatballs Cacciatore

Makes 4 to 6 servings

Active time: 25 minutes

Start to finish: 55 minutes

VARIATIONS

Replace the chicken with ground chuck for a heartier dish.

Substitute some Italian pork sausage for some of the ground turkey.

Cacciatore is Italian for "hunter's style." Any number of dishes from chicken to beef to veal can use cacciatore as a description, but all it means is that the dish is cooked with tomatoes, and frequently with wild mushrooms as well. The rest of the ingredients are up to the cook.

This dish contains both dried porcini mushrooms and chopped prosciutto for flavor.

½ ounce dried porcini mushrooms

1 cup boiling chicken stock

3 tablespoons olive oil

¼ pound prosciutto, finely chopped

1 large onion, chopped

4 garlic cloves, minced

½ pound mushrooms, wiped with a damp paper towel, and sliced

1 (28-ounce) can diced tomatoes, undrained

¼ cup chopped fresh parsley, divided

1 teaspoon Italian seasoning

1 bay leaf

1 large egg

2 tablespoons whole milk

½ cup seasoned Italian breadcrumbs

¼ cup freshly grated Parmesan

1¼ pounds ground chicken

Salt and freshly ground black pepper to taste

Vegetable oil spray

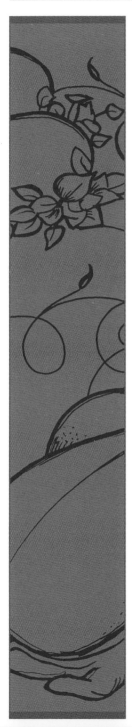

1. Soak porcini in boiling stock for 10 minutes. Drain, reserving soaking liquid. Discard stems and finely chop mushrooms. Set aside. Strain liquid through a paper coffee filter or paper towel. Reserve mushrooms and liquid.

2. While mushrooms soak, heat olive oil in large skillet over medium-high heat. Add prosciutto, onion, and garlic. Cook, stirring frequently, for 3 minutes, or until onion is translucent. Add mushrooms, and cook for 2 minutes, stirring frequently. Add chopped porcini, stock, tomatoes, 2 tablespoons parsley, Italian seasoning, and bay leaf to the pan. Bring to a boil, and cook over low heat, uncovered, for 10 minutes.

3. Preheat the oven broiler. Line a rimmed baking sheet with heavy-duty aluminum foil, and spray the foil with vegetable oil spray. Combine egg and milk in a mixing bowl, and whisk until smooth. Add breadcrumbs, Parmesan, and remaining parsley, and mix well. Add chicken, and season to taste with salt and pepper. Make mixture into 1½-inch meatballs, and arrange meatballs on the prepared pan. Spray tops of meatballs with vegetable oil spray.

4. Broil meatballs 6 inches from the broiler element, turning them with tongs to brown all sides. Remove meatballs from the baking pan with a slotted spoon, and add meatballs to sauce. Bring to a boil, and simmer meatballs, covered, over low heat, turning occasionally with a slotted spoon, for 15 minutes or until meatballs are cooked through and no longer pink. Season to taste with salt and pepper, and serve immediately.

Note: The chicken mixture can be prepared up to 1 day in advance and refrigerated, tightly covered. Also, the dish can be cooked up to 2 days in advance and refrigerated, tightly covered. Reheat it in a 350°F oven, covered, for 15 to 20 minutes, or until hot.

Prosciutto has been made for more than 2,000 years in the region of Italy near Parma and must come from Parma, San Daniele, or the Veneto to be authentic. If you've wondered why prosciutto, a famous Italian cured ham, seems to go so well with Parmesan, it's because the whey from Parmigiano-Reggiano is fed to the pigs.

Turkey and Basil Meatballs

Makes 4 to 6 servings

Active time:
20 minutes

Start to finish:
35 minutes

VARIATIONS

Replace the turkey with ground pork or ground veal.

Substitute some chopped fresh oregano for some of the basil.

I frequently make these meatballs during the summer when basil is bountiful in my garden.

2 tablespoons olive oil

2 shallots, chopped

2 garlic cloves, minced

1 cup mayonnaise

1 cup tightly packed chopped
    fresh basil

¼ cup chopped fresh parsley

¼ cup small capers, drained
    and rinsed

2 garlic cloves, minced

1 large shallot, chopped

2 teaspoons herbes de Provence

Salt and freshly ground black
    pepper to taste

1 large egg

½ cup plain breadcrumbs

1¼ pounds ground turkey

Vegetable oil spray

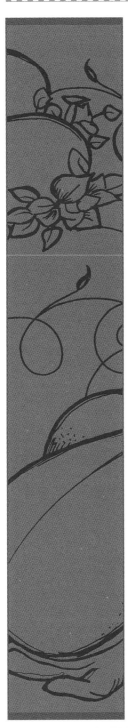

1. Preheat the oven to 450°F. Line a rimmed baking sheet with heavy-duty aluminum foil, and spray the foil with vegetable oil spray.

2. Heat oil in a small skillet over medium-high heat. Add shallots and garlic, and cook, stirring frequently, for 3 minutes, or until shallots are translucent. Combine shallot mixture, mayonnaise, basil, parsley, capers, garlic, shallot, herbes de Provence, salt, and pepper in a mixing bowl, and stir well.

3. Whisk egg, ½ cup mayonnaise mixture, and breadcrumbs in a mixing bowl, and mix well. Add turkey to the mixing bowl, season

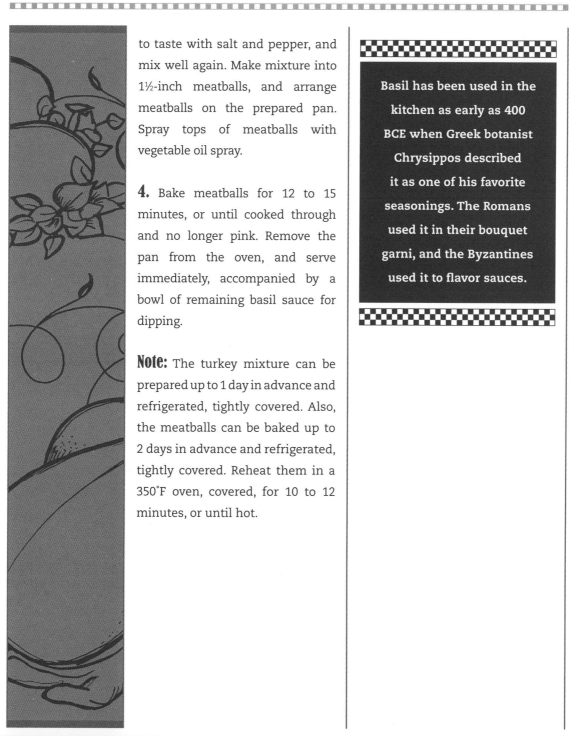

to taste with salt and pepper, and mix well again. Make mixture into 1½-inch meatballs, and arrange meatballs on the prepared pan. Spray tops of meatballs with vegetable oil spray.

4. Bake meatballs for 12 to 15 minutes, or until cooked through and no longer pink. Remove the pan from the oven, and serve immediately, accompanied by a bowl of remaining basil sauce for dipping.

Note: The turkey mixture can be prepared up to 1 day in advance and refrigerated, tightly covered. Also, the meatballs can be baked up to 2 days in advance and refrigerated, tightly covered. Reheat them in a 350°F oven, covered, for 10 to 12 minutes, or until hot.

Basil has been used in the kitchen as early as 400 BCE when Greek botanist Chrysippos described it as one of his favorite seasonings. The Romans used it in their bouquet garni, and the Byzantines used it to flavor sauces.

Sun-Dried Tomato and Herb Chicken Meatballs

Makes 4 to 6 servings

Active time: 20 minutes

Start to finish: 35 minutes

VARIATIONS

Replace the chicken with ground pork or ground veal.

Substitute some uncooked chicken sausage for some of the ground chicken.

Sun-dried tomatoes are one of my favorite ingredients; the process intensifies the fruit's natural sugars and succulent flavor. These meatballs, perfect as an hors d'oeuvre, also contain a variety of fresh herbs and some creamy mozzarella.

⅔ cup sun-dried tomatoes packed in olive oil

1 medium onion, chopped

2 garlic cloves, minced

1 celery rib, chopped

1 large egg

2 tablespoons whole milk

½ cup seasoned Italian breadcrumbs

½ cup grated whole milk mozzarella

2 tablespoons chopped fresh parsley

2 tablespoons chopped fresh rosemary or 2 teaspoons dried

1 tablespoon chopped fresh oregano or 1 teaspoon dried

1¼ pounds ground chicken

Salt and freshly ground black pepper to taste

Vegetable oil spray

For dipping:

1 cup Herbed Tomato Sauce (page 38) or purchased marinara sauce, heated

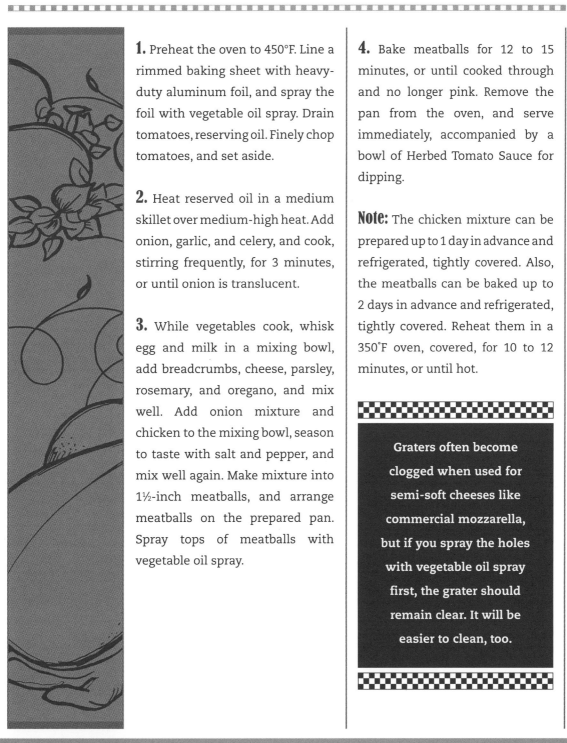

1. Preheat the oven to 450°F. Line a rimmed baking sheet with heavy-duty aluminum foil, and spray the foil with vegetable oil spray. Drain tomatoes, reserving oil. Finely chop tomatoes, and set aside.

2. Heat reserved oil in a medium skillet over medium-high heat. Add onion, garlic, and celery, and cook, stirring frequently, for 3 minutes, or until onion is translucent.

3. While vegetables cook, whisk egg and milk in a mixing bowl, add breadcrumbs, cheese, parsley, rosemary, and oregano, and mix well. Add onion mixture and chicken to the mixing bowl, season to taste with salt and pepper, and mix well again. Make mixture into 1½-inch meatballs, and arrange meatballs on the prepared pan. Spray tops of meatballs with vegetable oil spray.

4. Bake meatballs for 12 to 15 minutes, or until cooked through and no longer pink. Remove the pan from the oven, and serve immediately, accompanied by a bowl of Herbed Tomato Sauce for dipping.

Note: The chicken mixture can be prepared up to 1 day in advance and refrigerated, tightly covered. Also, the meatballs can be baked up to 2 days in advance and refrigerated, tightly covered. Reheat them in a 350°F oven, covered, for 10 to 12 minutes, or until hot.

Graters often become clogged when used for semi-soft cheeses like commercial mozzarella, but if you spray the holes with vegetable oil spray first, the grater should remain clear. It will be easier to clean, too.

Turkey Meatballs Tetrazzini

Makes 4 to 6 servings

Active time:
20 minutes

Start to finish:
50 minutes

The combination of mushrooms and turkey in a cream sauce laced with sherry and Parmesan is irresistible and a great dish for buffet entertaining. Serve atop orzo, a rice-shaped pasta.

This dish was named for Italian singer Luisa Tetrazzini, who was the toast of the American opera circuit in the early 1900s. Where the dish was created, and by whom, is not known; but the diva said she was served it all across America.

4 tablespoons unsalted butter, divided

2 tablespoons olive oil

2 shallots, chopped

2 garlic cloves, minced

1 celery rib, chopped

1 large egg

2 tablespoons whole milk

½ cup plain breadcrumbs

1¼ pounds ground turkey

Salt and freshly ground black pepper to taste

½ pound mushrooms, wiped with a damp paper towel and sliced

3 tablespoons all-purpose flour

½ cup medium dry sherry

1½ cups half-and-half

1 cup turkey or chicken stock

¾ cup freshly grated Parmesan

Vegetable oil spray

VARIATIONS

Replace the turkey with ground pork or ground veal.

Soak ½ cup dried porcini mushrooms in ½ cup boiling water for 10 minutes. Drain mushrooms, reserving soaking liquid. Chop mushrooms, and strain liquid through a paper coffee filter or paper towel. Add mushrooms to sauce, and use soaking liquid in place of ½ cup stock.

1. Preheat the oven broiler. Line a rimmed baking sheet with heavy-duty aluminum foil, and spray the foil with vegetable oil spray.

2. Heat 2 tablespoons butter and oil in a large skillet over medium-high heat. Add shallots, garlic, and celery, and cook, stirring frequently, for 3 minutes, or until shallots are translucent. While vegetables cook, whisk egg and milk in a mixing bowl, add breadcrumbs, and mix well.

3. Add vegetable mixture and turkey to the mixing bowl, season to taste with salt and pepper, and mix well again. Make mixture into 1½-inch meatballs, and arrange meatballs on the prepared pan. Spray tops of meatballs with vegetable oil spray.

4. Broil meatballs 6 inches from the broiler element, turning them with tongs to brown all sides.

5. While meatballs brown, heat remaining butter in the skillet over medium-high heat. Add mushrooms, and cook for 3 minutes, or until mushrooms begin to soften. Reduce the heat to low, stir in flour and cook, stirring constantly, for 2 minutes. Whisk in sherry, and bring to a boil over medium-high heat, whisking constantly. Simmer 3 minutes, then add half-and-half, stock, and Parmesan, and simmer 2 minutes.

6. Remove meatballs from the baking pan with a slotted spoon, and add meatballs to sauce. Bring to a boil, and simmer meatballs, covered, over low heat, turning occasionally with a slotted spoon, for 15 minutes or until meatballs are cooked through and no longer pink.

Note: The turkey mixture can be prepared up to 1 day in advance and refrigerated, tightly covered. Also, the dish can be cooked up to 2 days in advance and refrigerated, tightly covered. Reheat it in a 350°F oven, covered, for 15 to 20 minutes, or until hot.

Turkey Meatballs Provençal

Makes 4 to 6 servings

Active time: 20 minutes

Start to finish: 45 minutes

VARIATIONS

Replace the turkey with chopped fresh fish; look at the recipes in Chapter 9 for the procedure on how to chop fish.

Use celery in place of the fennel.

Olives and aromatic herbs are characteristic of the cooking in the sun-drenched French province of Provence, and you'll find them—along with crunchy fennel and tomatoes—in these meatballs.

1 large egg

1¼ cups chicken stock, divided

3 slices white bread, broken into small pieces

½ cup chopped oil-cured black olives

¼ cup chopped fresh parsley, divided

1 tablespoon herbes de Provence

1¼ pounds ground turkey

Salt and freshly ground black pepper to taste

3 tablespoons olive oil

2 leeks, white parts only, chopped and rinsed well

1 small fennel bulb, cored and diced

2 garlic cloves, minced

1 (14.5-ounce) can diced tomatoes, undrained

½ cup dry white wine

2 teaspoons grated orange zest

2 teaspoons cornstarch

Vegetable oil spray

1. Preheat the oven broiler. Line a rimmed baking sheet with heavy-duty aluminum foil, and spray the foil with vegetable oil spray.

2. Combine egg and 2 tablespoons stock in a mixing bowl, and whisk until smooth. Add bread, olives, 2 tablespoons parsley, and herbes de Provence, and mix well. Add turkey, and season to taste with salt and pepper. Make mixture into 1½-inch meatballs, and arrange meatballs on the prepared pan. Spray tops of meatballs with vegetable oil spray.

3. Heat oil in a large skillet over medium-high heat. Add leeks, fennel, and garlic, and cook, stirring frequently, for 3 minutes, or until leeks are translucent. Add remaining stock, remaining parsley, tomatoes, wine, and orange zest. Bring to a boil and simmer sauce, covered, for 5 minutes.

4. Broil meatballs 6 inches from the broiler element, turning them with tongs to brown all sides. Remove meatballs from the baking pan with a slotted spoon, and add meatballs to sauce. Bring to a boil, and simmer meatballs, covered, over low heat, turning occasionally with a slotted spoon, for 15 minutes or until meatballs are cooked through and no longer pink and fennel is crisp-tender. Combine cornstarch and 1 tablespoon cold water in a small cup, and stir well. Add mixture to the skillet, and simmer for 2 minutes, or until slightly thickened. Season to taste with salt and pepper, and serve immediately.

Note: The turkey mixture can be prepared up to 1 day in advance and refrigerated, tightly covered. Also, the dish can be cooked up to 2 days in advance and refrigerated, tightly covered. Reheat it in a 350°F oven, covered, for 15 to 20 minutes, or until hot.

Chicken-Vegetable Meatballs in Red Wine Sauce

Makes 4 to 6 servings

Active time:
25 minutes

Start to finish:
1¼ hours

This meatball stew contains hearty vegetables that are also cooked in a heady red wine sauce. Since potatoes are also included, serve the meatballs with a tossed salad.

When cooking with wine or any other acid such as lemon juice, use a stainless steel or coated steel pan rather than aluminum. When mixed with the wine or acid, an aluminum pan can impart a metallic taste to the dish.

1 large egg

¼ cup whole milk

½ cup plain breadcrumbs

¼ cup chopped fresh parsley, divided

2 teaspoons fresh thyme or
    ½ teaspoon dried

1¼ pounds ground chicken

Salt and freshly ground black
    pepper to taste

½ cup all-purpose flour

¼ pound bacon, cut into 1-inch
    pieces

2 garlic cloves, minced

½ pound small mushrooms,
    trimmed and diced

2 cups dry red wine

1 cup chicken stock

1 tablespoon fresh thyme or
    1 teaspoon dried

1 bay leaf

1 pound small new potatoes,
    scrubbed and cut into 1-inch
    cubes

½ (16-ounce) package frozen pearl
    onions, thawed

1. Preheat the oven to 375° F. Combine egg and milk in a mixing bowl, and whisk until smooth. Add breadcrumbs, 2 tablespoons parsley, and thyme, and mix well. Add chicken, and season to taste with salt and pepper. Mix well, and form mixture into 1½-inch balls. Roll balls in flour, and set aside.

2. Place bacon in a Dutch oven or roasting pan over medium-high heat. Cook, stirring often, until bacon is crisp. Remove bacon from the pan with a slotted spoon, and set aside. Add chicken balls to bacon fat, and brown well on all sides, turning gently with tongs, being careful to not crowd the pan. Remove chicken balls from the pan, and discard all but 2 tablespoons bacon fat.

3. Return the pan to the stove, and add garlic and mushrooms. Cook, stirring frequently, for 3 to 5 minutes, or until mushrooms are lightly brown. Add wine to the pan, and bring to a boil over high heat. Cook for 2 minutes, and then add stock, remaining parsley and

bay leaf to the pan. Bring to a boil, and add bacon, chicken balls, and potatoes.

4. Cover the pan, and bake for 45 minutes, or until potatoes are almost tender, and chicken balls are cooked through and no longer pink. Add onions to the pan, adjust seasoning with salt and pepper, and bake for an additional 10 minutes, or until potatoes are tender. Remove and discard bay leaf, and serve immediately.

Note: The chicken mixture can be prepared up to 1 day in advance and refrigerated, tightly covered. Also, the dish can be cooked up to 2 days in advance and refrigerated, tightly covered. Reheat it in a 350°F oven, covered, for 15 to 20 minutes, or until hot.

Basque Chicken Meatballs

Makes 4 to 6 servings

Active time: 20 minutes

Start to finish: 1 hour

VARIATIONS

Replace the chicken with ground pork, ground veal, or ground chuck.

Substitute some uncooked chicken sausage for some of the ground chicken.

The Basque region of the Pyrenees between France and Spain is known for its rustic, hearty fare. These chicken meatballs are delicate, but the seasonings in the sauce give them some punch. Serve the meatballs over pasta or a cooked grain such as farro or bulgur.

¼ cup olive oil
2 large onions, chopped
6 garlic cloves, minced
¼ pound baked ham, finely chopped
1 red bell pepper, seeds and ribs removed, and chopped
2 tablespoons smoked Spanish paprika
2 teaspoons fresh thyme or ½ teaspoon dried
1½ cups chicken stock, divided
¾ cup dry sherry
1 (14.5-oz.) can diced tomatoes, undrained
Crushed red pepper flakes to taste
1 large egg
½ cup plain breadcrumbs
1¼ pounds ground chicken
Salt and freshly ground black pepper to taste
Vegetable oil spray

1. Heat olive oil in a large skillet over medium-high heat. Add onions and garlic, and cook, stirring frequently, for 3 minutes, or until onions are translucent. Remove ⅓ of mixture, and set aside. Add ham

and red bell pepper, and cook for 3 minutes, stirring frequently. Stir in paprika and thyme and cook for 1 minute, stirring constantly.

2. Add 1¼ cups stock, sherry, tomatoes, and red pepper flakes. Bring to a boil and simmer sauce, uncovered, for 15 minutes, stirring occasionally.

3. Preheat the oven broiler. Line a rimmed baking sheet with heavy-duty aluminum foil, and spray the foil with vegetable oil spray.

4. While sauce simmers, whisk egg and remaining stock in a mixing bowl, add breadcrumbs, and mix well. Add reserved vegetable mixture and chicken to the mixing bowl, season to taste with salt and pepper, and mix well again. Make mixture into 1½-inch meatballs, and arrange meatballs on the prepared pan. Spray tops of meatballs with vegetable oil spray.

5. Broil meatballs 6-inches from the broiler element, turning them with tongs to brown all sides. Remove meatballs from the baking pan with a slotted spoon, and add meatballs to sauce. Bring to a boil, and simmer meatballs, covered, over low heat, turning occasionally with a slotted spoon, for 15 minutes or until meatballs are cooked through and no longer pink.

Note: The chicken mixture can be prepared up to 1 day in advance and refrigerated, tightly covered. Also, the dish can be cooked up to 2 days in advance and refrigerated, tightly covered. Reheat it in a 350°F oven, covered, for 15 to 20 minutes, or until hot.

The way you treat garlic determines the intensity of its flavor. Pushing the cloves through a garlic press is the way to extract the most punch. Mincing the cloves once they're peeled produces a milder flavor.

Chicken and Mushroom Meatballs

Makes 4 to 6 servings

Active time: 20 minutes

Start to finish: 35 minutes

VARIATIONS

Replace the ground chicken with ground turkey, ground pork, or ground veal.

Substitute some uncooked chicken sausage for some of the ground chicken.

Woodsy wild mushrooms and delicate white mushrooms are cooked and added to the ground chicken. These are great party meatballs; feel free to experiment with sauces other than the one suggested.

3 tablespoons olive oil

2 tablespoons unsalted butter

2 shallots, chopped

2 cloves garlic, minced

¼ pound white mushrooms, wiped with a damp paper towel, trimmed, and finely chopped

2 portobello mushroom caps, wiped with a damp paper towel, stemmed, and finely chopped

3 tablespoons chopped fresh parsley

2 teaspoons herbes de Provence

1 large egg

2 tablespoons whole milk

3 slices white bread, torn into small pieces

¼ cup grated whole milk mozzarella

1¼ pounds ground chicken

Salt and freshly ground black pepper to taste

Vegetable oil spray

For dipping:

1 cup Blue Cheese Sauce (page 41) or purchased blue cheese dressing

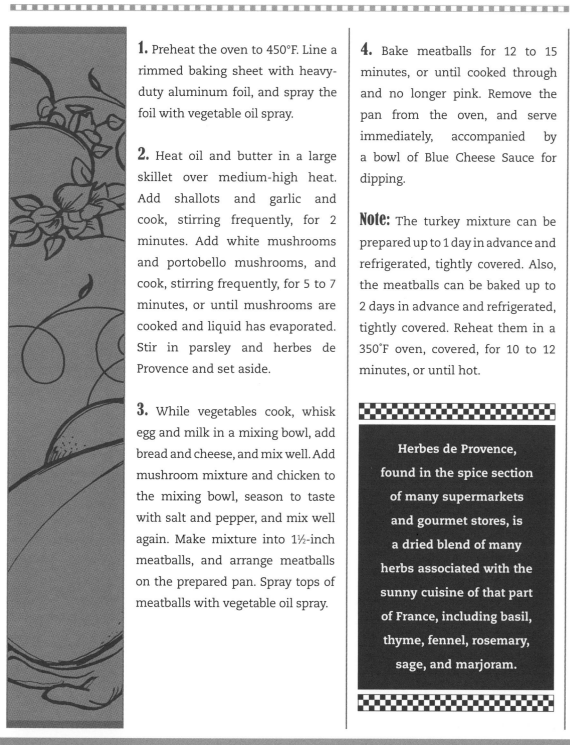

1. Preheat the oven to 450°F. Line a rimmed baking sheet with heavy-duty aluminum foil, and spray the foil with vegetable oil spray.

2. Heat oil and butter in a large skillet over medium-high heat. Add shallots and garlic and cook, stirring frequently, for 2 minutes. Add white mushrooms and portobello mushrooms, and cook, stirring frequently, for 5 to 7 minutes, or until mushrooms are cooked and liquid has evaporated. Stir in parsley and herbes de Provence and set aside.

3. While vegetables cook, whisk egg and milk in a mixing bowl, add bread and cheese, and mix well. Add mushroom mixture and chicken to the mixing bowl, season to taste with salt and pepper, and mix well again. Make mixture into 1½-inch meatballs, and arrange meatballs on the prepared pan. Spray tops of meatballs with vegetable oil spray.

4. Bake meatballs for 12 to 15 minutes, or until cooked through and no longer pink. Remove the pan from the oven, and serve immediately, accompanied by a bowl of Blue Cheese Sauce for dipping.

Note: The turkey mixture can be prepared up to 1 day in advance and refrigerated, tightly covered. Also, the meatballs can be baked up to 2 days in advance and refrigerated, tightly covered. Reheat them in a 350°F oven, covered, for 10 to 12 minutes, or until hot.

Herbes de Provence, found in the spice section of many supermarkets and gourmet stores, is a dried blend of many herbs associated with the sunny cuisine of that part of France, including basil, thyme, fennel, rosemary, sage, and marjoram.

Turkey Meatballs in Mexican Molé Sauce

Makes 4 to 6 servings

Active time: 15 minutes

Start to finish: 45 minutes

VARIATIONS

Replace the turkey with ground pork or ground veal.

Substitute some uncooked chicken sausage for some of the ground turkey.

There's an intensity to this classic Mexican sauce that comes from a combination of spices, ground nuts, and cocoa powder. Serve these meatballs over Mexican rice with a pile of warm tortillas on the side.

3 tablespoons olive oil
2 onions, chopped
6 garlic cloves, minced
3 tablespoons chili powder
1 tablespoon ground cumin
2½ cups chicken stock, divided
1 (14.5-oz.) can tomatoes, drained
¼ cup peanut butter
¼ cup chopped raisins
2 tablespoons granulated sugar
2 tablespoons unsweetened cocoa powder

Salt and cayenne to taste
1 large egg
¾ cup crushed tortilla chips
1¼ pounds ground turkey
Salt and freshly ground black pepper to taste

1. Heat oil in a large skillet over medium-high heat. Add onions and garlic and cook, stirring frequently, for 3 minutes, or until onions are translucent. Remove ⅓ of mixture, and set aside. Stir chili powder and cumin into the skillet, and cook, stirring constantly, for 1 minute.

2. Add 2¼ cups chicken stock, tomatoes, peanut butter, raisins, sugar, and cocoa powder. Stir well, and bring to a boil over high heat. Reduce the heat to low and simmer sauce, uncovered, for 20 minutes or until lightly thickened. Season to taste with salt and cayenne.

3. Preheat the oven broiler. Line a rimmed baking sheet with heavy-duty aluminum foil, and spray the foil with vegetable oil spray.

4. While sauce simmers, whisk egg and remaining ¼ cup stock in a mixing bowl, add crushed tortilla chips, and mix well. Add reserved vegetable mixture and turkey to the mixing bowl, season to taste with salt and pepper, and mix well again. Make mixture into 1½-inch meatballs, and arrange meatballs on the prepared pan. Spray tops of meatballs with vegetable oil spray.

5. Broil meatballs 6 inches from the broiler element, turning them with tongs to brown all sides. Remove meatballs from the baking pan with a slotted spoon, and add meatballs to sauce. Bring to a boil, and simmer meatballs, covered, over low heat, turning occasionally with a slotted spoon, for 15 minutes or until meatballs are cooked through and no longer pink.

Note: The turkey mixture can be prepared up to 1 day in advance and refrigerated, tightly covered. Also, the dish can be cooked up to 2 days in advance and refrigerated, tightly covered. Reheat it in a 350°F oven, covered, for 15 to 20 minutes, or until hot.

Molé, one of the oldest sauces in North America, dates back to the Aztec Indians of Mexico centuries before Columbus landed in America. Its most prominent feature is the inclusion of some sort of bitter chocolate, which adds richness to the dark, reddish-brown sauce without adding sweetness.

Grilled Middle Eastern Chicken Meatballs

Makes 4 to 6 servings

Active time:
15 minutes

Start to finish:
30 minutes

VARIATIONS

Replace the chicken with ground pork or ground veal.

Substitute some uncooked chicken sausage for some of the ground chicken.

The aromatic herbs and spices—ranging from garlic and parsley to cumin, coriander, and cinnamon—in these grilled skewers is reflective of the varied cultures of the Middle East. Serve these with a bowl of refreshing tabbouleh salad.

8 to 12 (8-inch) bamboo skewers

1 large egg

2 tablespoons water

2 tablespoons tomato paste

2 slices whole wheat bread, torn into small pieces

¼ cup chopped fresh parsley

2 shallots, chopped

2 garlic cloves, minced

1 tablespoon ground cumin

2 teaspoons ground coriander

½ teaspoon ground cinnamon

1¼ pounds ground chicken

Salt and cayenne to taste

For dipping:

1 cup Greek Feta Sauce (page 49), Tahini (page 50), or purchased hummus

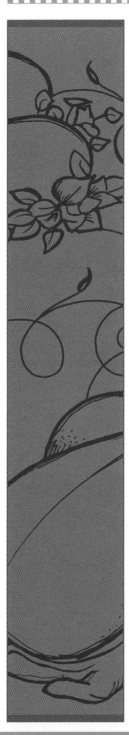

1. Soak the bamboo skewers in cold water to cover. Prepare a medium-hot charcoal or gas grill, or preheat the oven broiler.

2. Whisk egg, water, and tomato paste in a mixing bowl, add bread, parsley, shallots, garlic, cumin, coriander, and cinnamon, and mix well. Add chicken to the mixing bowl, season to taste with salt and cayenne, and mix well again.

3. Divide chicken mixture into 8 to 12 portions, and form each portion into a sausage shape. Insert a skewer into each sausage so that the tip of the skewer is almost at the top of the meat.

4. Grill skewers for a total of 8 to 10 minutes, uncovered if using a charcoal grill, turning them gently with tongs to cook all sides. Serve immediately, accompanied by a bowl of Greek Feta Sauce or Tahini for dipping.

Note: The meatball mixture can be prepared up to 1 day in advance and refrigerated, tightly covered. Also, the skewers can be grilled up to 2 days in advance and refrigerated, tightly covered. Reheat them in a 350°F oven, covered, for 10 to 12 minutes, or until hot.

In the Middle East, the word for meatball changes depending on how the minced morsels are cooked. If cooked in a sauce or stewed, they are called *kufteh*. If they are grilled, like these, they're referred to as *kal-e gonjeshki*, which literally means "sparrow's head."

Bombay Turkey Meatballs

Makes 4 to 6 servings

Active time:
20 minutes

Start to finish:
35 minutes

VARIATIONS

Replace the turkey with ground pork or ground veal.

Substitute some dried currants or dried cranberries for the chopped dried apricots.

Chopped dried apricots add sweetness and nuts add crunch to the curry-flavored turkey meatballs, which are then topped with a yogurt-based sauce. I serve the meatballs and sauce tucked into pita bread.

⅔ cup plain yogurt
¼ cup pine nuts
2 tablespoons vegetable oil
1 medium onion, finely chopped
2 garlic cloves, minced
1 large egg
2 tablespoons whole milk
2 slices white bread, broken into
    small pieces
½ cup finely chopped dried apricots
¼ cup chopped fresh cilantro
1 tablespoon curry powder
1¼ pounds ground turkey
Salt and freshly ground black
    pepper to taste
2 teaspoon ground cumin
1 medium tomato, rinsed, cored,
    seeded, and finely chopped
Vegetable oil spray

1. Preheat the oven to 450°F. Line a rimmed baking sheet with heavy-duty aluminum foil, and spray the foil with vegetable oil spray.

2. Place yogurt in a strainer set over a mixing bowl. Shake the strainer gently a few times, and allow yogurt to drain for at least 30 minutes at room temperature or up to 6 hours, refrigerated. Discard whey from the mixing bowl, and place yogurt in the bowl. Set aside.

3. While yogurt drains, place pine nuts in a small skillet over medium heat. Cook, stirring frequently, for 2 to 3 minutes, or until nuts brown. Remove nuts from the skillet with a slotted spoon, and set aside. Heat oil in the same skillet over medium-high heat. Add onion and garlic and cook, stirring frequently, for 5 minutes or until onion is soft.

4. While vegetables cook, whisk egg and milk in a mixing bowl, and add bread, dried apricots, cilantro, and curry powder, and mix well.

5. Add onion mixture and turkey to the mixing bowl, season to taste with salt and pepper, and mix well again. Make mixture into 1½-inch meatballs, and arrange meatballs on the prepared pan. Spray tops of meatballs with vegetable oil spray.

6. Bake meatballs for 12 to 15 minutes, or until cooked through and no longer pink. While meatballs bake, combine yogurt and cumin in a small bowl, and stir well. Gently fold in tomato. Remove the pan from the oven, and serve immediately, accompanied by the bowl of yogurt sauce for dipping.

Note: The turkey mixture can be prepared up to 1 day in advance and refrigerated, tightly covered. Also, the meatballs can be baked up to 2 days in advance and refrigerated, tightly covered. Reheat them in a 350°F oven, covered, for 10 to 12 minutes, or until hot.

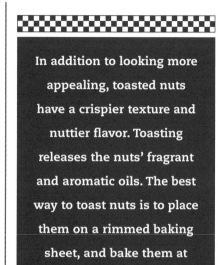

In addition to looking more appealing, toasted nuts have a crispier texture and nuttier flavor. Toasting releases the nuts' fragrant and aromatic oils. The best way to toast nuts is to place them on a rimmed baking sheet, and bake them at 350°F for 5 to 7 minutes.

Crunchy Asian Turkey Meatballs

Makes 4 to 6 servings

Active time: 20 minutes

Start to finish: 35 minutes

VARIATIONS

Replace the turkey with ground pork or ground veal.

Substitute cooked white rice for the panko.

Aromatic from heady toasted sesame oil and other Asian ingredients, these crispy balls are a great addition to any cocktail party menu. If serving them for dinner, accompany with stir-fried vegetables on the side.

2 tablespoons Asian sesame oil

4 scallions, white parts and
    3 inches of green tops, chopped

2 tablespoons grated fresh ginger

3 garlic cloves, minced

1 large egg

3 tablespoons fish sauce (nam pla)

1 cup panko breadcrumbs, divided

½ cup finely chopped water
    chestnuts

¼ cup chopped fresh cilantro

1¼ pounds ground turkey

Salt and red pepper flakes to taste

Vegetable oil spray

For dipping:

1 cup Thai Sweet and Spicy Dipping
    Sauce (page 58), Ponzu Sauce
    (page 59), or soy sauce

1. Preheat the oven to 450°F. Line a rimmed baking sheet with heavy-duty aluminum foil, and spray the foil with vegetable oil spray.

2. Heat sesame oil in a small skillet over medium-high heat. Add scallions, ginger, and garlic, and cook, stirring frequently, for 2 minutes, or until scallions are translucent.

3. While vegetables cook, whisk egg and fish sauce in a mixing bowl, and add ½ cup panko, water chestnuts, and cilantro, and mix well.

4. Add vegetable mixture and turkey to the mixing bowl, season to taste with salt and red pepper flakes, and mix well again. Make mixture into 1½-inch meatballs, roll meatballs in remaining ½ cup panko, and

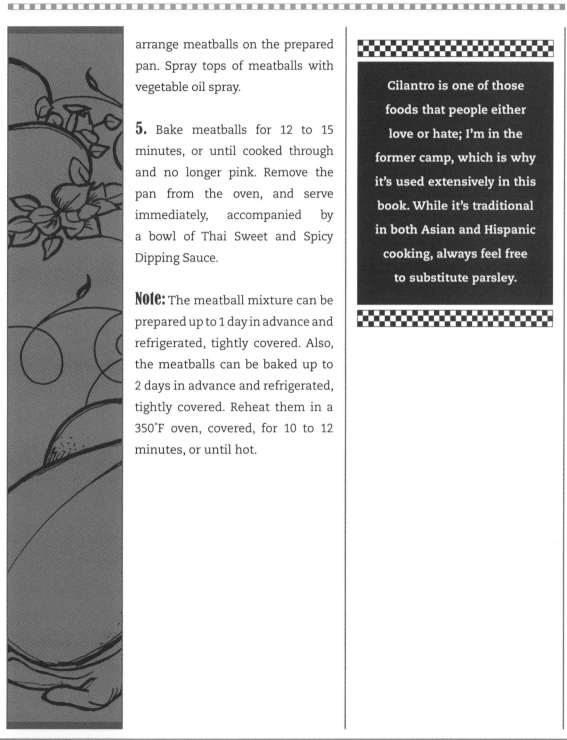

arrange meatballs on the prepared pan. Spray tops of meatballs with vegetable oil spray.

5. Bake meatballs for 12 to 15 minutes, or until cooked through and no longer pink. Remove the pan from the oven, and serve immediately, accompanied by a bowl of Thai Sweet and Spicy Dipping Sauce.

Note: The meatball mixture can be prepared up to 1 day in advance and refrigerated, tightly covered. Also, the meatballs can be baked up to 2 days in advance and refrigerated, tightly covered. Reheat them in a 350°F oven, covered, for 10 to 12 minutes, or until hot.

Cilantro is one of those foods that people either love or hate; I'm in the former camp, which is why it's used extensively in this book. While it's traditional in both Asian and Hispanic cooking, always feel free to substitute parsley.

Thai Chicken Meatballs

Makes 4 to 6 servings

Active time: 20 minutes

Start to finish: 35 minutes

VARIATIONS

Replace the turkey with ground pork or ground veal.

Substitute cooked white rice for the panko.

Aromatic lemongrass is the primary flavoring in these delicate chicken balls, made slightly spicy with both garlic and crushed red pepper flakes. But feel free to tone down the pepper; that's a matter of personal preference.

2 stalks fresh lemongrass
4 scallions, white parts only, sliced
2 garlic cloves, peeled
1 tablespoon Asian fish sauce
    (nam pla)
1 tablespoon water
½ teaspoon crushed red pepper
    flakes or to taste
1 large egg
2 tablespoons whole milk
3/4 cup cooked white rice
1¼ pounds ground chicken
Salt and freshly ground black
    pepper to taste

¾ cup panko breadcrumbs
Vegetable oil spray

For dipping:
1 cup Sweet and Sour Sauce (page
    56) or purchased duck sauce

1. Preheat the oven to 450°F. Line a rimmed baking sheet with heavy-duty aluminum foil, and spray the foil with vegetable oil spray.

2. Remove and discard leaves from lemongrass, and trim root end. Slice bottom 3 inches of root, and discard remainder. Combine lemongrass, scallions, garlic, fish sauce, water, and red pepper flakes in a blender, and puree until smooth. Set aside.

3. Whisk egg and milk in a mixing bowl, and add lemongrass mixture and rice, and mix well. Add chicken to the mixing bowl, season to taste with salt and pepper, and mix well again. Make mixture into 1½-inch meatballs, roll meatballs

in panko, and arrange meatballs on the prepared pan. Spray tops of meatballs with vegetable oil spray.

4. Bake meatballs for 12 to 15 minutes, or until cooked through and no longer pink. Remove the pan from the oven, and serve immediately, accompanied by a bowl of Sweet and Sour Sauce.

Note: The meatball mixture can be prepared up to 1 day in advance and refrigerated, tightly covered. Also, the meatballs can be baked up to 2 days in advance and refrigerated, tightly covered. Reheat them in a 350°F oven, covered, for 10 to 12 minutes, or until hot.

Lemongrass, technically an herb and used extensively in Thai and Vietnamese cooking, is characterized by a strong citrus flavor with a spicy finish similar to that of ginger. Fresh lemongrass is sold by the stalk. It looks like a pale, fibrous, woody scallion. Cut the lower bulb five inches from the stalk, discarding the fibrous upper part. Trim off the outer layers, as you would peel an onion; then bruise the stem to release the flavor. If you can't find lemongrass, substitute 1 teaspoon grated lemon zest plus 2 tablespoons lemon juice for each stalk of lemongrass specified in a recipe, along with a pinch of ginger powder.

AQUATIC ADVENTURES:

MEATBALLS WITH
FISH AND SEAFOOD

There's no question from increasing consumption figures that Americans are now eating more fish and seafood, both at home and off of restaurant menus.

With the exception of pre-minced clams, chopping fish and seafood is the responsibility of the cook, but it's an easy task with a food processor. Once cubes of fillet are partially frozen they can be chopped in a matter of seconds. In fact, there's one corner of my dishwasher reserved for the food processor work bowl because I use it so often.

While some of these recipes are fried, others are oven-baked or poached gently in a flavorful sauce. While it might take more time to create the mixtures from which the fish and seafood balls are made, they do not require any pre-browning so the total amount of cooking time is shorter.

Although these recipes were developed with specific fish, it is more important to use the freshest fish in the market rather than any particular species. Finned fish fall into three basic families, and you can easily substitute one species for another. Use the following table to make life at the fish counter easier.

A GUIDE TO FISH

DESCRIPTION	SPECIES	CHARACTERISTICS
Firm, lean fish	Black sea bass, cod family, flat fish (flounder, sole, halibut), grouper, lingcod, ocean perch, perch, pike, porgy, red snapper, smelt, striped bass, turbot, salmon, trout, drum family, tilefish	Low-fat, mild to delicate flavor, firm flesh, flake when cooked. Sold whole or as fillets.
Meaty fish	Catfish, carp, eel, monkfish (anglerfish), orange roughy, pike, salmon, shark, sturgeon, swordfish, some tuna varieties, mahi-mahi, whitefish, pompano, yellowtail	Low to high fat, diverse flavors and textures, usually available as thick steaks or fillets.
Fatty or strong-flavored fish	Bluefish, mackerel, some tuna varieties	High fat and pronounced flavor. Sold as fillets and steaks.

Cajun Shrimp Balls

Makes 4 to 6 servings

Active time:
20 minutes

Start to finish:
1¼ hours, including 30 minutes to chill mixture

Shrimp, caught in the Gulf of Mexico, are a favorite food in Louisiana, and these vibrantly flavored balls flecked with vegetables are an easy-to-make way to enjoy them.

2 tablespoons vegetable oil
1 small onion, chopped
2 garlic cloves, minced
1 celery rib, chopped
½ red bell pepper, seeds and ribs removed, and finely chopped
1½ pounds large raw shrimp (21 to 30 per pound), peeled and deveined, divided
2 large egg whites
¼ cup plain breadcrumbs
3 tablespoons chopped fresh chives
3 tablespoons chopped fresh parsley
½ teaspoon hot red pepper sauce or to taste
Cajun seasoning to taste
Vegetable oil spray

For dipping:
1 cup Tartar Sauce (page 44) or purchased tartar sauce

1. Preheat the oven to 400°F. Line a rimmed baking sheet with heavy-duty aluminum foil, and spray the foil with vegetable oil spray.

2. Heat oil in a medium skillet over medium heat. Add onion, garlic, celery, and red bell pepper. Cook, stirring frequently, for 5 to 7 minutes, or until vegetables are soft. Scrape mixture into a mixing bowl.

3. Finely chop ½ pound shrimp, and add to the mixing bowl. Puree remaining 1 pound shrimp and egg whites in a food processor. Add to the mixing bowl, along with breadcrumbs, chives, parsley, hot red pepper sauce, and Cajun seasoning, and mix well. Allow mixture to chill for a minimum of 30 minutes.

4. Make mixture into 1-inch balls, and arrange shrimp balls on the prepared pan. Spray tops of shrimp balls with vegetable oil spray. Bake shrimp balls for 12 to 15 minutes, or until cooked through. Remove the pan from the oven, and serve immediately, accompanied by a bowl of Tartar Sauce for dipping.

Note: The shrimp mixture can be prepared up to 1 day in advance and refrigerated, tightly covered. Also, the shrimp balls can be baked up to 2 days in advance and refrigerated, tightly covered. Reheat them in a 350°F oven, uncovered, for 8 to 10 minutes, or until hot.

Since Cajun seasoning includes salt as one of its ingredients, no additional salt is necessary. This is in contrast to an herb mix like Italian seasoning or herbes de Provence, which are salt-free.

Fried Chinese Shrimp Balls

Makes 4 to 6 servings

Active time: 20 minutes

Start to finish: 50 minutes, including 30 minutes to chill mixture

VARIATION

Substitute scallops or any firm-fleshed white fish like cod or tilapia for the shrimp.

These crunchy balls are similar to the topping on shrimp toast found on Chinese-American restaurant menus. They are light and fluffy and a perfect hors d'oeuvre for a party.

1½ pounds large raw shrimp (21 to 30 per pound), peeled and deveined
2 large egg whites
2 tablespoons cornstarch
½ cup chopped water chestnuts
3 scallions, white parts and 2 inches of green tops, chopped
2 tablespoons grated fresh ginger
2 tablespoons dry sherry
1 tablespoon soy sauce
1 tablespoon Asian sesame oil
Salt and freshly ground black pepper to taste
1½ cups panko breadcrumbs
3 cups vegetable oil for frying

For dipping:
1 cup Sweet and Sour Sauce (page 56) or purchased sweet and sour sauce

1. Finely chop ½ pound shrimp, and place in a mixing bowl. Puree remaining 1 pound shrimp, egg whites, and cornstarch in a food processor. Add to the mixing bowl, along with water chestnuts, scallions, ginger, sherry, soy sauce, sesame oil, salt, and pepper, and mix well. Allow mixture to chill for a minimum of 30 minutes.

2. Place panko in a shallow bowl. Make mixture into 1-inch balls, and roll balls in breadcrumbs, pressing gently so crumbs adhere.

3. Heat oil in a saucepan over medium-high heat to a temperature of 375°F. Add shrimp balls, being careful not to crowd the pan. Cook shrimp balls for a total of 2 to 3

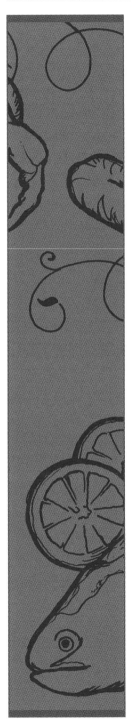

minutes, or until browned. Remove shrimp balls from the pan with a slotted spoon, and drain well on paper towels. Serve immediately, accompanied by a bowl of Sweet and Sour Sauce for dipping.

Note: The shrimp balls can be prepared for frying up to 1 day in advance and refrigerated, tightly covered. They can also be fried in advance; reheat them in a 400°F oven for 5 to 7 minutes, or until hot and crusty again.

To devein shrimp means to remove the black vein, actually the intestinal tract. To do this, hold the shrimp in one hand with the curved side up. Slice down the middle of the back with a paring knife, and pull out the black vein if one is present. This can also be done with a specialized tool called a deveiner.

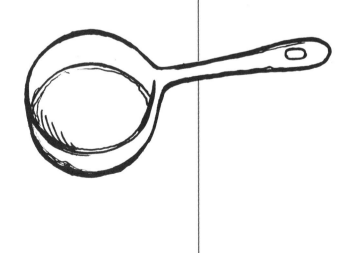

Shrimp Balls in Creole Sauce

Makes 4 to 6 servings

Active time: 25 minutes

Start to finish: 1¼ hours, including 30 minutes to chill mixture

VARIATIONS

Substitute scallops or any firm-fleshed white fish like cod or tilapia for the shrimp.

The Creole sauce is also delicious with ground chicken or turkey. Cook it in the same fashion.

This is one of my favorite dishes to serve on a buffet table at a party. The sauce is easy to make and full of flavor, and it's perfect served over boiled white rice.

1½ pounds large raw shrimp (21 to 30 per pound), peeled and deveined, divided
2 large egg whites
¼ cup plain breadcrumbs
2 tablespoons chopped fresh parsley
Hot red pepper sauce and Cajun seasoning to taste
2 tablespoons olive oil
1 large onion, diced
3 garlic cloves, minced
1 celery rib, diced
½ red bell pepper, seeds and ribs removed, and diced
1 (28-ounce) can diced tomatoes in tomato puree, undrained
1 tablespoon fresh thyme or 1 teaspoon dried
1 tablespoon chopped fresh oregano or 1 teaspoon dried
1 bay leaf
Salt and freshly ground black pepper to taste

1. Finely chop ½ pound shrimp, and place in a mixing bowl. Puree remaining 1 pound shrimp and egg whites in a food processor. Add to the mixing bowl, along with breadcrumbs, parsley, hot red pepper sauce, and Cajun seasoning, and mix well. Allow mixture to chill for a minimum of 30 minutes.

2. Heat oil in large covered skillet over medium-high heat. Add onion, garlic, celery, and red pepper. Cook, stirring frequently, for 3 minutes, or until onion is translucent. Add tomatoes, thyme, oregano, and bay leaf to the skillet, and bring to a boil over medium-high heat, stirring occasionally. Simmer sauce, uncovered, for 10 minutes.

3. Make shrimp mixture into 1-inch balls, and gently lower them into simmering sauce using a slotted spoon. Bring to boil, then reduce the heat to low, cover the pan, and simmer shrimp balls for 15 minutes, turning them gently with a slotted spoon after 10 minutes. Remove and discard bay leaf, season to taste with salt and pepper, and serve immediately.

Note: The shrimp mixture can be prepared up to 1 day in advance and refrigerated, tightly covered. Also, the dish can be cooked up to 2 days in advance and refrigerated, tightly covered. Reheat, covered, over low heat until hot.

In the eighteenth century, the Spaniards governing New Orleans named all residents of European heritage *Criollo*, which was transformed into *Creole* by the predominant French population. Creole cooking today reflects the amalgam of French, Spanish, and African cuisines that characterize food in Louisiana. In contrast to rural Cajun cooking, Creole food is more refined, and uses more tomatoes and less spices.

Southwestern Crab Balls

Makes 4 to 6 servings

Active time:
20 minutes

Start to finish:
35 minutes

VARIATIONS

In addition to cooked fish or seafood of any kind, try cooked and finely chopped chicken or pork.

Substitute 3 (6-ounce) cans of tuna fish, drained and flaked.

This recipe is a variation on traditional crab cakes, with the addition of cilantro and other seasonings. You can also make them into larger patties and serve them on buns like hamburgers.

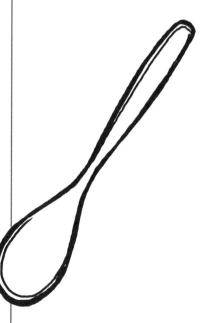

1 pound lump crab meat

3 tablespoons unsalted butter

4 scallions, white parts and
     2 inches of green tops, chopped

½ red bell pepper, seeds and ribs
     removed, and chopped

2 garlic cloves, minced

⅓ cup mayonnaise

1 large egg

3 tablespoons chopped fresh cilantro

1 tablespoon paprika

1 tablespoon chili powder

2 teaspoons Worcestershire sauce

½ teaspoon dried thyme

Salt and cayenne to taste

½ cup plain breadcrumbs

Vegetable oil spray

For dipping:

1 cup Creamy Chipotle Sauce
     (page 47) or purchased
     refrigerated salsa or guacamole

1. Preheat the oven to 425°F. Line a rimmed baking sheet with heavy-duty aluminum foil, and spray the foil with vegetable oil spray. Place crab on a dark surface and pick it over carefully to discard all shell fragments. Set aside.

2. Heat butter in a small skillet over medium-high heat. Add scallions, bell pepper, and garlic, and cook, stirring frequently, for 3 to 5 minutes, or until vegetables are soft. Set aside.

3. Combine mayonnaise, egg, cilantro, paprika, chili powder, Worcestershire sauce, thyme, salt, and cayenne in a mixing bowl, and whisk well. Stir in breadcrumbs, and then gently fold in crab.

4. Make mixture into 1½-inch balls, and arrange crab balls on the prepared pan. Spray tops of crab balls with vegetable oil spray. Bake crab balls for 12 to 15 minutes, or until cooked through. Remove the pan from the oven, and serve immediately, accompanied by a bowl of Creamy Chipotle Sauce for dipping.

Note: The crab mixture can be prepared up to 1 day in advance and refrigerated, tightly covered. Also, the crab balls can be baked up to 2 days in advance and refrigerated, tightly covered. Reheat them in a 350°F oven, uncovered, for 8 to 10 minutes, or until hot.

Picked-over crabmeat from the seafood department is a time-saver, but it's far from perfect. The best way to ensure that no shell fragments find their way into a dish is to spread out the crab on a dark-colored plate. Any bits of shell can easily be picked up against the dark background. Rub the morsels between your fingers, being careful not to break up large lumps, for any additional bits.

Scallop Balls in Tarragon Sauce

Makes 4 to 6 servings

Active time:
25 minutes

Start to finish:
1½ hours,
including
30 minutes to
chill mixture

VARIATION

Substitute shrimp or any firm-fleshed white fish like cod or tilapia for the scallops.

Seafood prepared with an herbed cream sauce is found in many European cuisines, and this delicate dish is drawn from classic French cooking. Serve it over rice, or place it in an ovenproof casserole with a pastry crust on top and bake it as a pot pie.

1½ pounds bay or sea scallops
4 tablespoons unsalted butter, divided
2 leeks, white parts only, trimmed, chopped, and rinsed well
1 carrot, chopped
1 celery rib, chopped
1 cup dry white wine
1 (8-ounce) bottle clam juice
1 bay leaf
2 large egg whites

1 cup half-and-half, divided
½ cup plain breadcrumbs
Salt and freshly ground black pepper to taste
3 tablespoons all-purpose flour
2 tablespoons chopped fresh parsley
2 tablespoons chopped fresh tarragon or 1 teaspoon dried tarragon

1. Rinse scallops and pat dry with paper towels; if using sea scallops, cut each into 8 pieces. Place scallops on a sheet of plastic wrap, and freeze for 20 to 30 minutes, or until firm but not frozen solid.

2. Heat 2 tablespoons butter in a large skillet over medium-high heat. Add leeks, carrot, and celery, and cook, stirring frequently, for 3 minutes, or until leeks are translucent. Add wine, clam juice, and bay leaf, and bring to a boil over medium-high heat, stirring occasionally. Reduce the heat to low, cover the pan, and cook mixture for 10 minutes. Strain

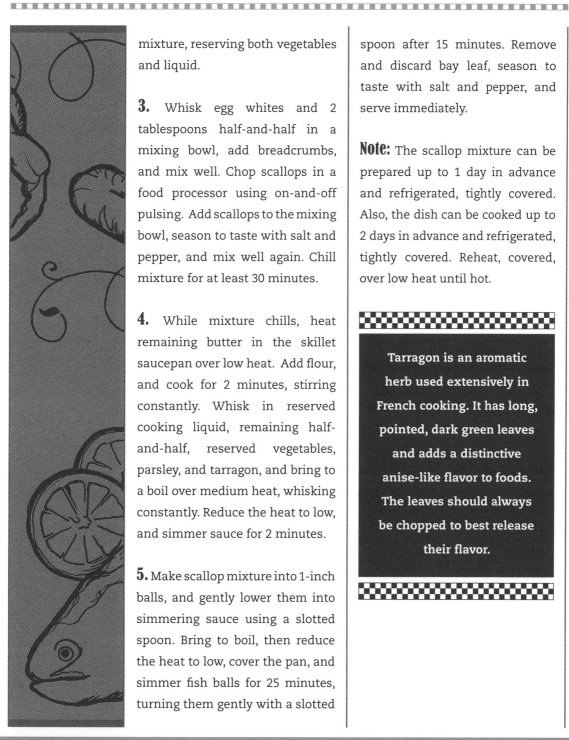

mixture, reserving both vegetables and liquid.

3. Whisk egg whites and 2 tablespoons half-and-half in a mixing bowl, add breadcrumbs, and mix well. Chop scallops in a food processor using on-and-off pulsing. Add scallops to the mixing bowl, season to taste with salt and pepper, and mix well again. Chill mixture for at least 30 minutes.

4. While mixture chills, heat remaining butter in the skillet saucepan over low heat. Add flour, and cook for 2 minutes, stirring constantly. Whisk in reserved cooking liquid, remaining half-and-half, reserved vegetables, parsley, and tarragon, and bring to a boil over medium heat, whisking constantly. Reduce the heat to low, and simmer sauce for 2 minutes.

5. Make scallop mixture into 1-inch balls, and gently lower them into simmering sauce using a slotted spoon. Bring to boil, then reduce the heat to low, cover the pan, and simmer fish balls for 25 minutes, turning them gently with a slotted

spoon after 15 minutes. Remove and discard bay leaf, season to taste with salt and pepper, and serve immediately.

Note: The scallop mixture can be prepared up to 1 day in advance and refrigerated, tightly covered. Also, the dish can be cooked up to 2 days in advance and refrigerated, tightly covered. Reheat, covered, over low heat until hot.

Tarragon is an aromatic herb used extensively in French cooking. It has long, pointed, dark green leaves and adds a distinctive anise-like flavor to foods. The leaves should always be chopped to best release their flavor.

Fried Mexican Scallop Balls

Makes 4 to 6 servings

Active time: 25 minutes

Start to finish: 55 minutes, including 30 minutes to chill mixture

Substitute shrimp or any firm-fleshed white fish like cod or tilapia for the scallops.

For Asian-inspired balls, omit the chili powder and cumin, substitute chopped scallions for the red onion, and add 2 tablespoons grated fresh ginger to the mixture.

While loaded with bright and clear flavors, these fried puffs are also delicate and fluffy. The batter is easy to make. Serve them with guacamole and stewed beans.

The English word scallop comes from the French *escalope*, which refers to the shell in which the mollusk lives.

1½ pounds bay scallops or
   sea scallops
2 large egg whites
3 tablespoons heavy cream
2 tablespoons cornstarch
¼ cup finely chopped red onion
¼ cup finely chopped red bell pepper
3 tablespoons chopped fresh cilantro
2 garlic cloves, minced
1 tablespoon chili powder
2 teaspoons ground cumin
Salt and freshly ground black
   pepper to taste
¾ cup plain breadcrumbs
3 cups vegetable oil for frying

For dipping:
1 cup Creamy Chipotle Sauce (page
   47) or purchased bottle salsa

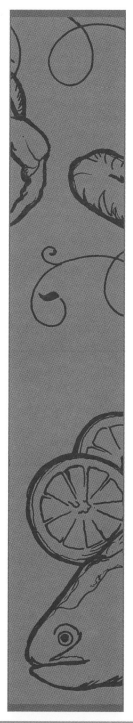

1. Finely chop ½ pound scallops, and place in a mixing bowl. Puree remaining 1 pound scallops, egg whites, cream, and cornstarch in a food processor. Add to the mixing bowl, along with onion, bell pepper, cilantro, garlic, chili powder, cumin, salt, and pepper, and mix well. Allow mixture to chill for a minimum of 30 minutes.

2. Place breadcrumbs in a shallow bowl. Make mixture into 1-inch balls, and roll balls in breadcrumbs, pressing gently so crumbs adhere.

3. Heat oil in a saucepan over medium-high heat to a temperature of 375°F. Add scallop balls, being careful not to crowd the pan. Cook scallop balls for a total of 2 to 3 minutes, or until browned. Remove scallop balls from the pan with a slotted spoon, and drain well on paper towels. Serve immediately, accompanied by a bowl of Creamy Chipotle Sauce for dipping.

Note: The scallop balls can be prepared for frying up to 1 day in advance and refrigerated, tightly covered. They can also be fried in advance; reheat them in a 400°F oven for 5 to 7 minutes, or until hot and crusty again.

Southwestern Clam and Corn Fritters

Makes 4 to 6 servings

Active time:
25 minutes

Start to finish:
25 minutes

VARIATION

Substitute chopped scallops, shrimp, or any firm-fleshed white fish like cod or tilapia for the clams.

Both clams and corn have an inherently sweet flavor, and they are delicious when cooked together, which is why many clam chowders also include corn. The inclusion of some Southwestern ingredients adds some sparkle.

1 pint minced clams
1 large egg
½ cup heavy cream
1½ cups all-purpose flour
1 tablespoon ground cumin
2 teaspoons dried oregano
1½ teaspoons baking powder
½ cup cooked corn kernels
2 scallions, finely chopped
2 garlic cloves, minced
2 tablespoons chopped fresh cilantro
2 tablespoons canned chopped mild
    green chiles, drained
Salt and cayenne to taste
3 cups vegetable oil for frying

For dipping:
1 cup Southwestern Barbecue Sauce
    (page 40) or purchased barbecue
    sauce, heated

1. Drain clams in a sieve over a bowl, reserving juice in the bowl. Press down with the back of a spoon to extract as much liquid as possible from clams.

2. Combine egg, cream, and ¼ cup reserved clam juice in a mixing bowl, and whisk well. Add flour, cumin, oregano, and baking powder, and whisk well. Stir in reserved clams, corn, scallions, garlic, cilantro, and chiles, and season to taste with salt and cayenne.

3. Preheat the oven to 150°F, and line a baking sheet with paper towels. Heat oil in a deep-sided saucepan over medium-high heat to a temperature of 375°F. Drop fritter batter by 1-tablespoon amounts into hot oil, and fry for 2 to 3 minutes, or until golden brown, turning as necessary with a slotted spoon. Remove fritters, and drain on paper towel–lined baking sheet. Place fritters in the oven, and repeat until all batter is fried. Serve immediately, accompanied by a bowl of Southwestern Barbecue Sauce for dipping.

Note: The fritters can be fried up to 1 day in advance, and refrigerated, tightly covered. Reheat them in a 400°F oven for 5 to 7 minutes, or until hot and crusty again.

The best way to judge the heat of oil is with a deep fat/candy thermometer attached to the side of the pot. Sold in kitchenware and department stores, these thermometers go up to very high temperatures and can accurately calibrate hot oil.

Gefilte Fish Balls

Makes 4 to 6 servings

Active time: 45 minutes

Start to finish: 4½ hours, including 2 hours to chill mixture

VARIATIONS

Add ¼ cup chopped dill to the fish mixture.

Add 2 garlic cloves, minced, to the fish mixture.

Gefilte fish dates from the Middle Ages in Germany, where it was conceived as way to stretch fresh fish to feed a crowd. It's served at many Jewish holidays, and it's always made from freshwater, rather than saltwater, fish.

1½ pounds fish fillets, some combination of whitefish, carp, and pike
3 large eggs
2 large onions, peeled, divided
2 celery ribs, divided
3 carrots, divided
½ cup matzo meal
Salt and freshly ground black pepper to taste
2 quarts fish stock or water

For serving:
½ cup prepared red or white horseradish

1. Rinse fish and pat dry with paper towels, and cut into 1-inch pieces. Place fish cubes on a sheet of plastic wrap, and freeze for 20 to 30 minutes, or until firm but not solid. Chop fish in a food processor using on-and-off pulsing.

2. Whisk eggs in a mixing bowl, and add chopped fish. Grate ½ onion, and finely chop 1 celery rib and 1 carrot. Add vegetables

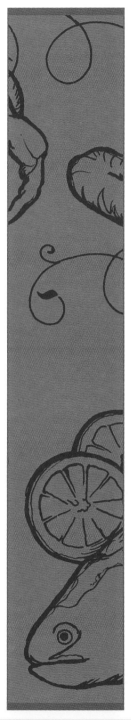

to mixing bowl along with matzo meal, salt, and pepper, and mix well. Refrigerate mixture for at least 2 hours, or up to 12 hours.

3. Place fish stock in a stockpot, season to taste with salt and pepper, and bring to a boil over medium-high heat. Slice remaining onion, celery, and carrots, and add vegetables to the pot.

4. Make fish mixture into 8 to 12 balls, and gently lower them into simmering stock using a slotted spoon. Bring to boil, then reduce the heat to low, cover the pot, and simmer fish for 1½ hours; add more fish stock or water if necessary to keep fish balls covered.

5. Remove fish balls and carrot slices from the pot, and allow to cool to room temperature. Refrigerate fish balls and carrots, tightly covered with plastic wrap, until very cold. Serve chilled with horseradish, with fish balls topped with carrot slices.

Note: The fish mixture can be prepared up to 1 day in advance and refrigerated, tightly covered. The dish can be prepared up to 3 days in advance, and refrigerated, tightly covered.

There are a few noted exceptions to the current situation that fish does not come pre-chopped. One is pre-minced clams and conch, and the other —if you live in a Jewish neighborhood—is a pre-ground mixture of fin fish for making gefilte fish around such holidays as Rosh Hashana and Passover.

Italian Cod Balls

Makes 4 to 6 servings

Active time: 20 minutes

Start to finish: 50 minutes

VARIATION

Substitute salmon or any firm-fleshed white fish like halibut or catfish for the cod.

This recipe is actually more Italian-American than authentically Italian; the addition of spinach and cheeses to the cod base gives the balls flavor and few calories. Serve these on top of spaghetti.

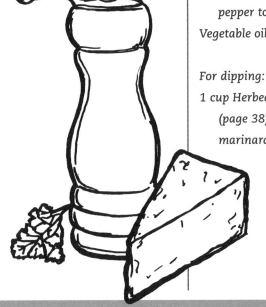

1¼ pounds cod fillet
1 large egg
2 tablespoons whole milk
1 cup seasoned Italian breadcrumbs, divided
¼ cup grated whole milk mozzarella
3 tablespoons freshly grated Parmesan
3 tablespoons chopped fresh parsley
1 tablespoon chopped fresh oregano or 1 teaspoon dried
½ (10-ounce) package frozen chopped spinach, thawed and squeezed dry
Salt and freshly ground black pepper to taste
Vegetable oil spray

For dipping:
1 cup Herbed Tomato Sauce (page 38) or purchased marinara sauce, heated

1. Rinse cod, pat dry with paper towels, and cut into 1-inch pieces. Place cod cubes on a sheet of plastic wrap, and freeze for 20 to 30 minutes, or until firm but not frozen solid.

2. Preheat the oven to 425°F. Line a rimmed baking sheet with heavy-duty aluminum foil, and spray the foil with vegetable oil spray.

3. Whisk egg and milk in a mixing bowl, add ½ cup breadcrumbs, mozzarella cheese, Parmesan, parsley, and oregano, and mix well. Chop cod in a food processor using on-and-off pulsing. Add cod and spinach, season to taste with salt and pepper, and mix well again.

4. Make mixture into 1½-inch balls, roll balls in remaining breadcrumbs, and arrange cod balls on the prepared pan. Spray tops of cod balls with vegetable oil spray.

5. Bake cod balls for 12 to 15 minutes, or until cooked through. Remove the pan from the oven, and serve immediately, accompanied by a bowl of Herbed Tomato Sauce for dipping.

Note: The cod mixture can be prepared up to 1 day in advance and refrigerated, tightly covered. Also, the cod balls can be baked up to 2 days in advance and refrigerated, tightly covered. Reheat them in a 350°F oven, uncovered, for 10 to 12 minutes, or until hot.

When a recipe calls for half a package of a frozen vegetable, allow the vegetable to thaw about half way. Then slice through the package with a serrated knife, and then cover and return the remainder to the freezer.

New England Cod Balls

Makes 4 to 6 servings

Active time:
20 minutes

Start to finish:
35 minutes

VARIATIONS

In addition to cooked fish or seafood of any kind, try cooked and finely chopped chicken or pork.

Substitute 3 (6-ounce) cans of tuna fish, drained and flaked.

While living on Nantucket I devised myriad recipes to use the surrounding ocean's famed cod, and this is one of them. The crunchy potato chips add texture. These can also be made into large patties for sandwiches.

2 tablespoons unsalted butter
1 small onion, finely chopped
½ green bell pepper, seeds and ribs removed, and finely chopped
1 large egg
1 cup Tartar Sauce (page 44) or purchased tartar sauce, divided
¾ cup finely crushed potato chips
2 tablespoons chopped fresh parsley
2 teaspoons fresh thyme or ½ teaspoon dried
Salt and freshly ground black pepper to taste
1¼ pounds cooked cod fillet, flaked
Vegetable oil spray

1. Preheat the oven to 425°F. Line a rimmed baking sheet with heavy-duty aluminum foil, and spray the foil with vegetable oil spray.

2. Heat butter in a small skillet over medium-high heat. Add onion and bell pepper, and cook, stirring frequently, for 3 to 5 minutes, or until onion is translucent. Set aside.

3. Combine egg and 2 tablespoons Tartar Sauce in a mixing bowl, and whisk well. Stir in crushed potato chips, parsley, thyme, salt, and pepper, and then gently fold in cod.

4. Make mixture into 1½-inch balls, and arrange cod balls on the prepared pan. Spray tops of cod balls with vegetable oil spray. Bake cod balls for 12 to 15 minutes, or until cooked through. Remove the pan from the oven, and serve immediately, accompanied by a bowl of remaining Tartar Sauce for dipping.

Note: The cod mixture can be prepared up to 1 day in advance and refrigerated, tightly covered. Also, the cod balls can be baked up to 2 days in advance and refrigerated, tightly covered. Reheat them in a 350°F oven, uncovered, for 8 to 10 minutes, or until hot.

Cod are so important to New England's history that Cape Cod became the official name for the Massachusetts sandbar that juts out into the Atlantic Ocean. Cod are omnivorous, bottom-dwelling fish that are caught both in Nantucket Sound and in offshore waters. Scrod is a fancier term for small cod, since the fillets are thinner and can be sautéed easier than those taken from larger fish. In some restaurants, scrod can also be haddock; the two are similar in taste and texture.

Tilapia Balls in Macadamia Coconut Sauce

Makes 4 to 6 servings

Active time: 25 minutes

Start to finish: 1½ hours, including 30 minutes to chill mixture

VARIATION

Substitute salmon or any firm-fleshed white fish like halibut or catfish for the tilapia.

The buttery richness of macadamia nuts, along with the coconut milk and Asian seasonings, make this a decadent treat.

1¼ pounds tilapia fillets

2 tablespoons Asian sesame oil

5 scallions, white parts and
    3 inches of green tops, chopped

3 garlic cloves, minced

3 tablespoons grated fresh ginger

1 large egg

1 (14-ounce) can coconut milk,
    divided

½ cup panko breadcrumbs

Salt and freshly ground black
    pepper to taste

2 tablespoons vegetable oil

⅓ pound fresh shiitake mushrooms,
    stemmed and sliced

1 cup chopped salted macadamia
    nuts

2 tablespoons fish sauce (nam pla)

2 teaspoons cornstarch

1 tablespoon cold water

¼ cup chopped cilantro

1. Rinse tilapia, pat dry with paper towels, and cut into 1-inch pieces. Place tilapia cubes on a sheet of plastic wrap, and freeze for 20 to 30 minutes, or until firm but not frozen solid.

2. Heat sesame oil in a large skillet over medium-high heat. Add scallions, garlic, and ginger, and cook, stirring frequently, for 3 minutes, or until scallions are translucent. Scrape mixture into a bowl, and set aside.

3. Whisk egg and 2 tablespoons coconut milk in a mixing bowl, add breadcrumbs, and mix well. Chop tilapia in a food processor using on-and-off pulsing. Add ⅓ of scallion mixture and tilapia, season to taste with salt and pepper, and mix well again. Chill mixture for at least 30 minutes.

4. While mixture chills, heat vegetable oil in the same skillet in which scallion mixture cooked over medium-high heat. Add mushrooms and cook, stirring frequently, for 3 minutes. Add macadamia nuts, and cook for

Cornstarch is a powdery substance obtained from finely grinding the endosperm of corn kernels and used as a thickening agent. Mix cornstarch with either a cold liquid (usually water) or another granular powder such as sugar to keep it from forming lumps in the finished dish.

1 minute, stirring constantly. Add remaining scallion mixture, remaining coconut milk, and fish sauce, and bring to a boil over medium heat, stirring frequently.

5. Make fish mixture into 1-inch balls, and gently lower them into simmering sauce using a slotted spoon. Bring to boil, then reduce the heat to low, cover the pan, and simmer fish balls for 25 minutes, turning them gently with a slotted spoon after 15 minutes. Combine cornstarch and water in a small cup,

and stir well. Add mixture to the skillet, and simmer for 2 minutes, or until slightly thickened. Season to taste with salt and pepper, stir in cilantro, and serve immediately.

Note: The fish mixture can be prepared up to 1 day in advance and refrigerated, tightly covered. Also, the dish can be cooked up to 2 days in advance and refrigerated, tightly covered. Reheat in a 350°F oven, covered, for 10 to 15 minutes, or until hot.

Halibut Balls with Gumbo Sauce

Makes 4 to 6 servings

Active time:
45 minutes

Start to finish:
1½ hours, including 30 minutes to chill mixture

VARIATION

Substitute salmon or any firm-fleshed white fish like sole or cod for the halibut.

Gumbo, from the Ethiopian word *gombo,* which means okra, is a classic ingredient used in Louisiana cooking, dating back to French and Spanish settlers and their African slaves. In this case, the gumbo sauce is not thickened with okra, but with filé powder, which is made from the ground roots of a sassafras tree.

⅓ cup vegetable oil

½ cup all-purpose flour

1½ pounds halibut fillet

2 tablespoons unsalted butter

1 medium onion, diced

½ green bell pepper, seeds and ribs removed, and diced

1 celery rib, diced

3 garlic cloves, minced

1 large egg

2 cups fish stock or bottled clam juice, divided

½ cup plain breadcrumbs

Salt and freshly ground black pepper to taste

1 tablespoon fresh thyme or 1 teaspoon dried

2 bay leaves

1 (14-ounce) can diced tomatoes, undrained

½ teaspoon hot red pepper sauce or to taste

1 tablespoon filé powder

1. Preheat the oven to 450° F. Combine oil and flour in a Dutch oven, and place the pan in the oven. Bake roux for 20 to 30 minutes, or until walnut brown, stirring occasionally.

2. Rinse halibut, pat dry with paper towels, and cut into 1-inch pieces. Place halibut cubes on a sheet of plastic wrap, and freeze for 20 to 30 minutes, or until firm but not frozen solid.

3. While roux bakes, heat butter in large skillet over medium-high heat. Add onion, green pepper, celery, and garlic. Cook, stirring frequently, for 3 minutes, or until onion is translucent. Set aside.

4. Whisk egg and 2 tablespoons fish stock in a mixing bowl, add breadcrumbs, and mix well. Chop halibut in a food processor using on-and-off pulsing. Add halibut to the mixing bowl, season to taste with salt and pepper, and mix well again. Chill mixture for at least 30 minutes.

5. Remove roux from the oven, and place the Dutch oven on the stove over medium heat. Add fish stock, and whisk constantly, until mixture comes to a boil and thickens. Add vegetable mixture, thyme, bay leaves, and tomatoes

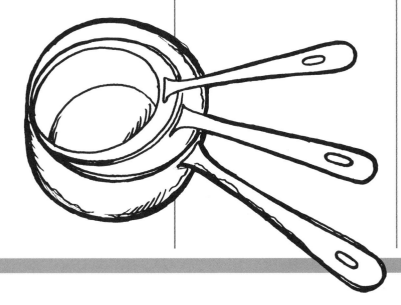

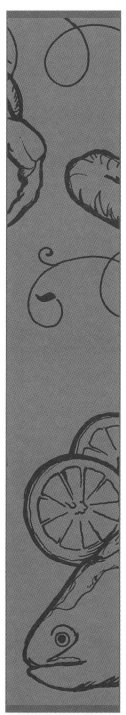

to pan. Season to taste with hot red pepper sauce, salt, and pepper. Bring to a boil, cover, and cook over low heat for 20 minutes, uncovered, stirring occasionally.

6. Make fish mixture into 1-inch balls, and gently lower them into simmering sauce using a slotted spoon. Bring to boil, then reduce the heat to low, cover the pan, and simmer fish balls for 25 minutes, turning them gently with a slotted spoon after 15 minutes. Remove and discard bay leaves. Remove the pan from the heat, and stir in filè powder. Stir well, season to taste with salt and pepper, and serve immediately. *Do not allow the mixture to boil or the filè powder will become stringy.*

Note: The fish mixture can be prepared up to 1 day in advance and refrigerated, tightly covered. Also, the dish can be cooked up to 2 days in advance and refrigerated, tightly covered. Reheat, covered, over low heat until hot.

A roux is a mixture of fat and flour used to thicken soups and sauces. The first step when making any roux is to cook the flour in the fat, so that the dish doesn't taste like library paste. For white sauces, this is done over low heat and the fat used is butter. Many Creole and Cajun dishes, such as gumbo, use a fuller-flavored brown roux made with oil or drippings and cooked to a deep brown. The dark roux gives dishes an almost nutty flavor.

Dill and Mustard Salmon Balls

Makes 4 to 6 servings

Active time:
25 minutes

Start to finish:
1¼ hours, including 30 minutes to chill mixture

VARIATION

Substitute tuna or any firm-fleshed white fish like halibut or cod for the salmon.

The use of aromatic fresh dill is part of many diverse cuisines; they range from Greek to all of the Scandinavian countries. This dish has northern European inspiration because it blends the fresh herb with sharp mustard for a contrast.

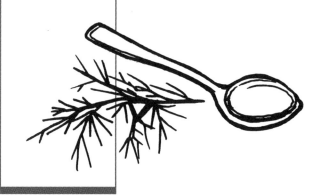

1¼ pounds skinned salmon fillet
1 large egg
½ cup mayonnaise, divided
⅓ cup Dijon mustard, divided
½ cup plain breadcrumbs
⅓ cup chopped fresh dill, divided
Salt and freshly ground black
    pepper to taste
¼ cup sour cream
2 teaspoons freshly squeezed
    lemon juice
Vegetable oil spray

1. Rinse salmon, pat dry with paper towels, and cut into 1-inch pieces. Place salmon cubes on a sheet of plastic wrap, and freeze for 20 to 30 minutes, or until firm but not frozen solid.

2. Preheat the oven to 425°F. Line a rimmed baking sheet with heavy-duty aluminum foil, and spray the foil with vegetable oil spray.

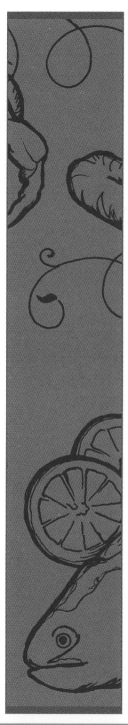

3. Whisk egg, 2 tablespoons mayonnaise, and 2 tablespoons mustard in a mixing bowl, add breadcrumbs and 3 tablespoons dill, and mix well. Chop salmon in a food processor using on-and-off pulsing. Add salmon, season to taste with salt and pepper, and mix well again.

4. Make mixture into 1½-inch balls, and arrange salmon balls on the prepared pan. Spray tops of salmon balls with vegetable oil spray.

5. Bake salmon balls for 12 to 15 minutes, or until cooked through. While salmon balls bake, combine remaining mayonnaise, sour cream, remaining mustard, remaining dill, and lemon juice in a mixing bowl, and whisk well. Remove the pan from the oven, and serve immediately, accompanied by the bowl of sauce for dipping.

Note: The salmon mixture can be prepared up to 1 day in advance and refrigerated, tightly covered. Also, the salmon balls can be baked up to 2 days in advance and refrigerated, tightly covered. Reheat them in a 350°F oven, uncovered, for 10 to 12 minutes, or until hot.

A vegetable peeler and a pair of tweezers are the best ways to get rid of those pesky little bones in fish fillets. Run a peeler down the center of the fillet, starting at the tail end. It will catch the larger pin bones, and with a twist of your wrist, you can pull them out. For finer bones, use your fingers to rub the flesh lightly and then pull out the bones with the tweezers.

Salmon Balls Niçoise

Makes 4 to 6 servings

Active time:
30 minutes

Start to finish:
1¼ hours,
including
30 minutes to
chill mixture

VARIATION

Substitute tuna or any firm-fleshed white fish like halibut or cod for the salmon.

These baked salmon balls, dotted with olives and other flavorful ingredients, are greatly improved from the salmon cakes I ate as a child. While those were made with canned salmon, fresh salmon makes them far more flavorful.

1¼ pounds skinless salmon fillet
1 large egg
2 tablespoons mayonnaise
1 tablespoon Dijon mustard
½ cup mashed potatoes
    (homemade or purchased)
¼ cup chopped oil-cured black olives
1 shallot, finely chopped
2 tablespoons chopped fresh parsley
2 tablespoons small capers,
    drained and rinsed
1 tablespoon herbes de Provence
Salt and freshly ground black
    pepper to taste
Vegetable oil spray

For dipping:
1 cup Sun-Dried Tomato Sauce
    (page 43)

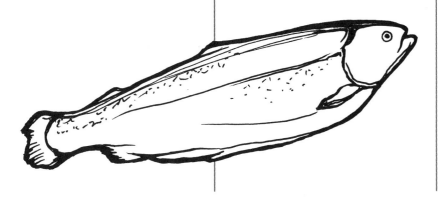

1. Rinse salmon, pat dry with paper towels, and cut into 1-inch pieces. Place salmon cubes on a sheet of plastic wrap, and freeze for 20 to 30 minutes, or until firm but not frozen solid.

2. Preheat the oven to 425°F. Line a rimmed baking sheet with heavy-duty aluminum foil, and spray the foil with vegetable oil spray.

3. Whisk egg, mayonnaise, and mustard in a mixing bowl, add potatoes, olives, shallot, parsley, capers, and herbes de Provence, and mix well. Chop salmon in a food processor using on-and-off pulsing. Add salmon to the mixing bowl, season to taste with salt and pepper, and mix well again.

4. Make mixture into 1½-inch balls, and arrange salmon balls on the prepared pan. Spray tops of salmon balls with vegetable oil spray.

5. Bake salmon balls for 12 to 15 minutes, or until cooked through. Remove the pan from the oven, and serve immediately, accompanied by a bowl of Sun-Dried Tomato Sauce for dipping.

Note: The salmon mixture can be prepared up to 1 day in advance and refrigerated, tightly covered. Also, the salmon balls can be baked up to 2 days in advance and refrigerated, tightly covered. Reheat them in a 350°F oven, uncovered, for 10 to 12 minutes, or until hot.

Most fish markets will remove the skin for you from a fish fillet, but here's how to do it yourself: Starting at the thin end of the fillet, slide a knife between the skin and flesh until you can grab hold of the skin with a paper towel. Use this "handle" to help steady the skin as you continue to cut the flesh away from it.

Asian Salmon Balls

Makes 4 to 6 servings

Active time: 20 minutes

Start to finish: 50 minutes, including 30 minutes to chill mixture

VARIATION

Substitute tuna or any firm-fleshed white fish like halibut or cod for the salmon.

The healthful Omega-3 fatty acids in salmon make this fish a popular choice. Enjoy these Asian-inspired salmon balls.

1¼ pounds skinned salmon fillet
1 large egg
2 tablespoons hoisin sauce
2 tablespoons mayonnaise
1 tablespoon Asian sesame oil
1 tablespoon soy sauce
1 cup panko breadcrumbs, divided
¼ cup chopped fresh cilantro
3 scallions, white parts and
   3 inches of green tops, chopped
1 tablespoon grated fresh ginger
2 garlic cloves, minced
Salt and freshly ground black
   pepper to taste
Vegetable oil spray

For dipping:
1 cup Ponzu Sauce (page 59) or
   purchased soy sauce

1. Rinse salmon, pat dry with paper towels, and cut into 1-inch pieces. Place salmon cubes on a sheet of plastic wrap, and freeze for 20 to 30 minutes, or until firm but not frozen solid.

2. Preheat the oven to 425°F. Line a rimmed baking sheet with heavy-duty aluminum foil, and spray the foil with vegetable oil spray.

3. Whisk egg, hoisin sauce, mayonnaise, sesame oil, and soy sauce in a mixing bowl, and add ½ cup breadcrumbs, cilantro, scallions, ginger, and garlic, and mix well. Chop salmon in a food processor using on-and-off pulsing. Add salmon, season to taste with salt and pepper, and mix well again.

4. Make mixture into 1½-inch balls, roll balls in remaining breadcrumbs, and arrange salmon balls on the prepared pan. Spray tops of salmon balls with vegetable oil spray.

5. Bake salmon balls for 12 to 15 minutes, or until cooked through. Remove the pan from the oven, and serve immediately, accompanied by a bowl of Ponzu Sauce for dipping.

Note: The salmon mixture can be prepared up to 1 day in advance and refrigerated, tightly covered. Also, the meatballs can be baked up to 2 days in advance and refrigerated, tightly covered. Reheat them in a 350°F oven, uncovered, for 10 to 12 minutes, or until hot.

Hoisin sauce is the ketchup of Chinese cooking. This thick sweet and spicy reddish-brown sauce is a mixture of soybeans, garlic, chiles, Chinese five-spice powder, and sugar. Like ketchup, it's used both as a condiment and as an ingredient.

Creamy Mexican Snapper Balls

Makes 4 to 6 servings

Active time:
30 minutes

Start to finish:
1½ hours, including 30 minutes to chill mixture

VARIATION

Substitute salmon or any firm-fleshed white fish like halibut, grouper, or cod for the snapper.

These lean and luscious balls made from red snapper from the Gulf of Mexico are poached in a brightly colored cream sauce laced with tequila. Serve them over Mexican rice with a tomato salad on the side.

Ancho are the sweetest of the dried chili peppers. They are the mild green poblano chiles in their fresh form, and they add a rich, almost fruity flavor to foods. They're about 3 to 4 inches long, and always need to be soaked before using.

1½ pounds red snapper fillets, skinned
4 large dried ancho chiles, stemmed, seeded, and broken into small pieces
½ cup boiling water
2 tablespoons olive oil
1 medium onion, chopped
1 large egg
1 cup half-and-half, divided
½ cup panko breadcrumbs
Salt and freshly ground black pepper to taste
2 tablespoons balsamic vinegar
4 garlic cloves, peeled
2 teaspoons dried oregano
⅓ cup tequila
2 teaspoons cornstarch
¼ cup chopped fresh cilantro

1. Rinse snapper, pat dry with paper towels, and cut into 1-inch pieces. Place snapper cubes on a sheet of plastic wrap, and freeze for 20 to 30 minutes, or until firm but not frozen solid. Combine chiles and boiling water in a small bowl, and allow chiles to soak for 15 minutes.

2. Heat oil in a large skillet over medium-high heat. Add onion, and cook, stirring frequently, for 3 minutes, or until onion is translucent. Whisk egg and 2 tablespoons half-and-half in a mixing bowl, add breadcrumbs, and mix well. Chop snapper in a food processor using on-and-off pulsing. Add ½ of onion and snapper to the mixing bowl, season to taste with salt and pepper, and mix well again. Chill mixture for at least 30 minutes.

3. While mixture chills, combine chiles and soaking water, vinegar, garlic, and oregano in a food processor, and puree until smooth. Add puree to the skillet along with tequila and remaining half-and-half. Bring to a boil over medium-high heat, stirring occasionally. Reduce the heat to low, and cook sauce for 10 minutes, uncovered, stirring occasionally.

4. Make fish mixture into 1-inch balls, and gently lower them into simmering sauce using a slotted spoon. Bring to boil, then reduce the heat to low, cover the pan, and simmer fish balls for 25 minutes, turning them gently with a slotted spoon after 15 minutes. Combine cornstarch and 1 tablespoon cold water in a small cup, and stir well. Add mixture to the skillet, and simmer for 2 minutes, or until slightly thickened. Season to taste with salt and pepper, stir in cilantro, and serve immediately.

Note: The fish mixture can be prepared up to 1 day in advance and refrigerated, tightly covered. Also, the dish can be cooked up to 2 days in advance and refrigerated, tightly covered. Reheat, covered, over low heat until hot.

Greek Tuna Balls

VARIATIONS

In addition to cooked fish or seafood of any kind, try cooked and finely chopped chicken or pork.

Substitute 3 (6-ounce) cans of salmon, drained, skin and bones discarded, and flaked.

While I prefer the imported Italian tuna packed in olive oil because it has more innate flavor and moisture, there's so much going on in the sauce that any brand of tuna will be fine.

The key word for the olives in this recipe is "pitted." Pitted kalamata olives can usually be found at the olive bar in supermarkets. If the only pitted olives are picholine or some other variety, go for those, choosing convenience over a specific olive.

2 tablespoons mayonnaise
1 large egg
½ cup seasoned Italian breadcrumbs
¼ cup freshly grated Parmesan
Salt and freshly ground black pepper to taste
3 (6-ounce) cans tuna, drained and flaked
2 tablespoons olive oil
1 small onion, chopped
3 garlic cloves, minced
1 celery rib, chopped
1 (28-ounce) can crushed tomatoes in tomato puree
½ cup dry white wine
¾ cup chopped pitted kalamata olives
¼ cup small capers, drained and rinsed
¼ cup chopped fresh parsley
3 tablespoons chopped fresh oregano or 1 tablespoon dried
1 bay leaf
Vegetable oil spray

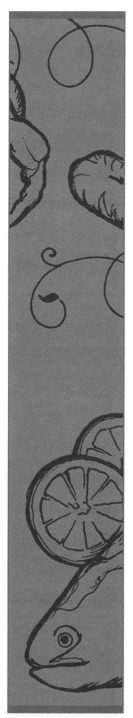

1. Preheat the oven to 425°F. Line a rimmed baking sheet with heavy-duty aluminum foil, and spray the foil with vegetable oil spray.

2. Combine mayonnaise and egg in a mixing bowl, and whisk well. Stir in breadcrumbs and cheese, season to taste with salt and pepper, and gently fold in tuna.

3. Make mixture into 1½-inch balls, and arrange tuna balls on the prepared pan. Spray tops of tuna balls with vegetable oil spray. Bake tuna balls for 8 to 10 minutes, or until lightly browned.

4. While tuna balls bake, heat oil in skillet over medium-high heat. Add onion, garlic, and celery. Cook, stirring frequently, for 3 minutes, or until onion is translucent. Add tomatoes, wine, olives, capers, parsley, oregano, and bay leaf. Bring to a boil, reduce the heat to medium, and simmer sauce, uncovered, for 15 minutes.

5. Remove the pan from the oven, and add tuna balls to sauce. Bring to a boil and simmer, uncovered, for 10 minutes. Remove and discard bay leaf, season to taste with salt and pepper, and serve immediately.

Note: The tuna mixture can be prepared up to 1 day in advance and refrigerated, tightly covered. Also, the dish can be cooked up to 2 days in advance and refrigerated, tightly covered. Reheat, covered, over low heat until hot.

Grilled Tuna Balls with Wasabi Mayonnaise

Makes 4 to 6 servings

Active time:
20 minutes

Start to finish:
1¼ hours,
including
30 minutes to
chill mixture

VARIATION

Substitute salmon or any firm-fleshed white fish like halibut or cod for the tuna.

Tuna steaks grilled rare have become popular, even with people who prefer other foods well done. There are so many luscious flavors joined with the succulent tuna in this recipe; it's a seared variation on the chopped po'ke appetizer popular in Hawaii.

8 to 12 (8-inch) bamboo skewers
1¼ pounds tuna steak
3 scallions, white parts only, chopped
2 garlic cloves, minced
2 tablespoons freshly grated ginger
2 tablespoons fish sauce (nam pla)
1 tablespoon mirin or sweet sherry
Salt and freshly ground black pepper to taste
1 tablespoon wasabi powder
2 tablespoons cold water
⅔ cup mayonnaise
3 tablespoons finely chopped pickled ginger
2 teaspoons Asian sesame oil

1. Soak the bamboo skewers in cold water to cover. Rinse tuna and pat dry with paper towels, and cut into 1-inch pieces, discarding sinews. Place tuna cubes on a sheet of plastic wrap, and freeze for 20 to 30 minutes, or until firm but not solid. Chop tuna in a food processor using on-and-off pulsing. Place tuna in a mixing bowl and add scallions, garlic, ginger, fish sauce, mirin, salt, and pepper.

2. Divide mixture into 8 to 12 portions, and form each portion into a sausage shape. Insert a skewer into each sausage so that the tip of the skewer is almost at the top of the tuna mixture. Cover skewers with plastic wrap, and refrigerate for at least 30 minutes.

3. While tuna skewers chill, prepare a hot charcoal or gas grill, or preheat the oven broiler. Combine wasabi and water in a mixing bowl to form a paste. Add mayonnaise, pickled ginger, and sesame oil. Stir well, and refrigerate until ready to use.

4. Grill skewers for a total of 4 to 6 minutes, uncovered if using a charcoal grill, turning them gently with tongs to brown all sides. Serve immediately, passing the bowl of wasabi sauce for dipping.

Note: The tuna mixture can be prepared up to 6 hours in advance and refrigerated, tightly covered.

> Wasabi is a fiery Japanese horseradish that comes from the root of an Asian plant and is far stronger and more pungent than even freshly grated white horseradish root. It is available both as a paste or a powder that is mixed with water to become a paste. I prefer the powder; using it means your wasabi is always fresh.

Grilled Tuna Balls with Aïoli

Makes 4 to 6 servings

Active time: 25 minutes

Start to finish: 1¼ hours, including 30 minutes to chill mixture

VARIATION

Substitute salmon or any firm-fleshed white fish like halibut or cod for the tuna.

This recipe is the next generation of tuna tartare from decades past. The addition of the herbs and flavorings to the tuna is delicious, and the contrast of the seared exterior and almost raw interior of these skewers makes them special.

8 to 12 (8-inch) bamboo skewers
1¼ pounds tuna steaks
½ cup chopped fresh parsley
2 shallots, chopped
3 tablespoons small capers, drained and rinsed
2 tablespoons prepared horseradish
2 tablespoons freshly squeezed lemon juice
2 tablespoons Dijon mustard
Salt and freshly ground black pepper to taste

For dipping:
1 cup Easy Aïoli (page 46)

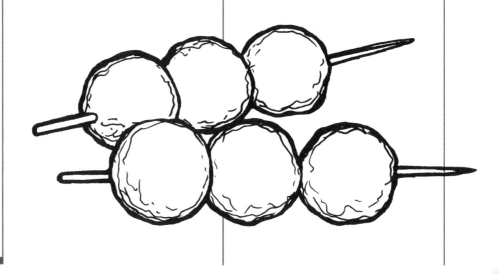

1. Soak the bamboo skewers in cold water to cover. Rinse tuna and pat dry with paper towels, and cut into 1-inch pieces, discarding sinews. Place tuna cubes on a sheet of plastic wrap, and freeze for 20 to 30 minutes, or until firm but not solid. Chop tuna in a food processor using on-and-off pulsing.

2. Place tuna in a mixing bowl and add parsley, shallots, capers, horseradish, lemon juice, mustard, salt, and pepper. Divide mixture into 8 to 12 portions, and form each portion into a sausage shape. Insert a skewer into each sausage so that the tip of the skewer is almost at the top of the tuna mixture. Cover skewers with plastic wrap, and refrigerate for at least 30 minutes.

3. While tuna skewers chill, prepare a hot charcoal or gas grill, or preheat the oven broiler. Grill skewers for a total of 4 to 6 minutes, uncovered if using a charcoal grill, turning them gently with tongs to brown all sides. Serve immediately, accompanied by the bowl of Easy Aïoli sauce for dipping.

Note: The tuna mixture can be prepared up to 6 hours in advance and refrigerated, tightly covered.

Capers are the flower buds of a low bush native to the Mediterranean, which are sun-dried after being harvested and then dried and pickled in vinegar or preserved in salt. The best capers are the tiny ones from France; always rinse capers well before using them.

Vibrant and Vegetarian:

Meatballs with Vegetables, Herbs, Legumes, and Grains

A ll of these recipes are for "meatballs" that contain no meat. Instead you'll find a wide range of foods bound together before being baked or fried. Many of them—such as dried beans—are an excellent source of protein and other nutrients too.

These recipes are all vegetarian, but most are not vegan because they include eggs and—frequently—cheese as well. A few uncooked cheese balls are included, too. In my carnivore household most of the recipes in this chapter are served as an hors d'oeuvre or a side dish to elevate a simple entree to elegance. But many are satisfying enough to be served as a light lunch with a tossed salad. I include variations to make these vegetarian dishes into non-vegetarian ones. Serving sizes are main dish portions to remain consistent with recipes in the rest of the book. If serving them as a side dish, they can easily feed twice that number.

You may wonder why so many recipes in this chapter require frying. Since vegetables don't have a high protein content like meats, poultry, and fish, the ground up vegetable mixtures won't hold together when baked.

Falafel

Makes 6 to 8 servings

Active time:
30 minutes

Start to finish:
2½ hours, 1½ to
soak beans

VARIATION

Omit the coriander and cumin, and add 2 tablespoons chili powder; substitute cilantro for the parsley. This will make these more American than Middle Eastern.

Falafel are the potato chips of the Middle East, and they're as popular in Israel as in Arab countries. While they can be made with fava beans, they are usually prepared with garbanzo beans, or chickpeas. What differentiates falafel from other bean balls is that the chickpeas are soaked—but not cooked—before they are ground into the paste. That is why dried beans are specified; canned beans would add too much moisture to the dish.

1 *pound dried garbanzo beans*
1 *small onion, diced*
3 *garlic cloves, peeled*
4 *tablespoons all-purpose flour*
2 *tablespoons chopped fresh parsley*
1 *tablespoon freshly squeezed*
   lemon juice
1 *tablespoon ground coriander*
2 *teaspoons ground cumin*
1 *teaspoon baking soda*
Salt and cayenne to taste
3 *cups vegetable oil for frying*

For dipping:
1 *cup Tahini (page 50) or*
   purchased hummus

1. Soak garbanzo beans in cold water to cover for a minimum of 6 hours, or preferably overnight. Or, place beans in a saucepan covered with water, and bring to a boil over high heat. Boil for 1 minute, turn off the heat, and cover the pan. Allow beans to soak for 1 hour, then drain. With either method, continue with the dish as soon as beans have soaked, or refrigerate beans.

2. Drain beans and place them in the work bowl of a food processor. Add onion, garlic, flour, parsley, lemon juice, coriander, cumin, baking soda, salt, and cayenne. Process until the mixture forms a smooth paste, scraping the sides of the work bowl as necessary.

3. Form mixture into 1-inch balls, and refrigerate for 20 minutes, tightly covered with plastic wrap. Heat oil in a saucepan over medium-high heat to a temperature of 375°F.

4. Add falafel balls, being careful not to crowd the pan. Cook falafel balls for 3 minutes, or until browned. Remove falafel balls from the pan with a slotted spoon, and drain well on paper towels. Serve immediately, accompanied by a bowl of Tahini for dipping.

Note: The falafel balls can be prepared for frying up to 1 day in advance and refrigerated, tightly covered. They can also be fried in advance; reheat them in a 400°F oven for 5 to 7 minutes, or until hot and crusty again.

Garbanzo beans, also called chickpeas and *ceci* in Italian, are legumes adored around the world for their nutlike flavor. Native to the Mediterranean, they found their way into dishes from India to Spain, with a lot of Middle Eastern cuisines included in the repertoire.

Black-Eyed Pea Balls

Makes 4 to 6 servings

Active time:

30 minutes

Start to finish:
2½ hours,
including 2 hours
to prepare beans

VARIATION

Replace the black-eyed peas with kidney beans or small navy beans.

Called *akla* in Ghana and *akara* in other parts of the African continent, these spicy morsels are a snack food equivalent to falafel. And like falafel, the beans are soaked but not cooked before frying. While they are traditionally eaten with a chile relish, I prefer a sauce.

1 cup dried black-eyed peas

1 medium onion, diced

3 garlic cloves, peeled

1 small jalapeño or serrano chile, seeds and ribs removed, and diced

1 large egg

3 tablespoons water

Salt and freshly ground black pepper to taste

3 cups vegetable oil for frying

For dipping:

1 cup Mexican Tomato Sauce (page 48) or bottled salsa, heated

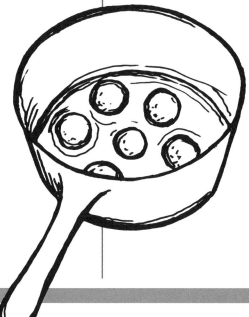

1. Soak black-eyed peas in cold water to cover for a minimum of 6 hours, or preferably overnight. Or, place beans in a saucepan covered with water, and bring to a boil over high heat. Boil for 1 minute, turn off the heat, and cover the pan. Allow beans to soak for 1 hour, then drain. With either method, continue with the dish as soon as beans have soaked, or refrigerate beans.

2. Drain beans and place them in the work bowl of a food processor. Add onion, garlic, chile, egg, water, salt, and pepper. Process until the mixture forms a smooth paste, scraping the sides of the work bowl as necessary.

3. Form mixture into 1-inch balls, and refrigerate for 20 minutes, tightly covered with plastic wrap. Heat oil in a saucepan over medium-high heat to a temperature of 375°F.

While dried beans and peas can keep for years in their dehydrated state, once they encounter water bacteria can grow on them. That's why when using either the "long" method of soaking the beans in cold water for a minimum of 6 hours or "short" method of bringing the beans to a boil and allowing them to sit, covered, for 1 hour, the beans should be cooked as soon as possible.

4. Add balls, being careful not to crowd the pan. Cook bean balls for 3 minutes, or until browned. Remove balls from the pan with a slotted spoon, and drain well on paper towels. Serve immediately, accompanied by a bowl of Mexican Tomato Sauce.

Note: The balls can be prepared for frying up to 1 day in advance and refrigerated, tightly covered. They can also be fried in advance; reheat them in a 400°F oven for 5 to 7 minutes, or until hot and crusty again.

Middle Eastern Lentil Balls

Makes 4 to 6 servings

Active time:
20 minutes

Start to finish:
1¼ hours, including 30 minutes to chill mixture

VARIATION

Substitute green or yellow split peas for the lentils; the split peas have a slightly sweeter flavor than lentils.

Lentils are the "meatiest" of the legumes, and you will find that even devout carnivores adore these flavorful fried balls. You can also make them as miniatures and serve them as an hors d'oeuvre.

2 cups lentils, picked over, rinsed, and drained
1 quart water
1 teaspoon salt
1 large egg
2 tablespoons tomato juice or water
1 tablespoon tomato paste
1 cup plain breadcrumbs, divided
¾ cup pine nuts
2 tablespoons olive oil
1 medium onion, chopped
2 garlic cloves, minced
2 teaspoons ground coriander
1 teaspoon ground cumin
Freshly ground black pepper to taste
Vegetable oil spray

For dipping:
1 cup Greek Feta Sauce (page 49) or purchased hummus

1. Place lentils in a 2-quart saucepan, cover with water, and add 1 teaspoon salt. Bring to a boil over medium-high heat, then reduce the heat to low and simmer lentils, covered, for 20 to 25 minutes or until cooked. Whisk egg, tomato juice, and tomato paste in a mixing bowl, add ½ cup breadcrumbs, and mix well. Drain lentils, and add to the mixing bowl.

2. Preheat the oven to 450°F. Line a rimmed baking sheet with heavy-duty aluminum foil, and spray the foil with vegetable oil spray. While lentils simmer, place pine nuts in a small dry skillet over medium-high heat. Toast nuts, shaking the pan frequently, for 2 to 3 minutes, or until browned. Remove nuts from the pan, and set aside.

3. Heat oil in the same small skillet over medium-high heat. Add onions and garlic, and cook, stirring frequently, for 3 minutes, or until onion is translucent. Add coriander and cumin, and cook, stirring constantly, for 1 minute. Add onion mixture to lentils, and stir well.

4. Puree ½ cup pine nuts and 1 cup lentil mixture in a food processor fitted with a metal blade. Scrape

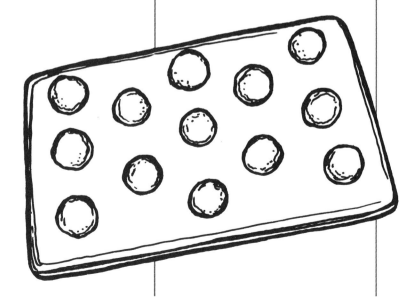

mixture back into mixing bowl, and add remaining pine nuts. Season to taste with salt and pepper. Refrigerate lentil mixture for at least 30 minutes.

5. Place remaining ½ cup breadcrumbs in a shallow bowl, make mixture into 1½-inch balls, roll balls in breadcrumbs, and arrange lentil balls on the prepared pan. Spray tops of lentil balls with vegetable oil spray.

6. Bake lentil balls for 12 to 15 minutes, or until cooked through and no longer pink. Remove the pan from the oven, and serve immediately, accompanied by a bowl of Greek Feta Sauce for dipping.

Note: The lentil mixture can be prepared up to 1 day in advance and refrigerated, tightly covered. Also, the meatballs can be baked up to 2 days in advance and refrigerated, tightly covered. Reheat them in a 350°F oven, covered, for 10 to 12 minutes, or until hot.

High in iron and vitamins A and B, lentils have long been used as a meat substitute in the Middle East and India, where they are called *dal*. These tiny, lens-shaped pulses (the dried seed of a legume) come in various colors, ranging from grayish-brown to fiery red and bright yellow. Due to their size, they are one of the few dried legumes that do not require any presoaking before cooking and can be used right from the bag.

Southwestern Black Bean Balls

Makes 4 to 6 servings

**Active time:
25 minutes**

**Start to finish:
1 hour, including
30 minutes to
chill mixture**

VARIATION

*Substitute kidney
beans, garbanzo
beans, or small
navy beans for
the black beans.*

These flavorful treats need no advance thought because the beans are already cooked. The cakes contain the pantheon of traditional Southwestern ingredients —including chili powder, chiles, and cilantro.

2 tablespoons olive oil

1 medium onion, chopped

3 garlic cloves, minced

2 jalapeño or serrano chiles, seeds
    and ribs removed, and chopped

2 tablespoons chili powder

1½ tablespoons ground cumin

2 (15-ounce) cans black beans,
    drained and rinsed

½ cup chopped fresh cilantro

½ cup water

Salt and freshly ground black
    pepper to taste

3 cups vegetable oil for frying

For dipping:

1 cup Creamy Chipotle Sauce
    (page 47) or bottled salsa

1. Heat olive oil in a heavy large skillet over medium-high heat. Add onion, garlic, and chiles and cook, stirring frequently, for 3 minutes, or until onion is translucent. Add chili powder and cumin and cook, stirring constantly, for 1 minute. Add black beans, cilantro, and water. Bring to a boil and simmer mixture, stirring frequently, for 3 minutes.

2. Transfer mixture to a food processor and puree. Scrape mixture into a mixing bowl, and season to taste with salt and pepper. Form mixture into 1-inch balls, and refrigerate for 30 minutes, tightly covered with plastic wrap. Heat oil in a saucepan over medium-high heat to a temperature of 375°F.

3. Add black bean balls, being careful not to crowd the pan. Cook black bean balls for 3 minutes, or until browned. Remove black bean balls from the pan with a slotted spoon, and drain well on paper towels. Serve immediately, accompanied by a bowl of Creamy Chipotle Sauce for dipping.

Note: The black bean balls can be prepared for frying up to 1 day in advance and refrigerated, tightly covered. They can also be fried in advance; reheat them in a 400°F oven for 5 to 7 minutes, or until hot and crusty again.

Chili powder is a spice blend you can make yourself. Combine 2 tablespoons ground red chile, 2 tablespoons paprika, 1 tablespoon ground coriander, 1 tablespoon garlic powder, 1 tablespoon onion powder, 2 teaspoons ground cumin, 2 teaspoons ground red pepper or cayenne, 1 teaspoon ground black pepper, and 1 teaspoon dried oregano. Store in a jar away from sunlight.

Kidney Bean and Sweet Potato Balls

Makes 4 to 6 servings

Active time: 30 minutes

Start to finish: 1¼ hours, including 30 minutes for mixture to chill

VARIATION

Substitute black-eyed peas, garbanzo beans, or small navy beans in place of the kidney beans.

These colorful balls combine brightly colored orange sweet potatoes with deep red beans. The seasoning is mild, and they make a great side dish with grilled meats and poultry.

½ pound sweet potatoes, cut into 2-inch pieces

3 scallions, white parts and 2 inches of green tops, chopped

2 tablespoons chopped fresh parsley

1 tablespoon chopped fresh sage or 1 teaspoon dried

1 (15-ounce) can kidney beans, drained and rinsed

2 garlic cloves, peeled

½ teaspoon baking powder

Salt and freshly ground black pepper to taste

3 cups vegetable oil for frying

For dipping: 1 cup Southern Barbecue Sauce (page 39) or purchased barbecue sauce, heated

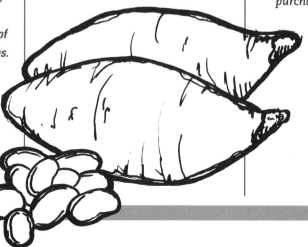

1. Cover sweet potatoes with salted water, and bring to a boil over high heat. Reduce the heat to medium, and cook potatoes for 15 minutes, or until tender. Drain potatoes, and when cool enough to handle, peel potatoes and place them in a mixing bowl.

2. Add scallions, parsley, and sage to the bowl, and mash potatoes with a potato masher until smooth.

3. Combine beans, garlic, baking powder, salt, and pepper in a food processor. Process until the mixture forms a smooth paste, scraping the sides of the work bowl as necessary. Add mixture to the mixing bowl, and mix well.

4. Form mixture into 1-inch balls, and refrigerate for 30 minutes, tightly covered with plastic wrap. Heat oil in a saucepan over medium-high heat to a temperature of 375°F.

5. Add balls, being careful not to crowd the pan. Cook balls for 3 minutes, or until browned. Remove balls from the pan with a slotted spoon, and drain well on paper towels. Serve immediately, accompanied by a bowl of Southern Barbecue Sauce for dipping.

The sweet potato provides proof for Thor Heyerdahl's theory that it was South American navigators who crossed the Pacific. The Maoris of New Zealand have a tradition that the sweet potato, native to the tropical Americas, came to them from "the country of our ancestors."

Italian Rice Balls

Makes 4 to 6 servings

Active time:
45 minutes

Start to finish:
3 hours, including
2 hours to chill
mixture

VARIATIONS

Add ½ teaspoon crushed saffron to the stock, and the rice balls will take on a bright yellow color.

Cook ⅓ pound chopped wild mushrooms in 2 tablespoons unsalted butter and add them to the risotto as it cooks.

In Italian, *arancini* means "little oranges," and these cheese-stuffed rice balls are a staple of Sicilian cooking. They go together quickly if you have some leftover risotto, so be sure to make some extra.

Risotto:

3 tablespoons unsalted butter

1 medium onion, chopped

2 garlic cloves, minced

2 cups arborio rice

¾ cup white wine

5 cups chicken stock, heated to just
    below simmer

¾ cup freshly grated Parmesan

Salt and freshly ground black
    pepper to taste

Rice balls:

2 large eggs

2 cups risotto, chilled

½ cup freshly grated Parmesan

1½ cups seasoned Italian
    breadcrumbs, divided

2 ounces whole milk mozzarella,
    cut into ½-inch cubes

3 cups vegetable oil for frying

Add 2 cups chopped fresh spinach or ½ of a 10-ounce package of frozen chopped spinach to the risotto as it cooks.

Stir 1 cup pureed cooked asparagus into the stock while making the risotto.

Add ¼ cup chopped fresh herbs (some combination of parsley, basil, oregano, thyme, and rosemary) to the risotto as it cooks.

Instead of mozzarella, form the rice balls around a cube of cooked Italian sausage.

1. For risotto, place butter in a heavy saucepan over medium-high heat. Add onion and garlic, and cook, stirring frequently, for 3 minutes, or until onion is translucent. Add rice, and stir to coat with butter.

2. Raise the heat to high, add wine, and cook for 2 minutes, stirring constantly. Reduce the heat to medium, and ladle 1 cup hot stock over rice. Stir constantly and wait for rice to absorb stock before adding next 1 cup, while stirring constantly. Repeat with stock until all 5 cups have been absorbed; this should take 12 to 15 minutes.

3. Stir cheese into rice, and season to taste with salt and pepper. Scrape rice into a 9 x 13-inch pan, and chill for at least 2 hours.

4. For rice balls, whisk eggs in a mixing bowl, and stir in risotto, cheese, and ½ cup breadcrumbs. Place remaining 1 cup breadcrumbs in a shallow bowl.

5. Measure out 1 tablespoon of rice mixture into your hand, and press a mozzarella cube into it. Top with another 1 tablespoon of rice mixture, and form into a ball; be careful to totally enclose cheese

cube. Roll balls in breadcrumbs, and repeat until all of rice mixture is used.

6. Heat oil in a deep-sided saucepan or deep-fryer to a temperature of 375°F. Preheat the oven to 150°F, and line a baking sheet with paper towels.

7. Add rice balls, being careful not to crowd the pan. Cook rice balls for 3 to 4 minutes, or until browned. Remove rice balls from the pan with a slotted spoon, and drain well on paper towel–lined baking sheet. Keep fried rice balls warm in the oven while frying remaining balls. Serve immediately.

Note: The rice balls can be prepared for frying up to 1 day in advance and refrigerated, tightly covered. They can also be fried in advance; reheat them in a 400°F oven for 5 to 7 minutes or until hot and crusty again.

Arborio is a medium-grain rice imported from Italy and used primarily in making risotto or risotto-based dishes such as fried rice balls stuffed with cheese. When the technique of adding liquid slowly while stirring constantly is used, the resulting risotto is creamy from the slow release of starch and the rice is still firm to the bite.

Rice and Cheddar Balls

Makes 4 to 6 servings

Active time: 30 minutes

Start to finish: 3½ hours, including 3 hours to chill mixture

These fried morsels are an Americanized version of Sicilian *arancini*. Much of their flavor comes from the liquid in which the rice is cooked.

1 cup whole milk

1 cup long-grain white rice

2 tablespoons paprika

1 teaspoon dry mustard

2 tablespoons unsalted butter

4 scallions, white parts and
    2 inches of green tops, chopped

½ red bell pepper, seeds and ribs
    removed, and finely chopped

2 large eggs

2 teaspoons fresh thyme or
    ½ teaspoon dried

2 cups grated cheddar cheese

Salt and freshly ground black
    pepper to taste

1 cup plain breadcrumbs

3 cups vegetable oil for frying

For dipping:

1 cup Herbed Tomato Sauce
    (page 38) or purchased
    marinara sauce, heated

VARIATIONS

Substitute Swiss or Gruyère for the cheddar.

Omit the paprika and mustard, add 2 tablespoons chili powder, and substitute jalapeño Jack for the cheddar.

Omit the red bell pepper, and add ½ cup frozen chopped spinach, thawed and squeezed dry.

1. Combine 1 cup water, milk, rice, paprika, and mustard in a saucepan, and stir well. Bring to a boil over medium-high heat, stirring occasionally. Cover the pan, reduce the heat to low, and cook for 15 to 18 minutes, or until liquid is absorbed and rice is tender. Remove the pan from the heat, and set aside.

2. While rice cooks, heat butter in a small skillet over medium-high heat. Add scallions and red pepper and cook, stirring frequently, for 5 minutes, or until vegetables soften.

3. Whisk eggs and thyme in a mixing bowl, and stir in rice, vegetable mixture, and cheese. Season to taste with salt and pepper, and mix well. Scrape mixture into a 9 x 13-inch pan, and refrigerate for at least 1 hour, or until well chilled.

4. Place breadcrumbs in a shallow bowl. Make mixture into 1½-inch balls, roll balls in breadcrumbs, and repeat until all of rice mixture is used.

5. Heat oil in a deep-sided saucepan or deep-fryer to a temperature of 375°F. Preheat the oven to 150°F, and line a baking sheet with paper towels.

6. Add rice balls, being careful not to crowd the pan. Cook rice balls for 3 to 4 minutes, or until browned. Remove balls from the pan with a slotted spoon, and drain well on paper towel–lined baking sheet. Keep fried rice balls warm in the oven while frying remaining balls. Serve immediately, accompanied by a bowl of Herbed Tomato Sauce for dipping.

Note: The rice balls can be prepared for frying up to 1 day in advance and refrigerated, tightly covered. They can also be fried in advance; reheat them in a 400°F oven for 5 to 7 minutes, or until hot and crusty again.

Rice is an ancient and venerable grain that has been cultivated since at least 5000 BCE. Archaeological explorations in China have uncovered sealed pots of rice that are almost 8,000 years old. Today, rice is a staple for half the world's population in parts of China, India, Japan, and Southeast Asia as well as in Latin America.

Corn Fritters

Makes 4 to 6 servings

Active time:
25 minutes

Start to finish:
25 minutes

VARIATIONS

Omit the scallions, garlic, cilantro, and coriander; add an additional 1 tablespoon granulated sugar. Serve them for breakfast with heated pure maple syrup.

Omit the cilantro and coriander, and add ¼ cup chopped pimiento and 1 teaspoon dried sage.

Crispy corn fritters are a wonderful hors d'oeuvre or side dish, and they are as at home on the breakfast table as the dinner table. The cornmeal in the recipe adds even more corn flavor.

1 pound whole corn kernels (either cut fresh from the cob or frozen and thawed; do not use canned corn)

2 large eggs

3 scallions, white parts only, chopped

1 garlic clove, minced

3 tablespoons chopped fresh cilantro

1 cup all-purpose flour

¼ cup yellow cornmeal

1 tablespoon granulated sugar

3 teaspoons baking powder

2 teaspoons ground coriander

Salt and freshly ground black pepper to taste

3 cups vegetable oil for frying

For dipping:

1 cup Southern Barbecue Sauce (see recipe page 39) or purchased barbecue sauce, heated

1. Place corn in a saucepan, and cover with salted water. Bring to a boil over high heat, and cook for 2 minutes. Drain, and place corn in a blender or in a food processor. Add eggs, and puree until smooth. Scrape mixture into a mixing bowl.

2. Stir scallions, garlic, and cilantro into corn. Combine flour, cornmeal, sugar, baking powder, coriander, salt, and pepper in another mixing bowl, and whisk well. Stir dry ingredients into corn mixture, stirring until just combined.

3. Heat oil in a deep-sided saucepan or deep-fryer to a temperature of 375°F. Preheat the oven to 150°F, and line a baking sheet with paper towels.

4. Using a rubber spatula push batter off carefully into hot fat, about 1 tablespoonful at a time. Fry fritters until they are a deep golden brown, turning them in the hot fat to brown both sides. Remove fritters from the pan with a slotted spoon, and drain on paper

towel–lined baking sheet. Keep fritters warm in the oven while frying remaining batter. Serve immediately, accompanied by a bowl of Southern Barbecue Sauce for dipping.

Note: The fritters can be prepared up to 2 days in advance and refrigerated, tightly covered. Reheat in a 375°F oven for 5 to 7 minutes, or until hot and crispy.

Baking powder does not last forever. If you haven't used it in a while, try this test: Mix 2 teaspoons of baking powder with 1 cup of hot tap water. If there's an immediate reaction of fizzing and foaming, the baking powder can be used. If the reaction is delayed or weak, throw the baking powder away and buy a fresh can.

Italian Eggplant Balls

Makes 4 to 6 servings

Active time:
30 minutes

Start to finish:
1½ hours

VARIATIONS

For Sicilian eggplant balls, add ½ cup toasted pine nuts and ½ cup dried currants (soaked in hot water for 10 minutes and then drained) to the eggplant mixture.

For Neapolitan eggplant balls, add ½ cup chopped pitted green or black olives to the eggplant mixture.

I n Southern Italy meat was quite scarce, so cooks invented dishes using eggplant and other vegetables. *Pitticelle di murignani* come from Calabria, the point of Italy's boot.

3 (1-pound) eggplants
2 large eggs
½ cup freshly grated Parmesan
1½ cups seasoned Italian
    breadcrumbs, divided
3 tablespoons chopped fresh parsley
2 tablespoons chopped fresh
    oregano or 2 teaspoons dried
Salt and freshly ground black
    pepper to taste
3 cups vegetable oil for frying

For dipping:
1 cup Herbed Tomato Sauce
    (page 38) or purchased
    marinara sauce, heated

1. Preheat the oven to 450°F, and line a rimmed baking sheet with heavy-duty aluminum foil. Prick eggplants with a meat fork, and bake for 20 minutes. Turn eggplants over and bake for an additional 20 minutes, or until eggplants are totally tender. Remove the pan from the oven, and cut eggplants in half. When cool enough to handle, scrape pulp away from skin, and puree in a food processor, adding juices that have accumulated in the pan. Scrape eggplant into a mixing bowl.

2. Whisk eggs in a mixing bowl, and add eggplant puree, cheese, ½ cup breadcrumbs, parsley, oregano, salt, and pepper. Add more breadcrumbs, if necessary, to form a cohesive dough.

3. Place remaining 1 cup breadcrumbs in a shallow bowl. Make mixture into 1½-inch balls, roll balls in breadcrumbs, and repeat until all of eggplant mixture is used.

4. Heat oil in a deep-sided saucepan or deep-fryer to a temperature of 375°F. Preheat the oven to 150°F, and line a baking sheet with paper towels.

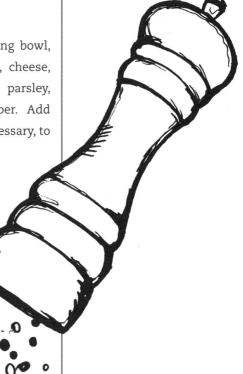

5. Add eggplant balls, being careful not to crowd the pan. Cook eggplant balls for 3 to 4 minutes, or until browned. Remove eggplant balls from the pan with a slotted spoon, and drain well on paper towel–lined baking sheet. Keep fried eggplant balls warm in the oven while frying remaining balls. Serve immediately, accompanied by a bowl of Herbed Tomato Sauce for dipping.

Note: The eggplant balls can be prepared for frying up to 1 day in advance and refrigerated, tightly covered. They can also be fried in advance; reheat them in a 400°F oven for 5 to 7 minutes, or until hot and crusty again.

Eggplants have male and female gender, and the males are preferable since they have fewer seeds and are less bitter in taste. To tell a male from a female, look at the stem end. The male is rounded and has a more even hole, and the female hole is indented.

Tofu Mushroom Balls

Makes 4 to 6 servings

Active time: 25 minutes

Start to finish: 40 minutes

VARIATION

Make the balls with portobello mushrooms for an even earthier flavor.

The meatiness here comes from the sautéed mushrooms. Serve on top of spaghetti.

3 tablespoons olive oil
1 medium onion, diced
3 garlic cloves, minced
2 cups diced mushrooms
Salt and freshly ground black
    pepper to taste
1 (14-ounce) package extra-firm
    tofu, drained and crumbled
1 large egg
¼ cup seasoned Italian breadcrumbs
3 tablespoons chopped fresh parsley
2 tablespoons chopped fresh
    rosemary or 2 teaspoons dried
Vegetable oil spray

For dipping:
1 cup Herbed Tomato Sauce
    (page 38) or purchased
    marinara sauce, heated

1. Preheat the oven to 425°F. Line a rimmed baking sheet with heavy-duty aluminum foil, and spray the foil with vegetable oil spray.

2. Heat oil in a medium skillet over medium-high heat. Add onion and garlic and cook, stirring frequently, for 3 minutes, or until onion is translucent. Add mushrooms, sprinkle with salt and pepper, and cook, stirring frequently, for 5 minutes, or until mushrooms give off water and it then evaporates. Scrape mixture into a mixing bowl, and set aside.

3. Combine tofu, egg, breadcrumbs, parsley, and rosemary in a food processor, and puree. Scrape mixture into the mixing bowl, and season to taste with salt and pepper. Mix well.

4. Make mixture into 1½-inch balls, and arrange balls on the prepared pan. Spray tops of balls with vegetable oil spray.

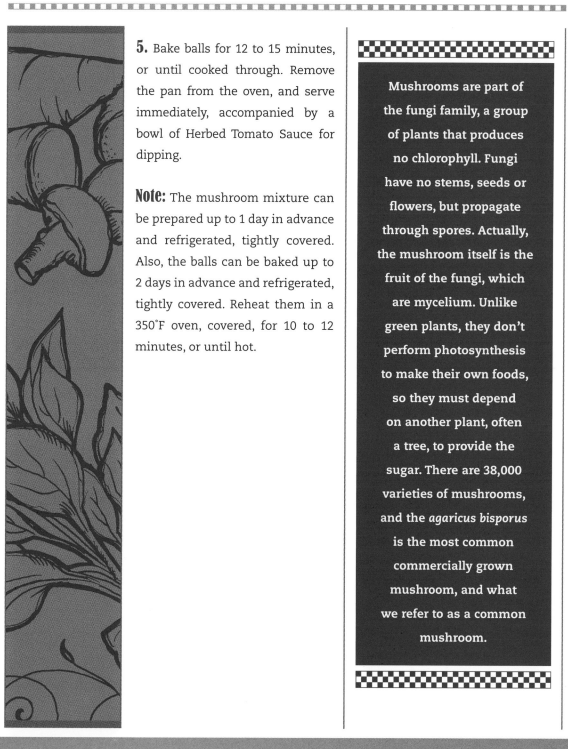

5. Bake balls for 12 to 15 minutes, or until cooked through. Remove the pan from the oven, and serve immediately, accompanied by a bowl of Herbed Tomato Sauce for dipping.

Note: The mushroom mixture can be prepared up to 1 day in advance and refrigerated, tightly covered. Also, the balls can be baked up to 2 days in advance and refrigerated, tightly covered. Reheat them in a 350°F oven, covered, for 10 to 12 minutes, or until hot.

Mushrooms are part of the fungi family, a group of plants that produces no chlorophyll. Fungi have no stems, seeds or flowers, but propagate through spores. Actually, the mushroom itself is the fruit of the fungi, which are mycelium. Unlike green plants, they don't perform photosynthesis to make their own foods, so they must depend on another plant, often a tree, to provide the sugar. There are 38,000 varieties of mushrooms, and the *agaricus bisporus* is the most common commercially grown mushroom, and what we refer to as a common mushroom.

German Sauerkraut Balls

Makes 4 to 6 servings

Active time:

30 minutes

Start to finish:

30 minutes

Add 1 cup chopped ham or cooked sausage, such as smoked kielbasa.

Add ½ cup grated cheese, such as cheddar or smoked cheddar.

Anyone who grew up in the Midwest knows about sauerkraut balls; they are an integral part of many parties and spring from the German tradition. Mashed potatoes hold them together.

1 pound potatoes, peeled

1 pound sauerkraut, drained well

2 large eggs

¾ cup grainy Dijon mustard, divided

3 scallions, white parts and
    2 inches of green tops, chopped

2 tablespoons chopped fresh parsley

1 tablespoon crushed caraway seeds

Salt and freshly ground black
    pepper to taste

1 cup plain breadcrumbs

3 cups vegetable oil for frying

½ cup mayonnaise

½ cup sour cream

1. Dice potatoes into 1-inch cubes, and boil in salted water for 10 to 15 minutes, or until very tender. Drain potatoes, shaking in a colander to get out as much water as possible. Mash potatoes until smooth, and set aside.

2. While potatoes boil, soak sauerkraut in cold water, changing the water every 3 minutes. Drain sauerkraut, pressing with the back of a spoon to extract as much liquid as possible, and coarsely chop sauerkraut.

3. Whisk eggs and ¼ cup mustard in a mixing bowl, and add potatoes, sauerkraut, scallions, parsley, and caraway seeds. Mix well, and season to taste with salt and pepper.

4. Place breadcrumbs in a shallow bowl. Make mixture into 1½-inch balls, roll balls in breadcrumbs, and repeat until all of sauerkraut mixture is used.

It's best to crush large seeds like caraway and fennel before adding them to a dish. The seeds release more flavor crushed, and they can be bitter if eaten whole. The easiest way to crush the seeds is with a mortar and pestle. If you don't have a mortar and pestle, place the seeds into a small, heavy plastic bag and pound them with the back of a small skillet or saucepan. This does the trick.

5. Heat oil in a deep-sided saucepan to a temperature of 375°F. Preheat the oven to 150°F, and line a baking sheet with paper towels.

6. While oil heats, mix remaining ½ cup mustard with mayonnaise and sour cream, and whisk well. Set aside.

7. Add sauerkraut balls, being careful not to crowd the pan. Cook sauerkraut balls for 3 to 4 minutes, or until browned. Remove balls from the pan with a slotted spoon, and drain well on paper towel–lined baking sheet. Keep fried sauerkraut balls warm in the oven while frying remaining balls. Serve immediately, accompanied by the bowl of sauce for dipping.

Note: The sauerkraut balls can be prepared for frying up to 1 day in advance and refrigerated, tightly covered. They can also be fried in advance; reheat them in a 400°F oven for 5 to 7 minutes or until hot and crusty again.

Golden Potato and Onion Balls

Makes 4 to 6 servings

Active time:
30 minutes

Start to finish:
45 minutes

VARIATIONS

Omit the onions, and add ¾ cup grated cheddar, Gruyère, or a smoked cheese.

These are my variation of *gougères*, a French hors d'oeuvre made with cream puff dough. The combination of sweet caramelized onion with potato is one of my favorites, and I serve these with any grilled or broiled entree.

2 tablespoons olive oil

2 tablespoons unsalted butter

2 large onions, diced

Salt and freshly ground black pepper to taste

2 teaspoons granulated sugar

2 pounds red potatoes, scrubbed

½ cup (1 stick) unsalted butter, cut into small cubes

1 cup all-purpose flour

2 large eggs

3 cups vegetable oil for frying

1. Heat oil and butter in a large skillet over medium heat. Add onions, and toss to coat. Cover the pan, and cook onions for 10 minutes, stirring occasionally. Sprinkle onions with salt, pepper, and sugar, and raise the heat to medium-high. Cook onions for 15 to 20 minutes, or until browned.

2. While onions cook, dice potatoes into 1-inch cubes, and boil in salted water for 10 to 15 minutes, or

until very tender. Drain potatoes, shaking in a colander to get out as much water as possible. Mash potatoes until smooth, and set aside.

3. Place 1 cup water in a saucepan, and bring to a boil over high heat. Add butter, and stir until melted. Add flour, and whisk until mixture comes together and leaves the

sides of the pan. Remove the pan from the stove and beat in eggs, 1 at a time, whisking well between each addition; this can be done in a food processor fitted with the steel blade.

4. Scrape mixture into a mixing bowl, and beat in potatoes and onions. Season to taste with salt and pepper, and roll mixture into 1-inch balls.

5. Heat oil in a deep-sided saucepan to a temperature of 375°F. Preheat the oven to 150°F, and line a baking sheet with paper towels.

6. Add potato balls, being careful not to crowd the pan. Cook potato balls for 3 to 4 minutes, or until browned. Remove balls from the pan with a slotted spoon, and drain well on paper towel–lined baking sheet. Keep fried potato balls warm in the oven while frying remaining balls. Serve immediately.

Note: The potato balls can be prepared for frying up to 1 day in advance and refrigerated, tightly covered. They can also be fried in advance; reheat them in a 400°F oven for 5 to 7 minutes, or until hot and crusty again.

The ancient Incas first started cultivating potatoes thousands of years ago, and the first conquistadors exported the tubers to Europe. Potatoes were not popular, however, until Sir Walter Raleigh planted them on his estate in Ireland in the eighteenth century.

Cheese-Spinach Balls

Makes 4 to 6 servings

Active time:
25 minutes

Start to finish:
40 minutes

Replace the spinach with finely chopped broccoli or asparagus.

Make these balls with cheddar instead of Parmesan.

These baked balls are a classic hors d'oeuvre. I serve them with a blue cheese sauce.

1 (10-ounce) package frozen chopped spinach, thawed

6 tablespoons (¾ stick) unsalted butter

1 medium onion, chopped

2 garlic cloves, minced

3 large eggs

¾ cup freshly grated Parmesan

2 tablespoons chopped fresh parsley

1 tablespoon fresh thyme or 1 teaspoon dried

1 cup seasoned Italian breadcrumbs, divided

Salt and freshly ground black pepper to taste

Vegetable oil spray

For dipping:

1 cup Blue Cheese Sauce (page 41) or purchased blue cheese dressing

1. Preheat the oven to 425°F. Line a rimmed baking sheet with heavy-duty aluminum foil, and spray the foil with vegetable oil spray. Place spinach in a colander and press with the back of a spoon to extract as much liquid as possible. Set aside.

2. Heat butter in a small skillet over medium-high heat. Add onion and garlic and cook, stirring frequently, for 3 minutes, or until onion is translucent. Set aside.

3. Whisk eggs well, and stir in spinach, onion mixture, cheese, parsley, thyme, ½ cup breadcrumbs, salt, and pepper. Mix well.

4. Place remaining ½ cup breadcrumbs in a shallow bowl, make mixture into 1½-inch balls, roll balls in breadcrumbs, and arrange spinach balls on the prepared pan. Spray tops of spinach balls with vegetable oil spray.

5. Bake spinach balls for 12 to 15 minutes, or until cooked through. Remove the pan from the oven, and serve immediately, accompanied by a bowl of Blue Cheese Sauce for dipping.

Note: The spinach mixture can be prepared up to 1 day in advance and refrigerated, tightly covered. Also, the balls can be baked up to 2 days in advance and refrigerated, tightly covered. Reheat them in a 350°F oven, covered, for 10 to 12 minutes, or until hot.

The best place to store eggs is in their cardboard carton. The carton helps prevent moisture loss, and it shields the eggs from absorbing odors from other foods. If you're not sure if your eggs are fresh, submerge them in a bowl of cool water. If they stay on the bottom, they're fine. If they float to the top, it shows they're old because eggs develop an air pocket at one end as they age.

Herbed Cheese Balls

Makes 4 to 6
servings

Active time:
20 minutes

Start to finish:
55 minutes,
including 30
minutes to chill

This is another "master recipe" from which endless variations can be made. I serve these little balls with a choice of crackers for spreading or with very thin carrot or celery sticks so guests can use them like toothpicks.

2 (8-ounce) packages cream cheese,
    softened
4 tablespoons unsalted butter,
    softened
½ cup chopped pimiento-stuffed
    green olives
3 scallions, white parts and
    2 inches of green tops, chopped
2 garlic cloves, minced
2 tablespoons Worcestershire sauce
2 teaspoons herbes de Provence
Salt and crushed red pepper flakes
    to taste
½ cup chopped fresh parsley

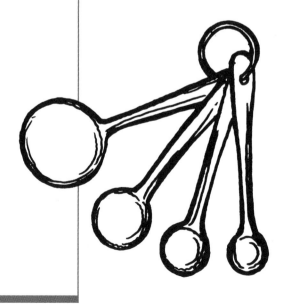

VARIATIONS

Add ½ cup chopped salami or other sausage instead of olives, and substitute horseradish for the Worcestershire sauce.

Roll the balls in toasted sesame seeds. Substitute soy sauce for the Worcestershire sauce and chopped rehydrated shiitake mushrooms for the olives.

Add ½ cup chopped pimiento in place of the olives, substitute bottled salsa for the Worcestershire sauce, and use ground cumin in place of the herbes de Provence.

1. Combine cream cheese and butter, and beat at medium speed with an electric mixer until light and fluffy. Stir in olives, scallions, garlic, Worcestershire sauce, and herbes de Provence, and mix well. Season to taste with salt and red pepper flakes and mix well again.

2. Make mixture into 1-inch balls. Roll balls in parsley. Refrigerate balls for at least 30 minutes before serving.

Note: The balls can be prepared up to 1 day in advance and refrigerated, tightly covered with plastic wrap.

The easiest way to soften cream cheese is in the microwave; take it out of the foil wrapper, cut it into 1 tablespoon amounts, and microwave the cream cheese at 20 percent power for 20 seconds. Repeat, if necessary.

Pesto-Pine Nut Cheese Balls

Makes 6 to 8 servings

Active time: 25 minutes

Start to finish: 55 minutes, including 30 minutes to chill

VARIATIONS

Replace the pesto with ½ cup sun-dried tomatoes packed in olive oil. Drain and puree the tomatoes.

Spoon the cheese into hollowed out cherry tomatoes, garnishing the tomatoes with the pine nuts.

These balls can be made in a matter of minutes with pesto sauce from the refrigerated aisle of the supermarket. These are so pretty when you put them out for guests, and because they're individual there's no messy look to the platter after some are gone as there is with a large cheese ball.

1 cup pine nuts, divided
2 garlic cloves, peeled
1 cup firmly packed fresh basil leaves
¼ cup olive oil
1 (8-ounce) package cream cheese, softened
Salt and freshly ground black pepper to taste

1. Preheat the oven to 350°F. Toast ¾ cup pine nuts for 5 to 7 minutes, or until lightly browned. Remove nuts from the oven, and set aside.

2. Combine remaining ¼ cup pine nuts, garlic, basil, and olive oil in a food processor, and puree until smooth. Scrape mixture into a mixing bowl, and add cream cheese. Blend until well combined, and season to taste with salt and pepper.

3. Roll mixture into ¾-inch balls, and then roll balls in toasted pine nuts, pressing gently so pine nuts adhere. Chill balls for a minimum of 30 minutes, then serve.

Note: The balls can be prepared up to 1 day in advance and refrigerated, tightly covered with plastic wrap.

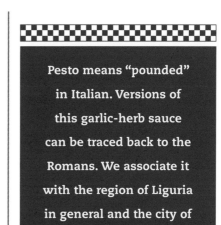

Pesto means "pounded" in Italian. Versions of this garlic-herb sauce can be traced back to the Romans. We associate it with the region of Liguria in general and the city of Genoa in particular, but the first recipe appeared in a Florentine cookbook in 1848.

The Final Round:

Desserts

This chapter stretches the definition of "meatball" to new meanings, but there are so many wonderful sweet things that are "ground and round" that it make sense to end this book on a sweet note.

These quick and easy-to-make recipes include homemade chocolate truffles, baby cream puffs filled with ice cream, baked and unbaked cookies, and some sweet fritters, which are bits of fried batter to be enjoyed hot. While many of these recipes are distinctly American, some come from cuisines around the world.

The key to the success in the recipes that use chocolate is to buy high-quality chocolate since it plays a starring role. While I like imported chocolate sold in big hunks, there are many excellent domestic brands now available. Look for a chocolate that contains at least 60 percent cocoa.

Basic Chocolate Truffles

Makes 3 dozen

**Active time:
30 minutes**

**Start to finish: 4½
hours, including
4 hours to chill**

VARIATIONS

*Instead of cocoa
powder, coat the
truffles in toasted
coconut, finely
chopped nuts,
or colored candy
sprinkles.*

*Add 2 to 4
tablespoons liquor
or liqueur to the
truffle mixture.*

*Add 1 to 2
tablespoons instant
coffee powder or
instant espresso
powder to make
mocha truffles.*

Once you learn how easy it is to make these truffles, you'll never buy those expensive ones again. See the many variations for making truffles in your favorite flavors—from coconut to espresso to orange.

1 pound good-quality bittersweet
    chocolate
1¼ cups heavy cream
Pinch of salt
½ cup unsweetened cocoa powder

Add 1 tablespoon grated orange zest to the mixture.

Form truffles around a small nut, such as a hazelnut or a peanut.

Coat truffles in dark chocolate or white chocolate or some combination of the two. To do this, melt chopped chocolate in a mixing bowl set over simmering water, or place chopped chocolate in a microwave safe bowl and microwave on 100% (HIGH) for 20 seconds, stir, and repeat as necessary until chocolate is smooth and melted. Place a small amount of melted chocolate in the palm of your hand, and roll formed balls in the chocolate.

1. Break chocolate into pieces no larger than a lima bean. Either chop chocolate in a food processor using on-and-off pulsing, or place it in a heavy resealable plastic bag, and smash it with the back of a heavy skillet.

2. Heat cream in a saucepan over medium heat, stirring frequently, until mixture comes to a simmer. Stir in salt, and add chocolate. Remove the pan from the heat, cover the pan, and allow chocolate to melt for 5 minutes. Whisk mixture until smooth, and transfer to a 9 x 9-inch baking pan. Chill mixture for at least 4 hours, or overnight.

3. Place cocoa powder in a shallow bowl. Using the large side of a melon baller, scoop out 2 teaspoons mixture, and gently form it into a ball. Roll balls in cocoa, and then refrigerate on a platter for 30 minutes to set cocoa.

Note: The truffles can be made up to 1 week in advance, and refrigerated, tightly covered with plastic wrap or in an airtight container. Allow them to sit at room temperature for 1 hour before serving.

Cold hands makes shaping the truffles easy. Keep a bowl of ice water and a roll of paper towels handy while rolling the truffles. Submerge your hands in the water until they are very cold. Then dry them and roll some truffles, repeating as necessary.

Chocolate Goat Cheese Truffles

Makes 4 dozen

Active time:
30 minutes

Start to finish: 2 hours, including 1½ hours to chill

VARIATIONS

Add 2 tablespoons of your favorite liqueur or liquor.

Roll the balls in shaved white chocolate instead of cocoa.

The sharpness of goat cheese balances the sweetness of the chocolate for these unusual confections.

½ *pound good-quality bittersweet chocolate, chopped or shaved*
½ *pound fresh goat cheese*
¼ *cup confectioners' sugar*
½ *teaspoon pure vanilla extract*
½ *cup unsweetened cocoa powder*

1. Break chocolate into pieces no larger than a lima bean. Either chop chocolate in a food processor using on-and-off pulsing, or place it in a heavy resealable plastic bag, and smash it with the back of a heavy skillet.

2. Melt chopped chocolate in a mixing bowl set over simmering water, or place chopped chocolate in a microwave safe bowl and microwave on 100% (HIGH) for 20 seconds, stir, and repeat as necessary until chocolate is smooth and melted.

3. Combine goat cheese, confectioners' sugar, and vanilla in a mixing bowl and beat at medium speed with an electric mixer until light and fluffy; this can also be done in a food processor. Slowly add chocolate, and beat until well mixed. Scrape mixture into a 9 x 9-inch baking pan, and refrigerate for at least 1 hour, or until firm.

4. Place cocoa powder in a shallow bowl. Using the large side of a melon baller, scoop out 2 teaspoons mixture, and gently form it into a ball. Roll balls in cocoa, and then refrigerate for 30 minutes to set cocoa.

Note: The truffles can be made up to 1 week in advance, and refrigerated, tightly covered with plastic wrap or in an airtight container. Allow them to sit at room temperature for 1 hour before serving.

Cocoa powder has a tendency to become lumpy when exposed to humidity, so sift the cocoa or shake it through a fine-meshed sieve before using it. Those little lumps are difficult to remove otherwise.

Extra-Chocolaty Truffles

Makes 2½ dozen

Active time:
30 minutes

Start to finish: 4½
hours, including
4 hours to chill

VARIATIONS

Use milk chocolate in place of bittersweet chocolate.

Add ½ cup chopped toasted nuts to the mixture.

These truffles are for those who like chocolate, but not too much sugar in their confections. Adding unsweetened cocoa powder to the mix increases the intense chocolate flavor.

½ pound good-quality bittersweet chocolate
½ cup heavy whipping cream
4 tablespoons (½ stick) unsalted butter, cut into small pieces
Pinch of salt
⅔ cup unsweetened cocoa powder, divided

1. Break chocolate into pieces no larger than a lima bean. Either chop chocolate in a food processor using on-and-off pulsing, or place it in a heavy resealable plastic bag, and smash it with the back of a heavy skillet.

2. Heat cream and butter in a saucepan over medium heat, stirring frequently, until mixture comes to a simmer. Stir in salt, and add chocolate and ¼ cup cocoa. Remove the pan from the heat, cover the pan, and allow chocolate to melt for 5 minutes. Whisk mixture until smooth, and transfer to a 9 x 9-inch baking pan. Chill mixture for at least 4 hours, or overnight.

3. Place remaining cocoa powder in a shallow bowl. Using the large side of a melon baller, scoop out 2 teaspoons mixture, and gently form it into a ball. Roll balls in cocoa, and then refrigerate for 30 minutes to set cocoa.

Note: The truffles can be made up to 1 week in advance, and refrigerated, tightly covered with plastic wrap or in an airtight container. Allow them to sit at room temperature for 1 hour before serving.

> When cooking, use butter that comes in sticks, not whipped butter sold in tubs. The air incorporated into whipped butter will throw off the recipe's measurements.

White Chocolate Almond Truffles

Makes 2½ dozen

Active time:
30 minutes

Start to finish: 4½ hours, including 4 hours to chill

Delicate almonds and creamy white chocolate are a winning combination in these easy to make truffles. Natural almond butter can be found in many supermarkets and health food stores.

1 pound good-quality white chocolate
1 cup whipping cream
1 cup natural almond butter
½ cup granulated sugar
Pinch of salt
1 cup blanched almonds

VARIATIONS

Use dark chocolate or milk chocolate instead of white chocolate.

Coat truffles in melted chocolate instead of nuts.

For peanut truffles, use natural peanut butter and chopped peanuts or commercial peanut butter and then omit the sugar from the recipe.

Wrap the truffle filling around a nut.

1. Break chocolate into pieces no larger than a lima bean. Either chop chocolate in a food processor using on-and-off pulsing, or place it in a heavy resealable plastic bag, and smash it with the back of a heavy skillet.

2. Heat cream, almond butter, sugar, and salt in a saucepan over medium heat, stirring frequently, until mixture comes to a simmer. Stir in chocolate. Remove the pan from the heat, cover the pan, and allow chocolate to melt for 5 minutes. Whisk mixture until smooth, and transfer to a 9 x 9-inch baking pan. Chill mixture for at least 4 hours, or overnight.

3. While mixture chills, preheat the oven to 350°F. Place almonds on a baking sheet, and toast for 5 to 7 minutes, or until lightly browned. Remove the pan from the oven, and finely chop almonds in a food processor using on-and-off pulsing, or by hand. Set aside.

4. Place chopped almonds in a shallow bowl. Using the large side of a melon baller, scoop out 2 teaspoons mixture, and gently form it into a ball. Roll balls in cocoa, and then refrigerate for 30 minutes or until firm.

Note: The truffles can be made up to 1 week in advance, and refrigerated, tightly covered with plastic wrap or in an airtight container. Allow them to sit at room temperature for 1 hour before serving.

Actually ivory in color, white chocolate is technically not chocolate at all; it is made from cocoa butter, sugar, and flavoring. It is difficult to work with and should only be used in recipes that are specifically developed for it. While other chocolate can be substituted for it, do not use white chocolate in lieu of dark chocolate in baking.

Booze-Laced Balls

Makes 5 dozen

Active time:
30 minutes

Start to finish: 4½ hours, including 4 hours to chill

VARIATIONS

Use rum instead of bourbon.

Use Frangelico instead of bourbon; hazelnuts rather than pecans. These can be made with or without the cocoa.

Use Grand Marnier instead of bourbon, omit the cocoa, and add 1 tablespoon grated orange zest.

These unbaked balls, popular at the holiday season for generations, are made from crushed cookies and have some sort of spirit or liqueur added to them.

1 cup pecan halves
1½ cups confectioners' sugar, divided
¼ cup unsweetened cocoa powder
½ cup bourbon
2 tablespoons light corn syrup
2½ cups finely crushed vanilla wafers

Add 1 cup finely chopped bittersweet chocolate or miniature chocolate chips.

Roll balls in additional finely chopped nuts instead of confectioners' sugar.

Use ginger snaps or crushed chocolate cookies instead of vanilla wafers.

Omit the cocoa, use rum and add ¾ cup toasted coconut.

Add ½ teaspoon ground cinnamon or apple pie spice.

Add ¾ cup finely chopped raisins or other dried fruit.

1. Preheat the oven to 350°F. Place pecans on a baking sheet, and toast for 5 to 7 minutes, or until lightly browned. Remove the pan from the oven, and finely chop nuts in a food processor using on-and-off pulsing, or by hand. Set aside.

2. Sift 1 cup sugar and cocoa powder into a mixing bowl, and whisk in bourbon and corn syrup. Stir in cookie crumbs and chopped nuts, and mix well. Refrigerate mixture for 30 minutes.

3. Sift remaining sugar into a low bowl. Make mixture into 1-inch balls, and roll balls in the sugar to coat evenly. Refrigerate balls for a minimum of 4 hours.

Note: The balls can be stored refrigerated up to 2 weeks. Place them in an airtight container with sheets of plastic wrap in between the layers.

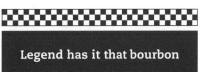

Legend has it that bourbon balls were first made before World War II in Kentucky, where, of course, bourbon was used. The "inventor" of mixing candy with bourbon was Ruth Hanly Booe, who, along with other former teacher Rebecca Gooch, began a candy company in Frankfort, Kentucky, in 1919.

Chocolate Kahlúa Balls

Makes 4 dozen

Active time:
30 minutes

Start to finish: 4½ hours, including 4 hours to chill

I ate confections similar to these in Hawaii a few years ago, and couldn't wait to come home to replicate them on this side of the Pacific. The combination of chocolate with coconut and laced with heady liqueur is a grown-up delight.

1 cup macadamia nuts
1½ cups shredded sweetened coconut
6 ounces good quality bittersweet chocolate
½ cup evaporated milk
Pinch of salt
2½ cups chocolate cookie crumbs
½ cup confectioners' sugar
½ cup Kahlúa liqueur
½ teaspoon pure vanilla extract

Use crushed ginger snap cookies or crushed vanilla cookies instead of chocolate cookie crumbs.

Use Grand Marnier and add ½ cup finely chopped dried apricots.

Use almonds, pecans, or hazelnuts rather than the macadamia nuts.

1. Preheat the oven to 350°F. Place macadamia nuts on a baking sheet, and toast for 5 to 7 minutes, or until lightly browned. Remove the pan from the oven, and finely chop nuts in a food processor using on-and-off pulsing, or by hand. Set aside. Place coconut on another baking pan, and toast for 10 to 12 minutes, or until browned. Remove the pan from the oven, and set aside.

2. Break chocolate into pieces no larger than a lima bean. Either chop chocolate in a food processor using on-and-off pulsing, or place it in a heavy resealable plastic bag, and smash it with the back of a heavy skillet.

3. Heat evaporated milk in a saucepan over medium heat, stirring frequently, until mixture comes to a simmer. Stir in salt, and add chocolate. Remove the pan from the heat, cover the pan, and allow chocolate to melt for 5 minutes.

4. Scrape chocolate mixture into a mixing bowl, and add nuts, cookie crumbs, confectioners' sugar, Kahlúa, and vanilla, and mix well. Refrigerate mixture for 30 minutes.

5. Place coconut in a low bowl. Make mixture into 1-inch balls, and roll balls in the coconut to coat evenly. Refrigerate balls for a minimum of 4 hours.

Note: The balls can be stored refrigerated up to 2 weeks. Place them in an airtight container with sheets of plastic wrap in between the layers.

The Aztecs first discovered chocolate, and our word comes from the Aztec xocolatl, which means "bitter water." Famed King Montezuma believed chocolate was an aphrodisiac and is reported to have consumed some 50 cups a day.

Crispy Peanut Butter Balls

Makes 2 dozen

Active time:
10 minutes

Start to finish:
40 minutes,
including 30
minutes to chill

The granola you choose to make these healthful snack balls changes the nature of the mixture. My favorite mixture contains nuts as well as dried cranberries.

½ cup peanut butter

3 tablespoons honey

2 cups granola cereal

2 to 4 tablespoons freshly squeezed
    orange juice

1 tablespoon grated orange zest

Vegetable oil spray

VARIATIONS

Use milk instead of orange juice, omit the orange zest, and add ½ teaspoon ground cinnamon to the peanut butter and honey mixture before adding the cereal.

Substitute almond butter for the peanut butter. If using natural almond butter, add ½ cup confectioners' sugar.

Add ¾ cup chopped dried fruit.

Add ¾ cup miniature chocolate chips or butterscotch chips.

1. Whisk peanut butter and honey in mixing bowl until smooth. Add granola, orange juice, and orange zest, and stir with a strong spatula until mixed well. Add additional orange juice, if necessary, so mixture stays together.

2. Spray your hands with vegetable oil spray. Make mixture into 1½-inch balls, and arrange balls on a baking sheet. Refrigerate for a minimum of 30 minutes.

Note: The balls can be stored refrigerated up to 1 week. Place them in an airtight container with sheets of plastic wrap in between the layers.

Peanuts, which are actually a legume and not a nut, are used in cuisines around the world, but peanut butter is an American invention, developed in 1890 and first promoted as a health food at the 1904 World's Fair in St. Louis.

Caramel Popcorn Balls

Makes 3 dozen

Active time:
15 minutes

Start to finish:
45 minutes,
including 30
minutes to chill

VARIATIONS

Substitute 1 cup chopped toasted nuts for 1 cup popped popcorn.

Add ½ cup chopped dried fruit to the mixture.

Substitute ground ginger for the cinnamon.

Children of all ages adore these. Make them any size you want. I've made them very large, wrapped them in cellophane, and hung them on my Christmas tree as edible ornaments. They were given as favors to guests as they left my holiday party.

1 cup firmly packed light brown sugar
½ cup water
½ cup light corn syrup
2 tablespoons unsalted butter
4 cups miniature marshmallows
½ teaspoon ground cinnamon
10 cups hot, salted popcorn
Vegetable oil spray

1. Combine sugar, water, and corn syrup in a saucepan, and bring to a boil over medium-high heat. Swirl the pan by the handle but do not stir. Allow syrup to cook until it reaches a walnut brown color, swirling the pot by the handle frequently.

2. Remove the pan from the heat, and stir in butter, marshmallows, and cinnamon. Return the pan to low heat and stir until lumps have melted and sauce is smooth.

3. Place popcorn in a large mixing bowl; go over it and discard any kernels that did not pop. Pour caramel mixture over popcorn, and stir with a heavy spatula to coat kernels evenly.

4. Spray your hands with vegetable oil spray. Make mixture into 3-inch balls, and arrange balls on a baking sheet. Refrigerate for a minimum of 30 minutes.

Note: The balls can be stored refrigerated up to 1 week. Place them in an airtight container with sheets of plastic wrap in between the layers.

Cinnamon, the inner bark of a tropical evergreen tree, is harvested during the rainy season, allowed to dry, and then sold as sticks or ground into powder. What we call cinnamon is cassia cinnamon, and there's also a Ceylon cinnamon that is less pungent.

Dried Fruit Coconut Balls

Makes 2½ dozen

- - - - - - - - - - - - - - - - - - -

Active time:
25 minutes

- - - - - - - - - - - - - - - - - - -

Start to finish:
55 minutes,
including 30
minutes to chill

VARIATIONS

Use any
combination
of dried fruits.

Substitute any
variety of nut.

Substitute
crushed ginger
snaps for the
graham cracker
crumbs.

Not all calories are created equal, and the fat calories in these treats are monounsaturated from the nuts, so they can be eaten without much guilt. The combination of fruits along with the sweet honey is really satisfying.

1 cup cashew pieces

1½ cups shredded sweetened coconut

½ cup finely chopped dried apricots

½ cup dried currants

½ cup finely chopped dried dates

½ cup graham cracker crumbs

⅓ cup honey

Vegetable oil spray

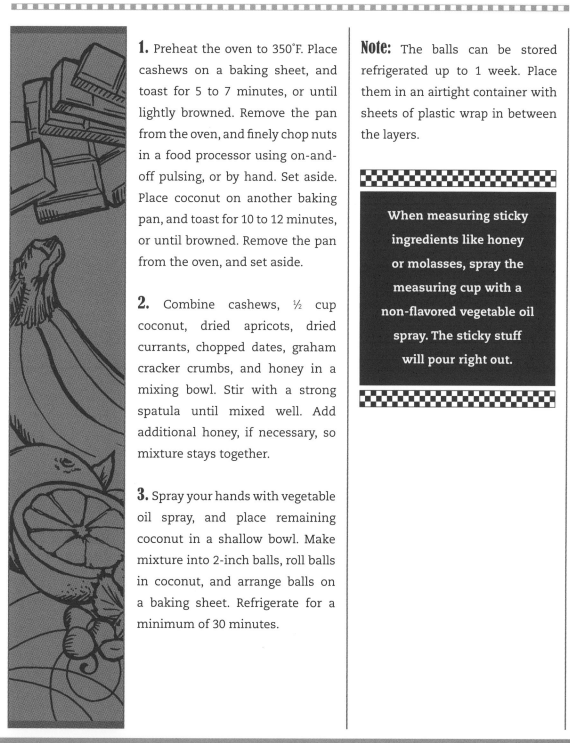

1. Preheat the oven to 350°F. Place cashews on a baking sheet, and toast for 5 to 7 minutes, or until lightly browned. Remove the pan from the oven, and finely chop nuts in a food processor using on-and-off pulsing, or by hand. Set aside. Place coconut on another baking pan, and toast for 10 to 12 minutes, or until browned. Remove the pan from the oven, and set aside.

2. Combine cashews, ½ cup coconut, dried apricots, dried currants, chopped dates, graham cracker crumbs, and honey in a mixing bowl. Stir with a strong spatula until mixed well. Add additional honey, if necessary, so mixture stays together.

3. Spray your hands with vegetable oil spray, and place remaining coconut in a shallow bowl. Make mixture into 2-inch balls, roll balls in coconut, and arrange balls on a baking sheet. Refrigerate for a minimum of 30 minutes.

Note: The balls can be stored refrigerated up to 1 week. Place them in an airtight container with sheets of plastic wrap in between the layers.

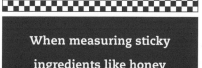

When measuring sticky ingredients like honey or molasses, spray the measuring cup with a non-flavored vegetable oil spray. The sticky stuff will pour right out.

Hazelnut Balls

Makes 4 dozen

Active time:
20 minutes

Start to finish:
45 minutes

Buttery, aromatic hazelnuts are my favorite. They perfume as well as flavor these delicious cookies.

1½ cups skinned hazelnuts

1 cup (2 sticks) unsalted butter, softened

1 teaspoon pure vanilla extract

2 cups confectioners' sugar, divided

2¼ cups all-purpose flour

Pinch of salt

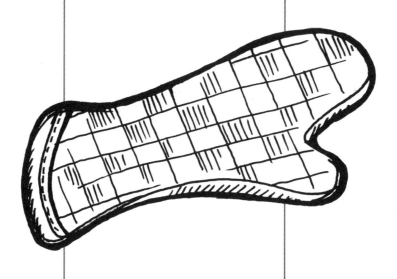

VARIATIONS

Omit the vanilla and add 1 tablespoon grated lemon zest.

Add finely chopped white chocolate.

Rather than hazelnuts, use chopped almonds, peanuts, or cashews.

Instead of nuts, use 1 cup chopped apricots, candied cherries, or some combination of dried and candied fruits.

1. Preheat the oven to 350°F, and grease 2 baking sheets with butter or shortening. Place hazelnuts on a baking sheet, and toast for 5 to 7 minutes, or until lightly browned. Remove the pan from the oven, and finely chop nuts in a food processor using on-and-off pulsing, or by hand. Set aside.

2. Combine butter, vanilla, and ⅔ cup sugar in a mixing bowl, and beat at medium speed with an electric mixer until light and fluffy. Reduce the speed to low, and add flour and salt. Beat until just combined. Stir in chopped nuts.

3. Form dough into ¾-inch balls, and place them 1 inch apart on the prepared baking sheets. Bake for 15 to 18 minutes, or until firm. Remove the pans from the oven.

4. Sift remaining confectioners' sugar into a low bowl, and add a few cookies at a time, rolling them around in the sugar to coat them well. Transfer cookies to a rack to cool completely.

Note: The cookies can be stored in an airtight container at room temperature up to 3 days, or they can be frozen up to 3 months.

The skins of hazelnuts are bitter and must be removed before using them. Look for hazelnuts that are already skinned. If you can't find them, arrange hazelnuts in a single layer on a baking sheet. Bake them at 350°F for 25 minutes; watch them so they don't burn. Pour the hot nuts in a tea towel and rub them back and forth until the skins come off.

Mocha Balls

Makes 3 dozen

Active time:
20 minutes

Start to finish:
45 minutes

VARIATIONS

For coffee cookies, increase the instant espresso powder to 2 tablespoons and omit the cocoa.

For an intensely flavored cookie, increase the instant espresso powder to 1½ tablespoons and increase the cocoa to ¼ cup.

Whoever came up with the glorious combination of chocolate and coffee for a flavor dubbed mocha should have a special place in cooks' heaven. If you're a mocha fan, then these cookies are for you.

1 tablespoon instant espresso powder

2 tablespoons boiling water

8 tablespoons (1 stick) unsalted butter, softened and cut into small pieces

⅓ cup granulated sugar

1 large egg

½ teaspoon pure vanilla extract

3 tablespoons unsweetened cocoa powder

1⅓ cups all-purpose flour

Pinch of salt

1 cup confectioners' sugar

1. Preheat the oven to 350°F, and grease 2 baking sheets with butter. Combine coffee powder and water in a small bowl, and stir well to dissolve coffee. Set aside.

2. Combine butter and sugar in a mixing bowl, and beat at medium speed with an electric mixer until light and fluffy. Add egg and vanilla, and beat well. Add cocoa powder and coffee mixture, and beat well, scraping the sides of the bowl as necessary. Reduce the speed to low, and add flour and salt. Beat until just combined.

3. Form dough into 1-inch balls, and place them 1 inch apart on the prepared baking sheets. Bake for 15 to 18 minutes, or until firm. Remove the pans from the oven.

4. Sift confectioners' sugar into a low bowl, and add a few cookies at a time, rolling them around in the sugar to coat them well. Transfer cookies to a rack to cool completely.

Note: The cookies can be stored in an airtight container at room temperature up to 3 days, or they can be frozen up to 3 months.

Instant espresso powder, imported from Italy, is becoming easier to find in North America. It's made from real espresso coffee, which is then dehydrated and ground. Look for it in the supermarket near other instant coffees.

Mexican Wedding Cookies

Makes 3 dozen

Active time:
20 minutes

Start to finish:
45 minutes

VARIATION

Use pecans or walnuts in place of the almonds. Toast them in a 350°F oven for 5 to 7 minutes before chopping them.

Sometimes called *polvarones*, these rich and buttery cookies are similar to shortbread. In Mexico they are made with lard, but I prefer unsalted butter.

½ *pound (2 sticks) unsalted butter, softened*
1¾ *cups confectioners' sugar, divided*
1 *cup cake flour*
1 *cup self-rising flour*
1 *cup blanched almonds, very finely chopped*
½ *teaspoon pure vanilla extract*

1. Preheat the oven to 350°F. Grease 2 baking sheets with butter.

2. Place butter in a mixing bowl with 1¼ cups sugar, and beat well at medium speed with an electric mixer until light and fluffy. Add cake flour, self-rising flour, almonds, and vanilla to the bowl, and mix briefly until just combined. The dough will be very stiff; add a few drops of hot water, if necessary, to make it pliable.

3. Form dough into ¾-inch balls, and place them 1 inch apart on the prepared baking sheets. Bake for 15 to 18 minutes, or until firm. Remove the pans from the oven.

4. Sift remaining sugar into a low bowl, and add a few cookies at a time, rolling them around in the sugar to coat them well. Transfer cookies to a rack to cool completely.

Note: The cookies can be stored in an airtight container at room temperature up to 3 days, or they can be frozen up to 3 months.

If your butter is too cold to work into dough, don't soften it in the microwave oven. A few seconds too long and you've got a melted mess. Grate cold butter on the large holes of a box grater. It will soften in a matter of minutes.

Banana Fritters

Makes 2 dozen

Active time:
20 minutes

Start to finish:
20 minutes

VARIATIONS

Use any juicy fruit; I've used a combination of banana and mango or pineapple and peaches with fresh raspberries.

Replace 2 tablespoons of milk with rum or a liqueur.

I love dessert fritters with their crispy coating! Serve them with ice cream, whipped cream, or plain—the way they're presented here.

1 large egg
½ cup whole milk
1½ cups chopped ripe bananas
1⅓ cups all-purpose flour
3 tablespoons granulated sugar
1½ teaspoons baking powder
½ teaspoon ground cinnamon
½ teaspoon ground ginger
Pinch of salt
3 cups vegetable oil for frying
Confectioners' sugar for dusting
    the fritters

1. Whisk egg and milk in a mixing bowl, and stir in bananas. Combine flour, sugar, baking powder, cinnamon, ginger, and salt in another mixing bowl, and whisk well. Stir dry ingredients into banana mixture, stirring until just combined.

2. Heat oil in a deep-sided saucepan or deep-fryer to a temperature of 375°F. Preheat the oven to 150°F. Line a baking sheet with paper towels.

3. Using a rubber spatula push batter off carefully into hot fat, about 1 tablespoonful at a time. Fry fritters until they are a deep golden brown, turning them in the hot fat to brown both sides. Remove fritters from the pan with a slotted spoon, and drain on paper towel–lined baking sheet. Keep fritters warm in the oven while frying remaining batter. Serve immediately dusted with confectioners' sugar.

Note: The fritters can be prepared up to 2 days in advance and refrigerated, tightly covered. Reheat in a 375°F oven for 5 to 7 minutes, or until hot and crispy.

> If bananas are too ripe to eat, they are still perfect for cakes or banana breads. But you don't have to use them in baking right at that second. Freeze the bananas in their skins, then defrost and mash them as necessary.

Eggnog Fritters with Maple Sauce

Makes 2 dozen

Active time:
20 minutes

Start to finish:
20 minutes

VARIATIONS

Use Grand Marnier and 2 teaspoons orange zest in place of the brandy and apples.

Want a lighter flavor than maple? Try a fruit puree sauce sweetened with the same flavor as apple pie spice.

Eggnog, flavored with spices and brandy, is not only a holiday treat, it lends flavor to these crispy fritters any time of year.

2 large eggs

1 cup whole milk

¼ cup brandy, divided

1¼ teaspoons pure vanilla extract, divided

2½ cups all-purpose flour

½ cup granulated sugar

2 teaspoons baking powder

1 teaspoon baking soda

1 teaspoon apple pie spice

Pinch of salt

1 cup pure maple syrup

½ teaspoon ground cinnamon

3 cups vegetable oil for frying

1. Whisk eggs, milk, 2 tablespoons brandy, and ¾ teaspoon vanilla in a mixing bowl. Combine flour, sugar, baking powder, baking soda, apple pie spice, and salt in another mixing bowl, and whisk well. Stir dry ingredients into wet ingredients, stirring until just combined.

2. Combine maple syrup, remaining 2 tablespoons brandy, remaining ½ teaspoon vanilla, and cinnamon in a small saucepan, and whisk well. Heat to a simmer, and set aside.

3. Heat oil in a deep-sided saucepan or deep-fryer to a temperature of 375°F. Preheat the oven to 150°F, and line a baking sheet with paper towels.

4. Using a rubber spatula, push batter off carefully into hot fat, about 1 tablespoonful at a time. Fry fritters until they are a deep golden brown, turning them in the hot fat to brown both sides. Remove fritters from the pan with a slotted spoon, and drain on paper towel–lined baking sheet. Keep fritters warm in the oven while frying remaining batter. Serve immediately, passing maple sauce separately.

Note: The fritters can be prepared up to 2 days in advance and refrigerated, tightly covered. Reheat in a 375°F oven for 5 to 7 minutes, or until hot and crispy.

Early New England settlers sweetened foods with maple syrup because expensive white sugar had to be imported. Tapping the sugar maple trees native to North America and cooking syrup from the sap is another skill the Native Americans taught the settlers.

Italian Sweet Ricotta Fritters

Makes 2 dozen

Active time:
20 minutes

Start to finish:
20 minutes

VARIATIONS

Omit the orange zest and add ½ teaspoon ground cinnamon and a pinch of ground nutmeg.

Add ½ cup finely chopped dried fruit to the fritter batter.

Rather than dusting the fritters with confectioners' sugar, drizzle heated honey over the top.

If you live in a neighborhood with an Italian grocery store, see if it carries fresh ricotta cheese; it has a creamy flavor and texture not found in commercial cheeses. These fritters are light and delicious, with just a hint of orange.

4 large eggs
⅓ cup granulated sugar
1 pound ricotta cheese
2 teaspoons grated orange zest
½ teaspoon pure vanilla extract
1 tablespoon baking powder
Pinch of salt
1 cup all-purpose flour
3 cups vegetable oil for frying
½ cup confectioners' sugar

1. Combine eggs, sugar, ricotta, orange zest, and vanilla in the bowl of an electric mixer, and beat at medium speed until smooth. Add baking powder and salt, and mix well. Add flour and mix at low speed until just combined.

2. Heat oil in a deep-sided saucepan or deep-fryer to a temperature of 375°F. Preheat the oven to 150°F, and line a baking sheet with paper towels.

3. Using a rubber spatula, push batter off carefully into hot fat, about 1 tablespoonful at a time. Fry fritters until they are a deep golden brown, turning them in the hot fat to brown both sides. Remove fritters from the pan with a slotted spoon, and drain on paper towel–lined baking sheet. Keep fritters warm in the oven while frying remaining batter. Serve immediately dusted with confectioners' sugar.

Note: The fritters can be prepared up to 2 days in advance and refrigerated, tightly covered. Reheat in a 375°F oven for 5 to 7 minutes, or until hot and crispy.

Ricotta is a fresh cheese with a smooth consistency and a slightly sweet flavor. In Italy, it's made with the whey from cheeses like mozzarella. The name means "recooked," which comes from the fact that the cheese is made by heating the whey.

Profiteroles with Ice Cream and Caramel Sauce

Makes 3 dozen

Active time:

30 minutes

Start to finish:

1 hour

VARIATIONS

Fill them with any flavor of mousse or pudding.

Top them with Chocolate Sauce (page 00) to warm jam.

For a savory version, omit the sugar, add a pinch of freshly ground black pepper, and fill them with egg salad, smoked salmon, or chive cream cheese.

Profiteroles are baby cream puffs filled with ice cream and topped with a sauce or a glaze of chocolate. The dough is called *pâte a choux* in classic French cooking; it's a useful one to have in your repertoire.

1 cup water

6 tablespoons (¾ stick) unsalted butter

2 teaspoons granulated sugar

½ teaspoon salt

¼ teaspoon pure vanilla extract

¾ cup all-purpose flour

5 large eggs, divided

1½ pints ice cream (your favorite flavor), softened

1½ cups Caramel Sauce (page 476) or purchased caramel sauce

1. Preheat the oven to 425° F, and line 2 cookie sheets with parchment paper.

2. Combine water, butter, sugar, salt, and vanilla in a saucepan, and bring to a boil over medium-high heat, stirring occasionally. Remove the pan from the heat, and add flour all at once. Using a wooden paddle or wide wooden spoon, beat flour into the liquid until it is smooth. Then place the saucepan over high heat and beat mixture constantly for 1 to 2 minutes, until it forms a mass that leaves the sides of the pan and begins to film the bottom of it.

3. Transfer mixture to a food processor fitted with the steel blade. Add 4 of the eggs, 1 at a time, beating well between each addition and scraping the sides of the work bowl between each addition. This can also be done by hand.

4. Scrape dough into a pastry bag fitted with a ½-inch round nozzle. Pipe mounds 1-inch in diameter and ½-inch high onto the baking sheets, allowing 2 inches between puffs.

5. Beat remaining egg with a pinch of salt, and brush only tops of dough mounds with a small pastry brush or rub gently with a finger dipped in the egg wash. (Be careful not to drip egg wash onto the baking sheet or egg may prevent dough from puffing.)

6. Bake puffs for 20 to 25 minutes, or until the puffs are golden brown and crusty to the touch. Remove the pans from the oven, and using the tip of a paring knife, cut a slit in the side of each puff to allow steam to escape. Turn off the oven, and place baked puffs back into the oven with the oven door ajar for 5 minutes. Remove puffs, and transfer to a wire rack to cool.

7. To serve, split puffs with a serrated knife, and fill with ice cream. Top puffs with Caramel Sauce, and serve immediately.

Note: The puffs can be made up to 1 day in advance and kept covered at room temperature.

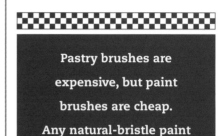

Pastry brushes are expensive, but paint brushes are cheap. Any natural-bristle paint brush can be used as a pastry brush.

Fried Ice Cream Balls

Makes 4 to 6 servings

Active time: 30 minutes

Start to finish: 8½ hours, including a total of 8 hours to chill

VARIATIONS

Roll the balls in crushed puffed rice cereal, graham cracker crumbs, or cookie crumbs Instead of cornflakes.

This is hardly a spur-of-the-moment dessert; the ice cream balls spend many hours freezing between steps, so start preparation the day before you plan to fry and serve them. They are always a hit and are easy to make. The contrast between the crispy coating and chilly ice cream is unique.

1 quart high-quality ice cream
(your choice of flavor), softened
3 large eggs
2 tablespoons granulated sugar
1 teaspoon pure vanilla extract
6 cups cornflakes (about 7 ounces)
4 cups vegetable oil for frying

To serve:
1½ cups Chocolate Sauce (page 478)
or purchased fudge sauce,
heated

1. Line a baking sheet with plastic wrap, and freeze the sheet for 10 minutes. Scoop ice cream with a 1-ounce scoop; you should have 12 balls. Freeze balls, covered with plastic wrap, for at least 3 hours, or until very hard.

2. Combine eggs, sugar, and vanilla in a mixing bowl, and whisk well. Place cornflakes in a food processor fitted with the steel blade, and chop very finely using on-and-off pulsing; this can also be done by placing cornflakes in a heavy resealable plastic bag and hitting the bag with the bottom of a heavy skillet. Place corn flakes in a shallow bowl.

3. Dip balls in egg, allowing excess to drip off, and roll in cornflakes to coat well. Return balls to the freezer, covered, and freeze for at least 1 hour and up to 4 hours. Reserve remaining cornflakes, and

refrigerate remaining egg mixture. Repeat coating process, and freeze for a minimum of 4 hours after second coating.

4. Heat oil in a deep-sided saucepan or deep-fryer to a temperature of 375°F. Working in batches of 2 or 3 balls, fry balls for 30 seconds or until golden. Remove balls from the pan with a slotted spoon, and drain on paper towels. Repeat with remaining balls, and serve immediately, passing a bowl of Chocolate Sauce separately.

Note: The ice cream balls can be made up to 2 days in advance of frying them. Keep them covered with plastic wrap in a single layer in the freezer.

To meet the standards set by the Food and Drug Administration, pure vanilla extract must contain about 1 pound of vanilla beans per gallon, which is why it's twice as expensive as imitation extract. Pure extract is worth the money, considering how little you use. Read the label carefully before you buy.

Caramel Sauce

Makes 3 cups

Active time:
15 minutes

Start to finish:
15 minutes

VARIATION

Decrease the vanilla to ½ teaspoon and add 2 tablespoons brandy, rum, or a liqueur.

Caramel is sugar and water cooked together to a high temperature until syrupy. Once that's done, just add some butter and cream and you've got caramel sauce. Be very careful, however, as the mixture is quite hot.

3 cups granulated sugar

1 cup water

6 tablespoons (¾ stick) unsalted butter, cut into small pieces

2 cups heavy cream

2 teaspoons pure vanilla extract

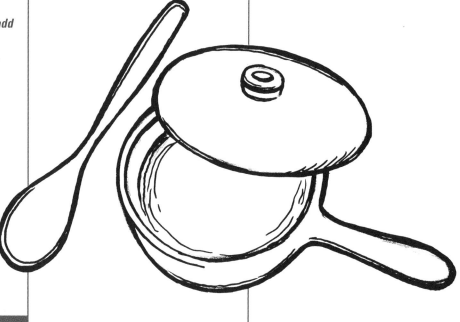

1. Combine sugar and water in a 2-quart saucepan, and bring to a boil over medium-high heat. Swirl the pan by the handle but do not stir. Raise the heat to high, and allow syrup to cook until it reaches a walnut brown color, swirling the pot by the handle frequently.

2. Remove the pan from the heat, and stir in butter and cream with a long-handled spoon; the mixture will bubble furiously at first. Return the pan to low heat and stir until lumps melt and sauce is smooth. Stir in vanilla, and transfer to a jar. Serve hot, room temperature, or cold

Note: The sauce can be refrigerated up to 1 week, tightly covered.

To clean a pan that has been used to make caramel sauce, fill the pan with water and place it back on the stove. Stir as the water comes to a boil and all the caramel bits will dissipate.

Chocolate Sauce

Makes 3 cups

Active time:
15 minutes

Start to finish:
15 minutes

VARIATIONS

Add 2 tablespoons instant coffee powder along with the cocoa for mocha sauce.

Add 2 tablespoons of your favorite liquor or liqueur.

Add ½ cup chopped toasted nuts.

Homemade chocolate sauce is so much better than any you can buy and it's easy to make. This version offers pure chocolate flavor from the combination of chocolate and cocoa.

10 ounces good-quality bittersweet chocolate

1 cup heavy cream

¼ cup cocoa powder

½ teaspoon pure vanilla extract

Pinch of salt

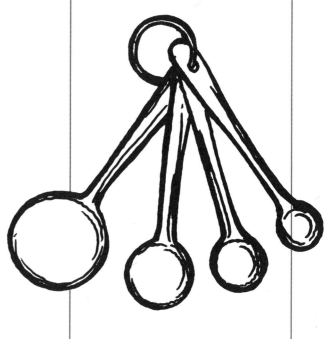

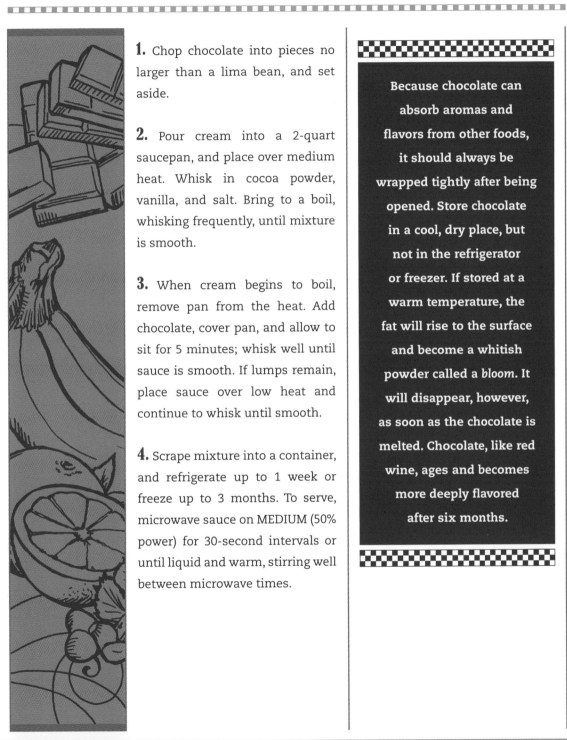

1. Chop chocolate into pieces no larger than a lima bean, and set aside.

2. Pour cream into a 2-quart saucepan, and place over medium heat. Whisk in cocoa powder, vanilla, and salt. Bring to a boil, whisking frequently, until mixture is smooth.

3. When cream begins to boil, remove pan from the heat. Add chocolate, cover pan, and allow to sit for 5 minutes; whisk well until sauce is smooth. If lumps remain, place sauce over low heat and continue to whisk until smooth.

4. Scrape mixture into a container, and refrigerate up to 1 week or freeze up to 3 months. To serve, microwave sauce on MEDIUM (50% power) for 30-second intervals or until liquid and warm, stirring well between microwave times.

Because chocolate can absorb aromas and flavors from other foods, it should always be wrapped tightly after being opened. Store chocolate in a cool, dry place, but not in the refrigerator or freezer. If stored at a warm temperature, the fat will rise to the surface and become a whitish powder called a *bloom*. It will disappear, however, as soon as the chocolate is melted. Chocolate, like red wine, ages and becomes more deeply flavored after six months.

ACKNOWLEDGMEMTS

While writing a book is a solitary task, its always takes a team to bring it to fruition. My thanks go:

To John Whalen of Cider Mill Press for envisioning such a fun addition to the world's collection of cookbooks.

To Ed Claflin, my agent, for his constant support, encouragement, and great humor.

To Harriet Bell, a wonderful old friend with whom it was so nice to work again, for her editorial guidance.

To Ellen Urban, for her eagle-eyed editing and insights.

To many dear friends who recalled their favorite meatballs and shared them with me, including Vicki Veh, Kenn Speiser, Kim Montour, Janet Morell, Suzanne Cavedon, Karen Davidson, Nick Brown, John Mariani, Pam Parmal, Bill Van Siclen, and Catherine Morrison Golden.

And to Tigger-Cat Brown and Patches-Kitten Brown, who kept me company from their perch in the office each day, and approved all the fish and seafood meatball recipes.

METRIC
CONVERSION
TABLES

The scientifically precise calculations needed for baking are not necessary when cooking conventionally. The tables in this appendix are designed for general cooking. If making conversions for baking, use your calculator to compute the exact amounts.

CONVERTING OUNCES TO GRAMS

The numbers in the following table are approximate. To reach the exact amount of grams, multiply the number of ounces by 28.35.

OUNCES	GRAMS	OUNCES	GRAMS
1 ounce	30 grams	9 ounces	250 grams
2 ounces	60 grams	10 ounces	285 grams
3 ounces	85 grams	11 ounces	300 grams
4 ounces	115 grams	12 ounces	340 grams
5 ounces	140 grams	13 ounces	370 grams
6 ounces	180 grams	14 ounces	400 grams
7 ounces	200 grams	15 ounces	425 grams
8 ounces	225 grams	16 ounces	450 grams

CONVERTING QUARTS TO LITERS

The numbers in the following table are approximate. To reach the exact amount of liters, multiply the number of quarts by 0.95.

QUARTS	LITER	QUARTS	LITER
1 cup (¼ quart)	¼ liter	4 quarts	3¾ liter
1 pint (½ quart)	½ liter	5 quarts	4¾ liter
1 quart	1 liter	6 quarts	5½ liter
2 quarts	2 liter	7 quarts	6½ liter
2½ quarts	2½ liter	8 quarts	7½ liter
3 quarts	2¾ liter		

CONVERTING POUNDS TO GRAMS AND KILOGRAMS

The numbers in the following table are approximate. To reach the exact amount of grams, multiply the number of pounds by 453.6.

POUNDS	GRAMS; KILOGRAMS	POUNDS	GRAMS; KILOGRAMS
1 pound	450 grams	4½ pounds	2 kilograms
1½ pounds	675 grams	5 pounds	2¼ kilograms
2 pounds	900 grams	5½ pounds	2½ kilograms
2½ pounds	1,125 grams;	6 pounds	2¾ kilograms
	1¼ kilograms	6½ pounds	3 kilograms
3 pounds	1,350 grams	7 pounds	3¼ kilograms
3½ pounds	1,500 grams;	7½ pounds	3½ kilograms
	1½ kilograms	8 pounds	3¾ kilograms
4 pounds	1,800 grams		

CONVERTING FAHRENHEIT TO CELSIUS

The numbers in the following table are approximate. To reach the exact temperature, subtract 32 from the Fahrenheit reading, multiply the number by 5, and then divide by 9.

DEGREES FAHRENHEIT	DEGREES CELSIUS	DEGREES FAHRENHEIT	DEGREES CELSIUS
170°F	77°C	350°F	180°C
180°F	82°C	375°F	190°C
190°F	88°C	400°F	205°C
200°F	95°C	425°F	220°C
225°F	110°C	450°F	230°C
250°F	120°C	475°F	245°C
300°F	150°C	500°F	260°C
325°F	165°C		

CONVERTING INCHES TO CENTIMETERS

The numbers in the following table are approximate. To reach the exact number of centimeters, multiply the number of inches by 2.54.

INCHES	CENTIMETERS	INCHES	CENTIMETERS
½ inch	1.5 centimeters	7 inches	18 centimeters
1 inch	2.5 centimeters	8 inches	20 centimeters
2 inches	5 centimeters	9 inches	23 centimeters
3 inches	8 centimeters	10 inches	25 centimeters
4 inches	10 centimeters	11 inches	28 centimeters
5 inches	13 centimeters	12 inches	30 centimeters
6 inches	15 centimeters		

TABLE OF WEIGHTS AND MEASURES
OF COMMON INGREDIENTS

FOOD	QUANTITY	YIELD
Apples	1 pound	2½ to 3 cups sliced
Avocado	1 pound	1 cup mashed fruit
Bananas	1 medium	1 cup, sliced
Bell Peppers	1 pound	3 to 4 cups sliced
Blueberries	1 pound	3⅓ cups
Butter	¼ pound (1 stick)	8 tablespoons
Cabbage	1 pound	4 cups packed shredded
Carrots	1 pound	3 cups diced or sliced
Chocolate, bulk	1 ounce	3 tablespoons grated
Chocolate, morsels	12 ounces	2 cups
Cocoa powder	1 ounce	¼ cup
Coconut, flaked	7 ounces	2½ cups
Cream	½ pt = 1 cup	2 cups whipped
Cream cheese	8 ounces	1 cup
Flour	1 pound	4 cups
Lemons	1 medium	3 tablespoons juice

FOOD	QUANTITY	YIELD
Lemons	1 medium	2 teaspoons zest
Milk	1 quart	4 cups
Molasses	12 ounces	1½ cups
Mushrooms	1 pound	5 cups sliced
Onions	1 medium	½ cup chopped
Peaches	1 pound	2 cups sliced
Peanuts	5 ounces	1 cup
Pecans	6 ounces	1½ cups
Pineapple	1 medium	3 cups diced fruit
Potatoes	1 pound	3 cups sliced
Raisins	1 pound	3 cups
Rice	1 pound	2 to 2½ cups raw
Spinach	1 pound	¾ cup cooked
Squash, summer	1 pound	3½ cups sliced
Strawberries	1 pint	1½ cups sliced
Sugar, brown	1 pound	2¼ cups, packed
Sugar, confectioner's	1 pound	4 cups
Sugar, granulated	1 pound	2¼ cups
Tomatoes	1 pound	1½ cups pulp
Walnuts	4 ounces	1 cup

TABLE OF LIQUID MEASUREMENTS

Dash	=	less than ⅛ teaspoon
3 teaspoons	=	1 tablespoon
2 tablespoons	=	1 ounce
8 tablespoons	=	½ cup
2 cups	=	1 pint
1 quart	=	2 pints
1 gallon	=	4 quarts

INDEX

W

ABOUT THE AUTHOR

Ellen Brown, the author of more than 20 cookbooks, gained the national limelight in 1982 as the founding food editor of *USA Today*. Her books include *Gourmet Gazelle Cookbook*, winner of the IACP Award, and *Cooking with the New American Chefs*, a Tastemaker Award finalist.

From 2003 to 2008 she was allied with Alpha Books as an author for its popular series on basic instruction, *The Complete Idiot's Guides*. Her nine books covered topics as diverse as slow cooker cooking and fondues to juicing and a dictionary of cooking substitutions. Just released by Lyons Press is a series of five regional American grilling books, and other topics she has written about range from sushi to smoothies.

Her writing has appeared in more than two dozen publications, including *The Washington Post, The Los Angeles Times* syndicate, the Prodigy computer network, *Bon Appetit, Art Culinaire, The Baltimore Sun, The San Francisco Chronicle, Tables, Good Food, Showcase,* and *Diversion*.

In 1985, she was honored by *Cook's* magazine, who selected her for inclusion in the prestigious "Who's Who of Cooking in America." Profiles of her have appeared in *The Washington Post, The Detroit News, Coastal Living,* and *The Miami Herald.* She was also shown in an episode on *Food Finds,* shown nationally on the Television Food Network. She lives in Providence, Rhode Island.

ABOUT CIDER MILL PRESS BOOK PUBLISHERS

Good ideas ripen with time. From seed to harvest, Cider Mill Press strives to bring fine reading, information, and entertainment together between the covers of its creatively crafted books. Our Cider Mill bears fruit twice a year, publishing a new crop of titles each spring and fall.

Visit us on the web at
www.cidermillpress.com
or write to us at
12 Port Farm Road

Kennebunkport, Maine 04046